INTRODUCTION

This revision guide is matched to the AQA Modular specifications for Double Award Science.

Everything you need to know is contained within this slim volume but in addition, to make things even easier for you, we've condensed each module down to a single page of last minute 'Key Points' for that final recap before your tests.

The new layout and improved diagrams make the pages seem even more spacious and user-friendly and there's a set of multiple choice summary questions relating to each module.

Although the guide mostly follows the syllabus order, a few topics have been sympathetically relocated for better understanding. However, the contents page links each page to its specification reference number to allow pages to be easily cross-referenced to their location on the AQA specification.

Please make sure that you turn to page 4 and read the section entitled **'How To Use This Revision Guide'**.

This guide will give you a definite edge – make the most of it!

Good luck in your forthcoming exams.

Mary James

Mary James – **Editor**

The second volume of this guide concentrates on the six modules that will be tested in the **TERMINAL EXAMINATION**. It is available from the address on the opposite page.

CONTENTS

Covered in Class | Revised | Revised | Page No.

Humans As Organisms

Maintenance Of Life

Metals

CONTENTS

Covered in Class | Revised | Revised | Page No.

Earth Materials

Energy

Electricity

* Numbers in brackets refer to Specification reference numbers.

HOW TO USE THIS REVISION GUIDE

- In certain places, we have included slightly more than you actually need to know, in order to aid understanding. In particular, 'Conscious Action' is included on p30 to help you understand the reason for 'Reflex Action'. Similarly, we have included a small 'Facts' section on p12 and 13 to illustrate the essential difference between 'Aerobic' and 'Anaerobic Respiration'.
  Other than this, the guide contains, 'everything you need to know, and nothing else', in a highly refined, user-friendly format.

- Don't just read the guide! LEARN ACTIVELY! Constantly test yourself ...
  WITHOUT LOOKING AT THE TEXT.

- When you have revised a small sub-section or a diagram, PLACE A BOLD TICK AGAINST IT, and also tick the 'Covered In Class' and 'Revised' sections of the Contents page as you progress.
  This is great for your self-confidence.

- Jot down anything that you think will help you to remember – no matter how trivial it may seem.

> REMEMBER! Don't throw away this guide at the end of year 10! You will need to revise all the sections OUTLINED IN RED in this volume, as well as the SIX modules in Volume Two, before you take your final exam at the end of year 11.

SOME IMPORTANT FACTS ABOUT YOUR MODULE TESTS

- You will take 6 module tests over the duration of your course.

- The specified occasions are LATE NOVEMBER/EARLY DECEMBER, EARLY MARCH and MID/LATE JUNE, on dates which are announced each year. You may also do tests in year 11.

- You will be entered for each of these tests at either HIGHER or FOUNDATION TIER.
  You don't have to stick to one tier for all six tests.

- The tests will be entirely MULTIPLE CHOICE and similar in style to the summary questions in this guide.

- There is a maximum of 36 marks for either tier, and in previous tests 18 of the marks have been for questions common to both tiers.

NOTES

ANIMAL CELLS

Animal Cell Structure

All animals and plants are made up of cells. Most human cells, like most other animal cells, have the following parts:

CELL MEMBRANE
Controls movement of substances into and out of the cell.

CYTOPLASM
Most chemical reactions take place here.

NUCLEUS
Controls what the cell does and contains the genetic information.

MITOCHONDRIA
Where most of the energy is released via respiration.

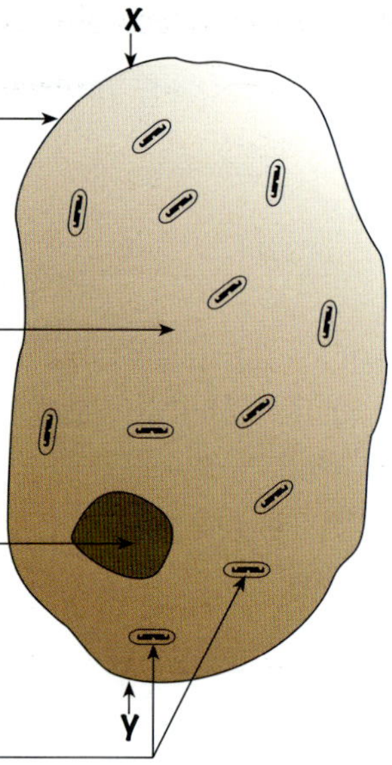

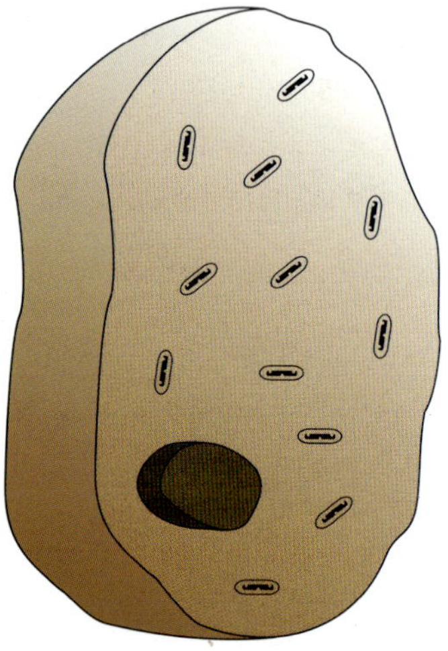

This shows the cell as it would look if it had been cut along the line XY.

Most cells are made up mainly of water containing dissolved substances. These substances are usually in the process of being made into something which the cell needs. This involves chemical reactions taking place, under the control of enzymes.

Types Of Animal Cell

Some cells are highly SPECIALISED to do a particular job ...

The OVUM or egg cell is much larger than other cells so that it can carry massive food reserves for the developing embryo.

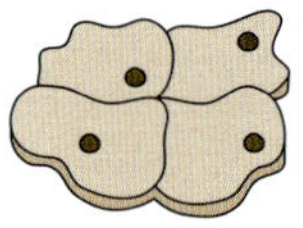

EPITHELIAL CELLS are flattened in shape and joined together at the edges, so that they can form covering layers eg. skin.

The SPERM CELL is the most mobile cell because of its tail. It has to travel from the vagina to the ovum.

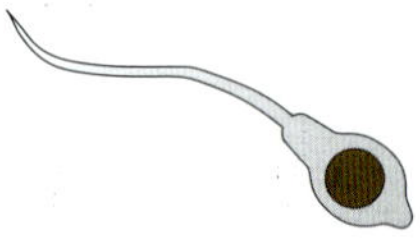

GLANDULAR CELLS have a large cavity into which substances are emptied before being released. They are found in the digestive system.

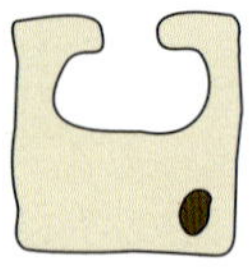

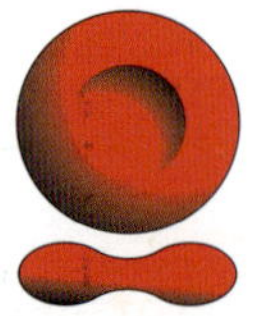

RED BLOOD CELLS lose their nucleus so that they can be packed full of haemoglobin in order to carry lots of oxygen.

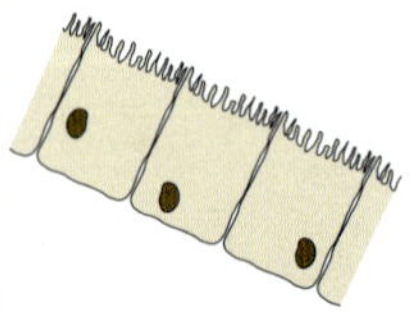

CILIATED EPITHELIAL CELLS move mucus along our windpipe, trapping and carrying away debris which we have breathed in.

WHITE BLOOD CELLS can change their shape in order to engulf and destroy microbes which have invaded the body.

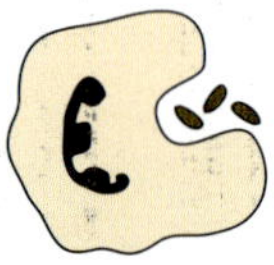

NERVE CELLS (Neurones) have long slender processes which can carry nerve impulses over distances as long as 1 metre.

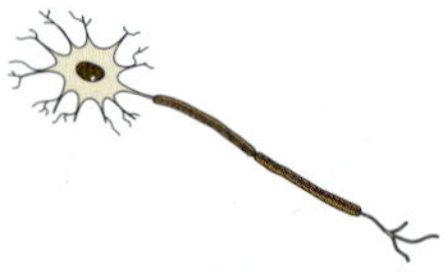

CELLS → TISSUES → ORGANS → ORGAN SYSTEMS → ORGANISM

Diffusion

Because cells are living things, they have to constantly replace substances which are used up (food, oxygen) and remove other substances which would otherwise accumulate (carbon dioxide, waste products).

These substances, plus simple sugars and ions, pass easily through cell membranes.

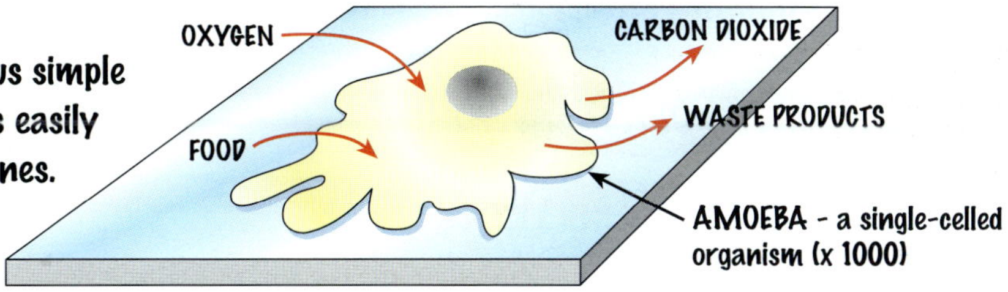

Even simple, single-celled animals, like the amoeba above, need to do this. Happily, this can take place automatically, without the need for energy, in a process called DIFFUSION.

DIFFUSION is ...
... the spreading of the particles of a gas, or of any substance in solution, ...
... resulting in a net movement from a region where they are at a higher concentration ...
... to a region where they are at a lower concentration.

Diffusion can be demonstrated in the following ways...

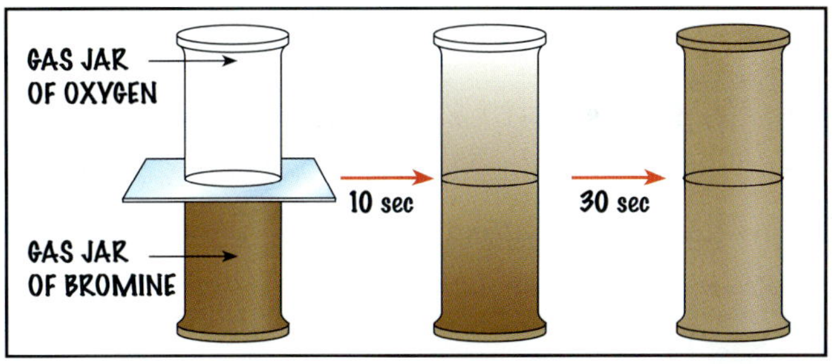

The greater the difference in concentration, the faster the rate of diffusion.

So in the example of oxygen and the amoeba, there's lots of oxygen outside the amoeba but much less inside, because it's being used up in respiration. So the higher concentration outside results in oxygen 'spreading' (DIFFUSING) into the amoeba across the cell membrane.

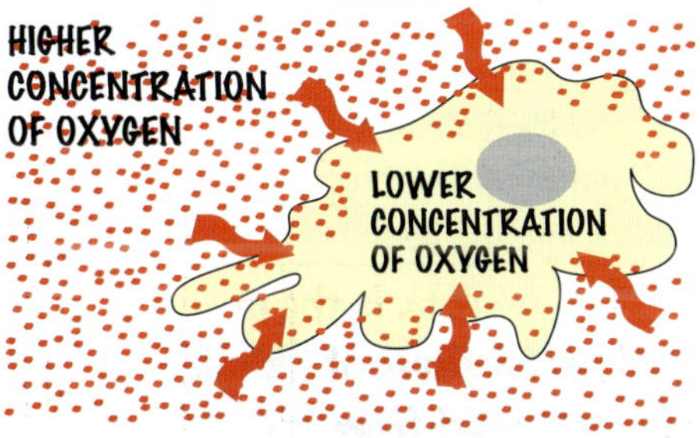

Examples In Humans

Surfaces across which gases are exchanged are often specialised in humans by having LARGE SURFACE AREAS to increase the rate at which diffusion can occur.
These are examples of ADAPTATION.

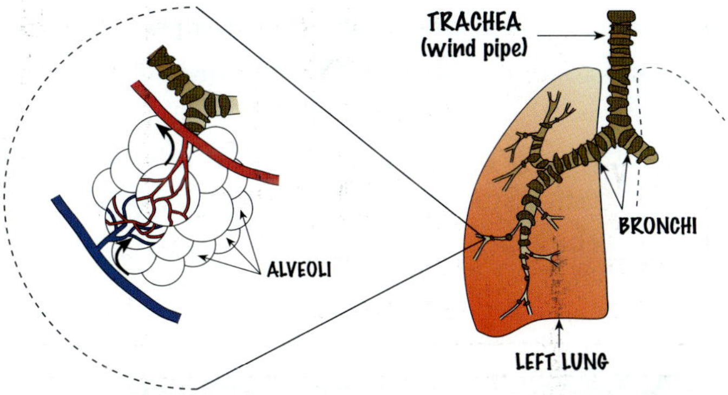

The ALVEOLI in the lungs provide a massive surface area for exchange of oxygen and carbon dioxide.

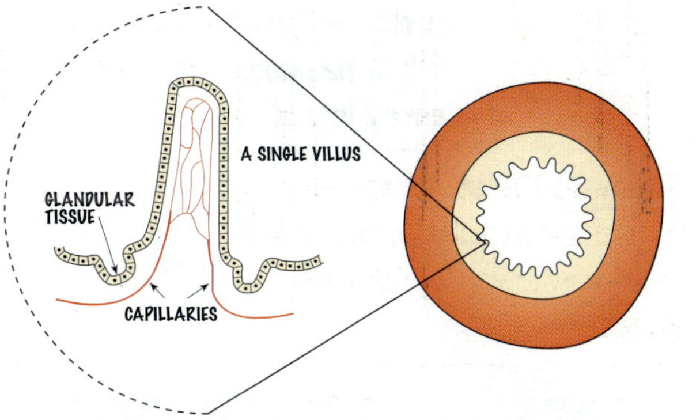

The VILLI in the small intestine provide a massive surface area for absorption of digested food.

THE DIGESTIVE SYSTEM

The **DIGESTIVE SYSTEM** is really made up of a long **MUSCULAR TUBE** in which **ENZYMES** speed up (catalyse) the breakdown of **LARGE INSOLUBLE MOLECULES** eg. starch, proteins and fats into **SMALLER SOLUBLE MOLECULES** so that they can pass through the walls of the small intestine and into the bloodstream. Reabsorption of water takes place in the large intestine leaving indigestible food which leaves the body as faeces via the anus.

The Human Digestive System

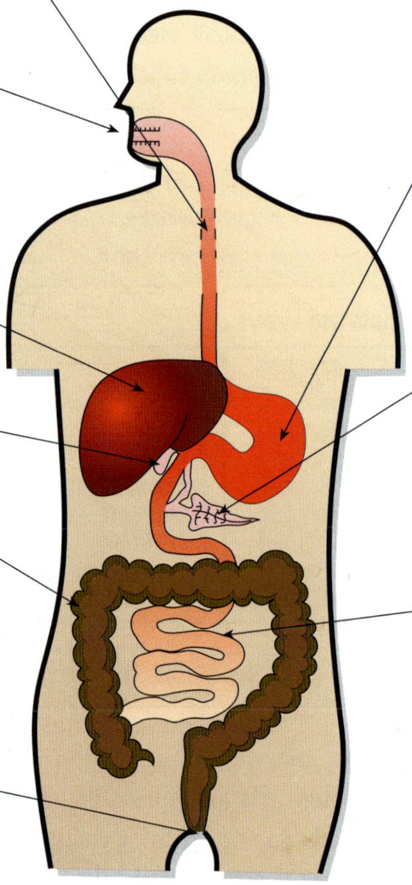

The Function Of Bile

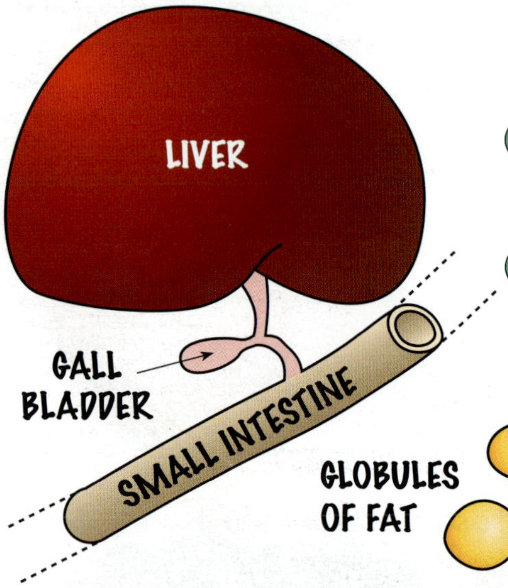

Bile is produced in the **LIVER** and then stored in the **GALL BLADDER** ...
... before being released into the **SMALL INTESTINE**.
Bile has 2 functions ...

1. ... it neutralises the acid, which was added to food in the stomach, to produce **ALKALINE** conditions in which the enzymes of the small intestine work best.
2. ... it **EMULSIFIES** fats ie. it breaks large drops of fat into small droplets to increase their surface area. This enables the lipase enzymes to work much faster.

Enzyme Summary

Three enzymes PROTEASE, LIPASE and AMYLASE are produced in four separate regions of the digestive system. They digest Proteins, Fats and Carbohydrates to produce molecules which can be absorbed.

SALIVARY GLANDS

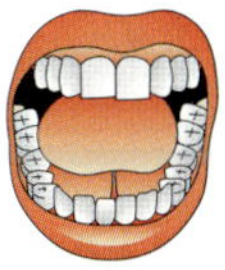

AMYLASE	CARBOHYDRATES →	SUGARS

STOMACH

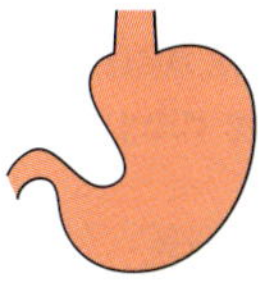

PROTEASE	PROTEINS →	AMINO ACIDS

PANCREAS
(These enzymes are released into the small intestine).

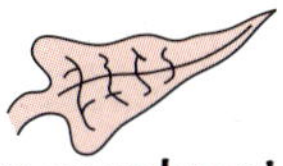

AMYLASE	CARBOHYDRATES →	SUGARS
PROTEASE	PROTEINS →	AMINO ACIDS
LIPASE	LIPIDS (fats & oils) →	FATTY ACIDS + GLYCEROL

SMALL INTESTINE

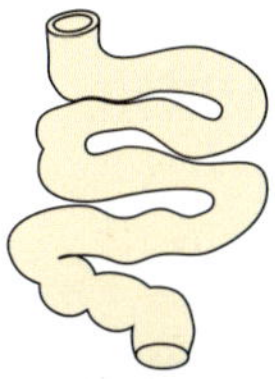

AMYLASE	CARBOHYDRATES →	SUGARS
PROTEASE	PROTEINS →	AMINO ACIDS
LIPASE	LIPIDS (fats & oils) →	FATTY ACIDS + GLYCEROL

Absorption In The Small Intestine

The three enzymes catalyse the breakdown of LARGE INSOLUBLE MOLECULES into SMALL SOLUBLE MOLECULES which then diffuse through the walls of the small intestine into the bloodstream.

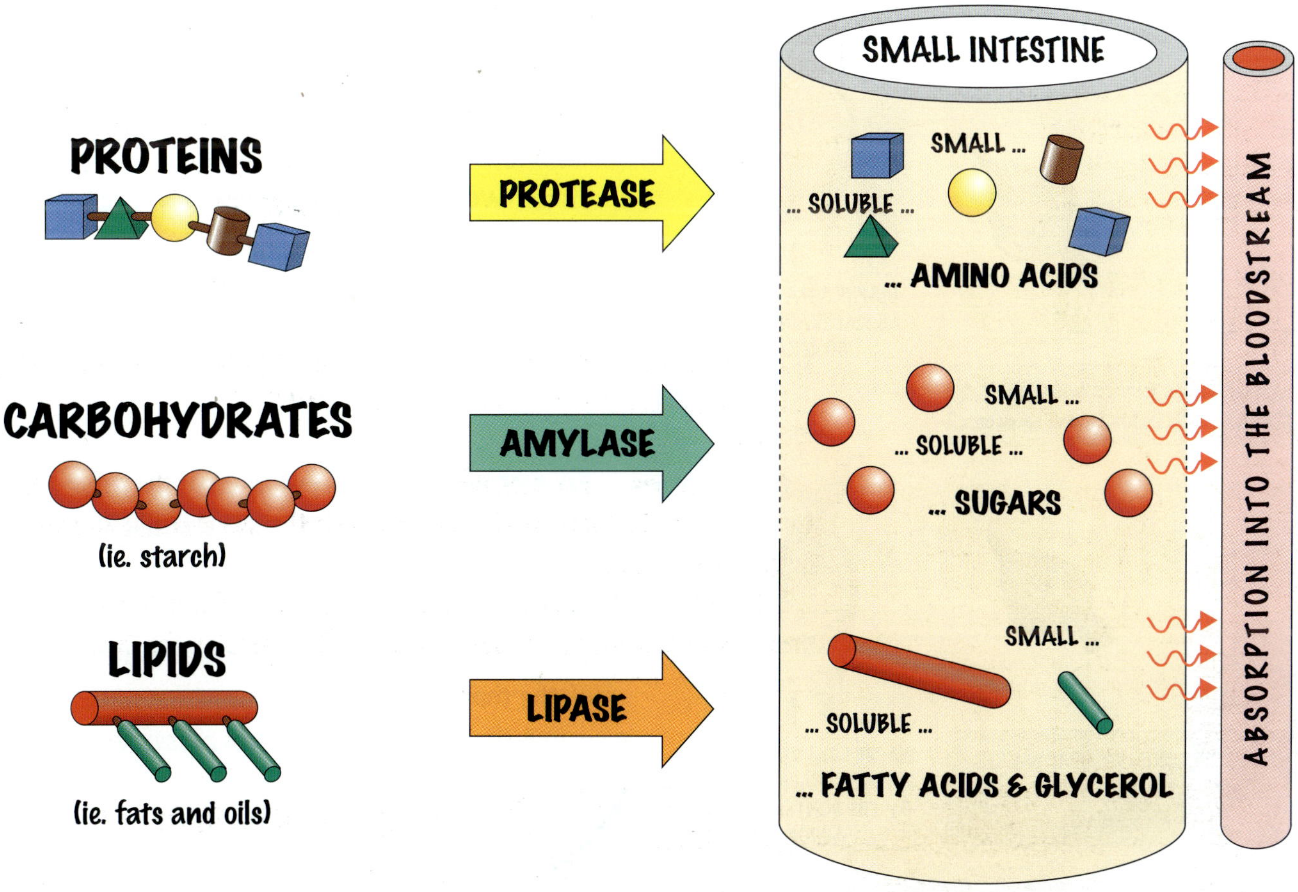

The Breathing System

The most important structures in the breathing system are shown in the diagram below...

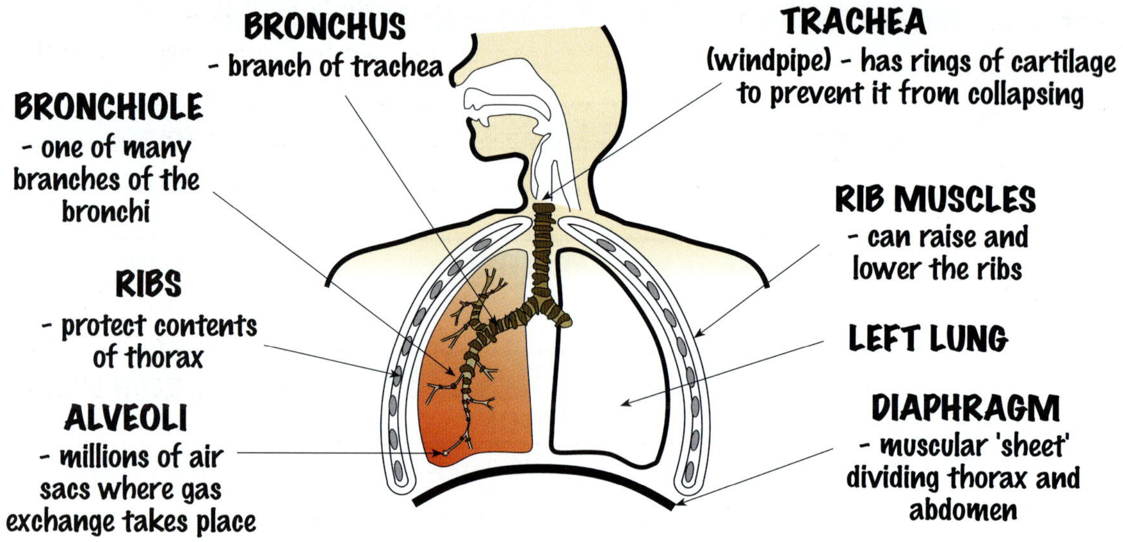

- The **RIBCAGE** protects the contents of the **THORAX** ie. the **HEART** and **LUNGS**.

Ventilation

The breathing system is designed to allow oxygen and carbon dioxide to be efficiently exchanged. For this to happen, however, the lungs have to be constantly 'refreshed' by atmospheric air. This happens by increasing and then decreasing the volume of the thorax (chest cavity).

It's the same principle with the SYRINGE and the BELLOWS ...

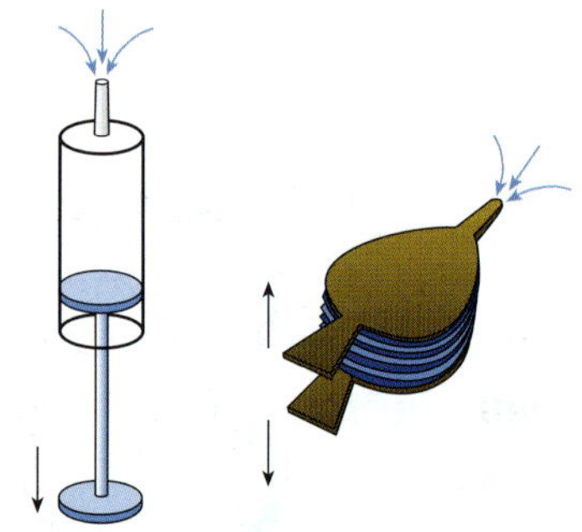

... AN INCREASE IN VOLUME CAUSES A DECREASE IN PRESSURE - and air enters.

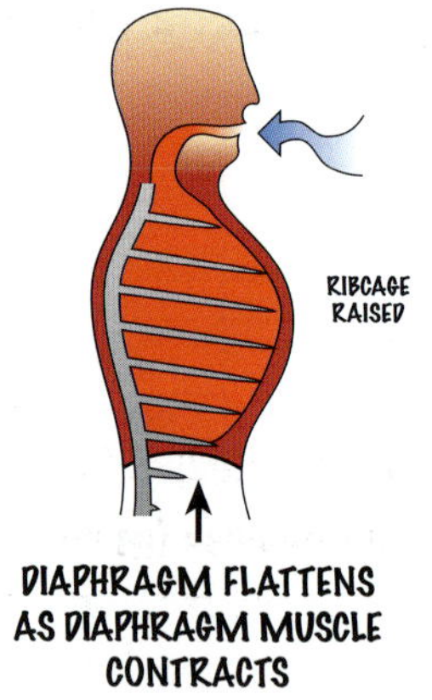

To inhale:

- The muscles between the ribs contract, pulling the ribcage upwards and outwards.
- At the same time the diaphragm muscles contract causing the diaphragm to flatten.
- These two movements cause an increase in the volume of the thorax ...
- ... and therefore a decrease in pressure which results in atmospheric air entering.

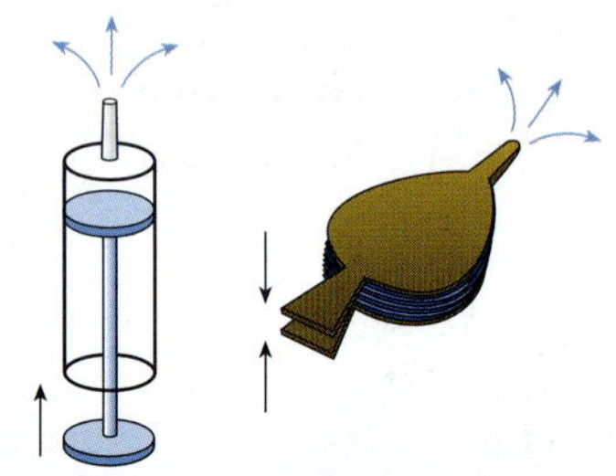

... A DECREASE IN VOLUME CAUSES AN INCREASE IN PRESSURE - and air is forced out.

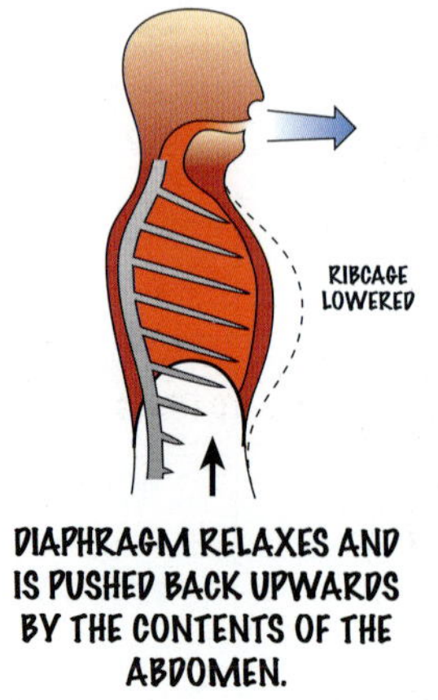

To exhale:

- The muscles between the ribs relax allowing them to fall.
- The diaphragm muscles also relax.
- These movements cause a decrease in the volume of the thorax ...
- ... and therefore an increase in pressure resulting in air being forced out.

Diffusion Of Oxygen And Carbon Dioxide In The Alveoli

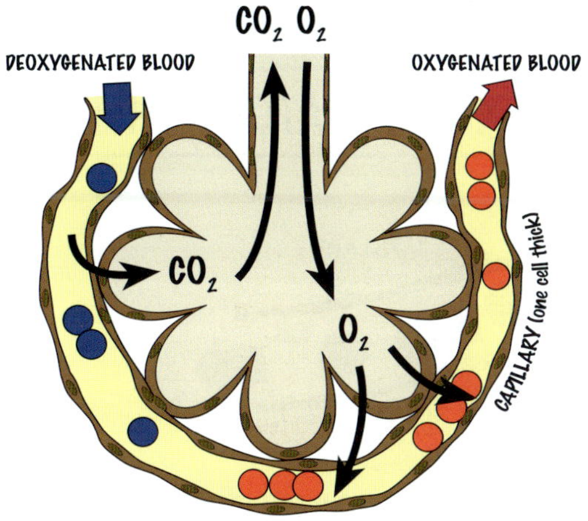

A SINGLE ALVEOLUS AND A CAPILLARY.

- The TRACHEA divides into two tubes ...
- ... called the BRONCHI, which divide again, several times, ...
- ... to form the BRONCHIOLES which continue to divide ...
- ... until they end as air sacs called ALVEOLI (there are millions of these) ...
- ... which are very close to the blood CAPILLARIES.

and here, ...

- ... CARBON DIOXIDE diffuses from the BLOOD into the ALVEOLI.
- ... OXYGEN diffuses from the ALVEOLI into the blood.

This means the blood has swapped its CARBON DIOXIDE for OXYGEN and is now OXYGENATED.

Features Which Make The Lungs An Excellent Exchange Surface

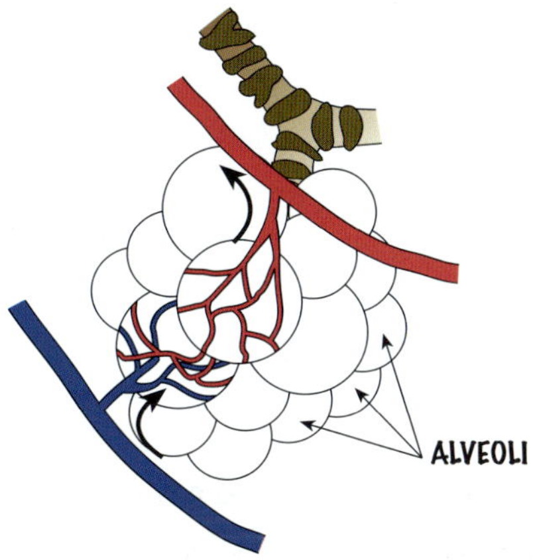

The arrangement of alveoli and capillaries in the lungs makes the lungs very EFFICIENT at exchanging OXYGEN and CARBON DIOXIDE,

because ...

- ... they have a **LARGE, MOIST SURFACE AREA.**
- ... they have an **EXCELLENT CAPILLARY BLOOD SUPPLY.**

Providing Energy For Cells

- Once oxygen has diffused into the bloodstream, it must be transported to all the cells of the body so that it can be used to release energy from glucose (in respiration).
- This relies on three body systems working together: THE RESPIRATORY SYSTEM, THE DIGESTIVE SYSTEM and THE CIRCULATORY SYSTEM.

- The respiratory system and ...
  ... the digestive system provide the reactants for respiration.
- These pass into the bloodstream and are carried to the CELLS of the body.
- CARBON DIOXIDE is transported, by blood, back to the lungs where it is breathed out.

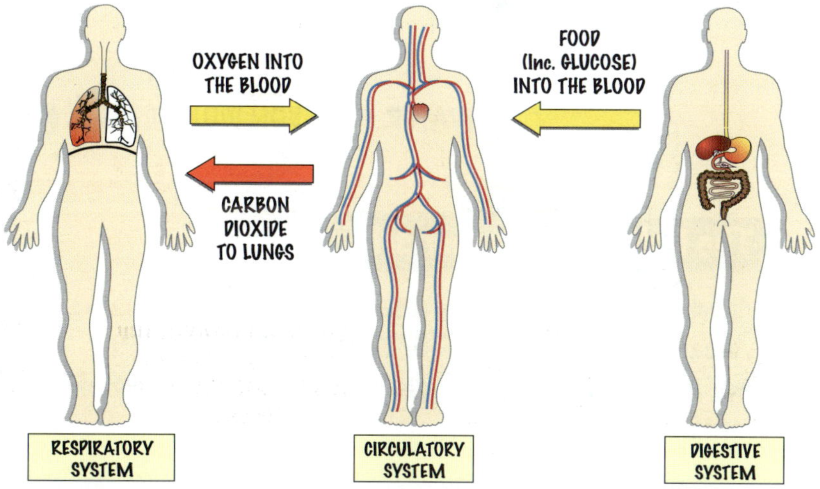

Aerobic Respiration

... 'is the release of energy from the breakdown of glucose, ...
... by combining it with OXYGEN inside living cells.'
(The energy is actually contained inside the glucose molecule.)

THE EQUATION: **GLUCOSE + OXYGEN ⟹ CARBON DIOXIDE + WATER + ENERGY**

EXAMPLE:
a working muscle cell

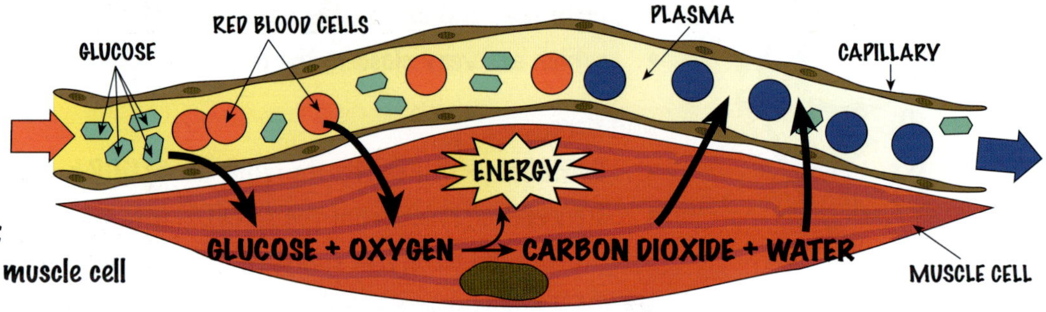

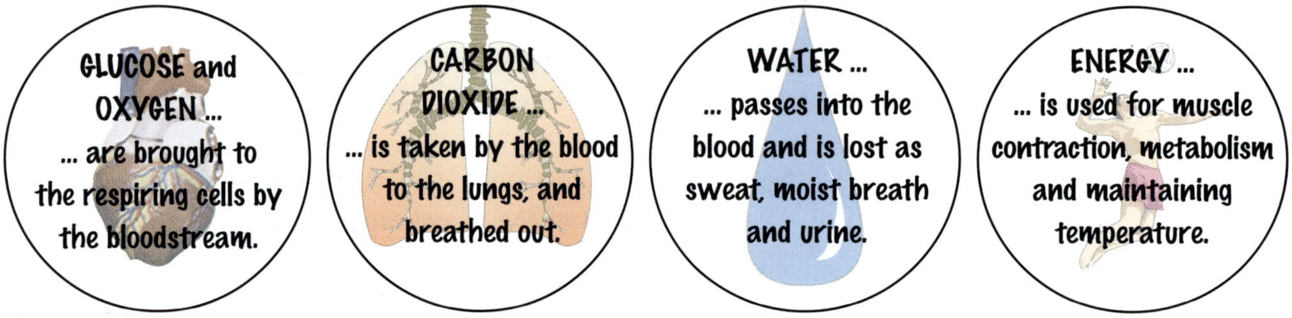

Some Facts About Aerobic Respiration

- This is a very efficient method of producing energy, and one molecule of glucose can provide twenty times as much energy as ANAEROBIC RESPIRATION (see next page).
- It occurs during normal day to day activity and accounts for our energy production up to about 60% of maximum effort.
- The drawback is that it doesn't produce energy anything like as quickly as ANAEROBIC RESPIRATION.

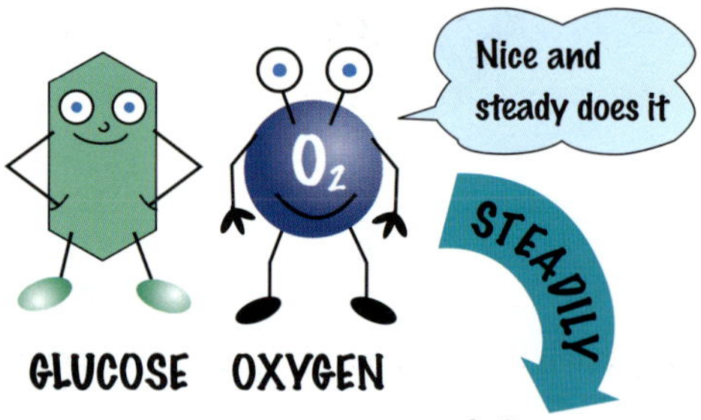

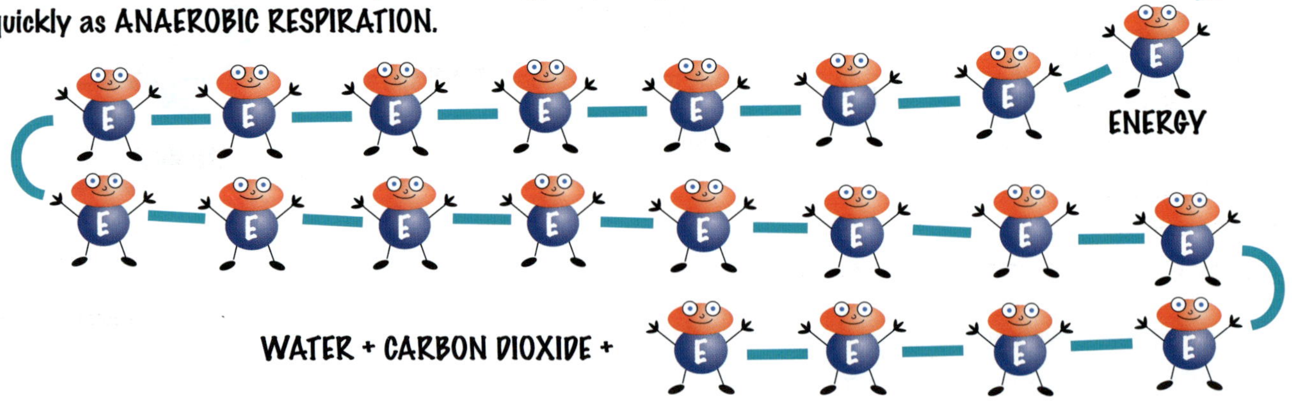

The Role Of Mitochondria

Mitochondria are found in greater numbers in fast respiring cells...
... because they are the SITE OF AEROBIC RESPIRATION.
They absorb glucose and oxygen and provide energy which is transferred in cells.

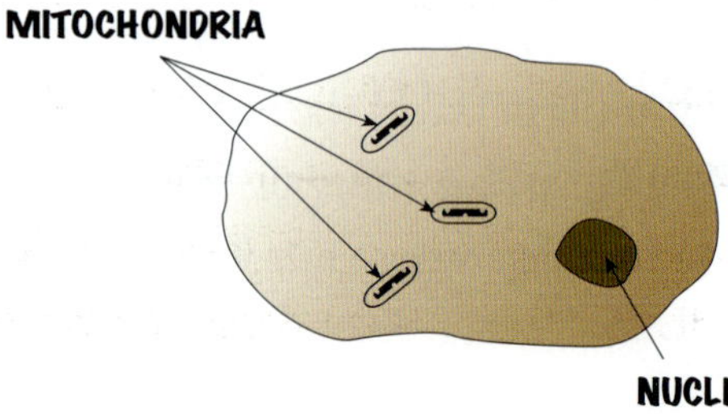

Anaerobic Respiration

... is the release of a little bit of energy, <u>very quickly</u>, inside living cells, from the INCOMPLETE breakdown of glucose in the ABSENCE OF OXYGEN.

THE EQUATION: **GLUCOSE → LACTIC ACID + A BIT OF ENERGY**

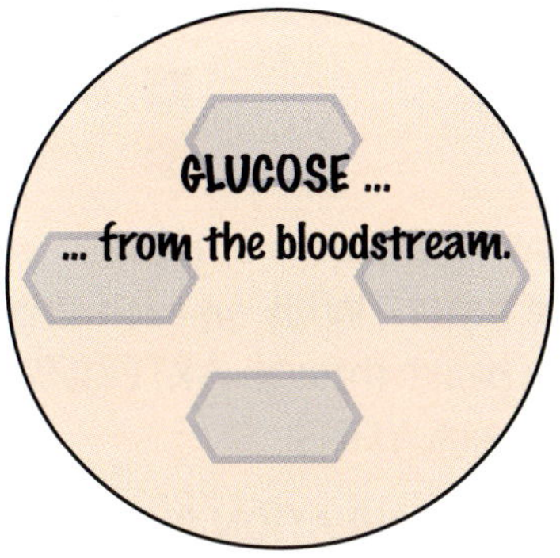

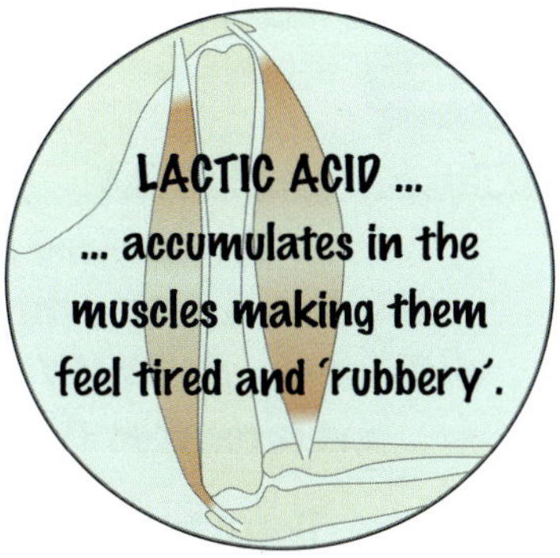

- This happens when the muscles are working so hard that...
- ...the lungs and bloodstream can't deliver enough OXYGEN, to respire the available glucose aerobically.
- Therefore the GLUCOSE can only be partly broken down, releasing a much smaller amount of energy...
- ... and LACTIC ACID as a waste product. It can only operate for a short time.
- Build up of lactic acid during vigorous activity causes acute fatigue in muscles, and results in 'OXYGEN DEBT'. This causes them to stop contracting efficiently.
- This 'debt' must be 'repaid' by continued deep breathing after exercise in order to provide enough oxygen to oxidise the lactic acid to carbon dioxide and water.

Some Facts About Anaerobic Respiration

- Anaerobic respiration is an inefficient process since it produces only $^1/_{20}$th as much energy as aerobic respiration (see previous page).
- However it produces energy MUCH FASTER and so is used during high intensity (explosive) activity over a <u>short period</u>.
- After a relatively short time, the build up of lactic acid affects the performance of the muscles.

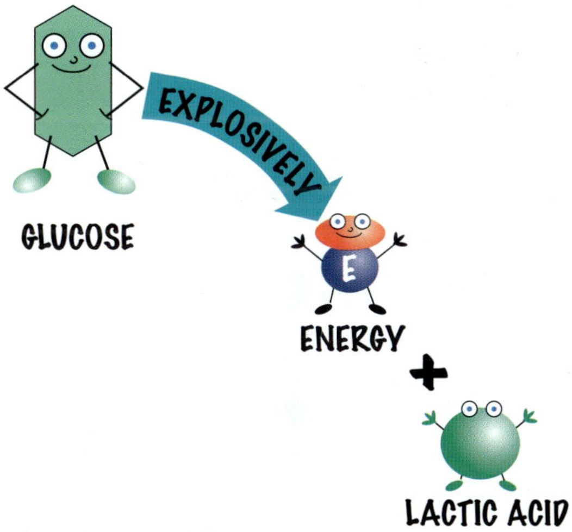

What Cells Do With Their Energy

The energy released during respiration is used in the following ways ...

- To build larger **MOLECULES** using smaller ones.
- To enable **MUSCLES** to contract.
- To **MAINTAIN TEMPERATURE** in colder surroundings.
- To actively transport materials across **MEMBRANES**.

They all begin with **M**. (Remember the 'M's')

The Function Of The Circulatory System

■ = DEOXYGENATED
■ = OXYGENATED

The circulatory system is the body's transport system.

- It carries blood from the heart to all the cells of the body ...
- ... to provide them with FOOD and OXYGEN, and ...
- ... carries WASTE PRODUCTS including CARBON DIOXIDE away from the cells.
- Blood is pumped to the lungs so that CARBON DIOXIDE can be exchanged for OXYGEN.
- The system consists of THE HEART, THE BLOOD VESSELS, and THE BLOOD.

The Heart And Major Blood Vessels

The heart acts as a PUMP in a DOUBLE CIRCULATORY SYSTEM.

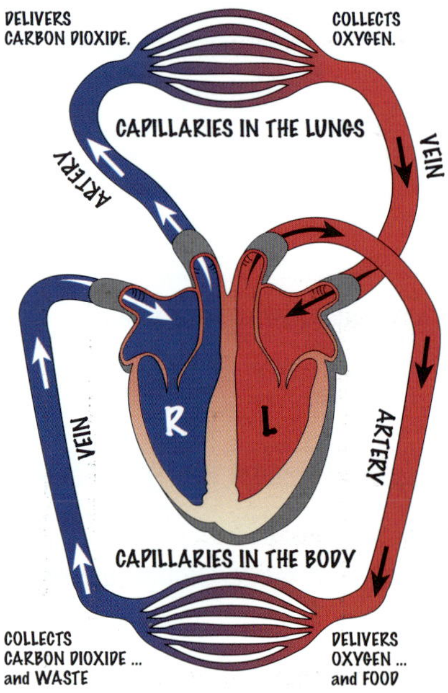

■ Blood low in oxygen (DEOXYGENATED)
■ Blood rich in oxygen (OXYGENATED)

- As you can see blood flows around a 'figure of eight' circuit and passes through the heart TWICE on each circuit.
- Blood travels AWAY from the heart through ARTERIES, ...
- ... and returns to the heart through VEINS.

There are TWO SEPARATE CIRCULATION SYSTEMS, ...

... one 'loop' carries blood from the HEART to the LUNGS and then back to the HEART ...

... and the other carries blood from the HEART to ALL OTHER PARTS OF THE BODY and then back to the HEART.

The RIGHT SIDE of the heart pumps blood which is LOW IN OXYGEN to the LUNGS, to pick up OXYGEN.

The LEFT SIDE of the heart pumps blood which is RICH IN OXYGEN to all other parts of the BODY.

The Blood

If blood is allowed to stand without clotting, it separates out into its 4 components ...

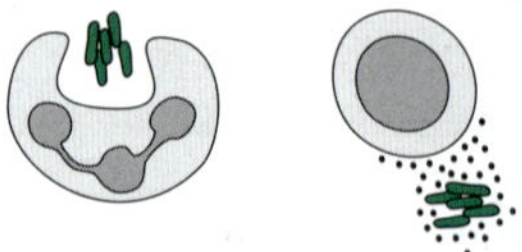

PLASMA is a straw-coloured liquid which transports ...

- ... carbon dioxide from the organs to the lungs ...
- ... glucose from the small intestine to the organs ...
- ... other wastes (eg. urea) from the liver to the kidneys.

WHITE CELLS have a nucleus which is variable in shape.

- Some engulf invading microbes to defend the body ...
- ... while others produce ANTIBODIES to attack them.
- There's 1 white cell for every 600 red cells!!

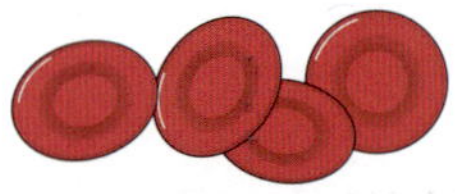

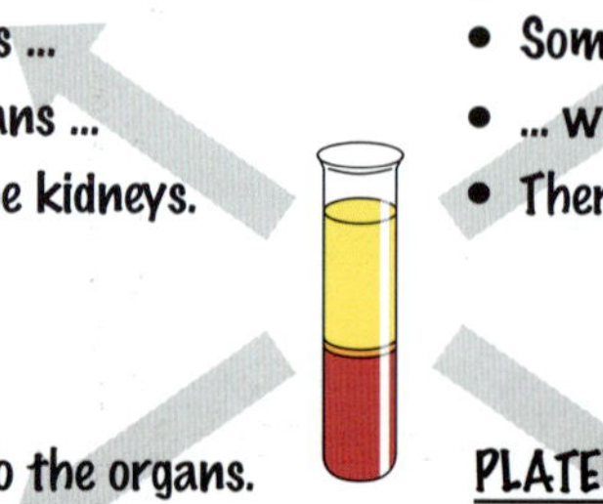

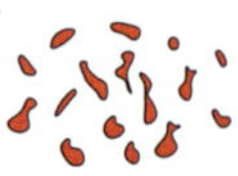

RED CELLS transport OXYGEN from the lungs to the organs.

- They have NO NUCLEUS so that they can contain lots of HAEMOGLOBIN, (a red pigment which can carry oxygen).
- In the lungs HAEMOGLOBIN combines with oxygen to form OXYHAEMOGLOBIN. In other organs OXYHAEMOGLOBIN splits up into HAEMOGLOBIN plus OXYGEN.

PLATELETS are tiny pieces of cell which have no nucleus.

- They clump together when a blood vessel is damaged ...
- ... and form a meshwork of fibres to produce a CLOT.

The Heart In More Detail

The HEART is a muscular organ in the circulatory system and PUMPS BLOOD around the body.

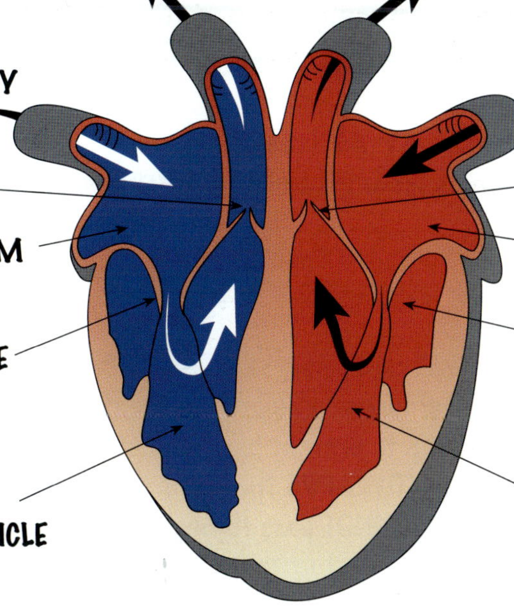

- Most of the wall of the heart is made of MUSCLE.
- ATRIA are the smaller, LESS MUSCULAR upper chambers, which receive blood coming back to the heart through VEINS.
- VENTRICLES are the larger, MORE MUSCULAR lower chambers.
  The LEFT is more muscular than the right since it has to pump blood around the whole body.
- VALVES make sure that the blood flows in the right direction, and can't flow backwards.

How The Heart Pumps Blood

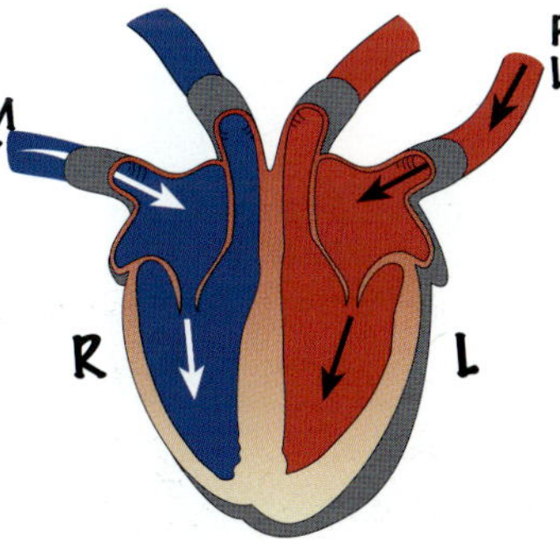

- When the HEART MUSCLE RELAXES, blood flows into the ATRIA, through veins, from the LUNGS and the rest of the BODY.
- The ATRIA then CONTRACT squeezing blood into the VENTRICLES.

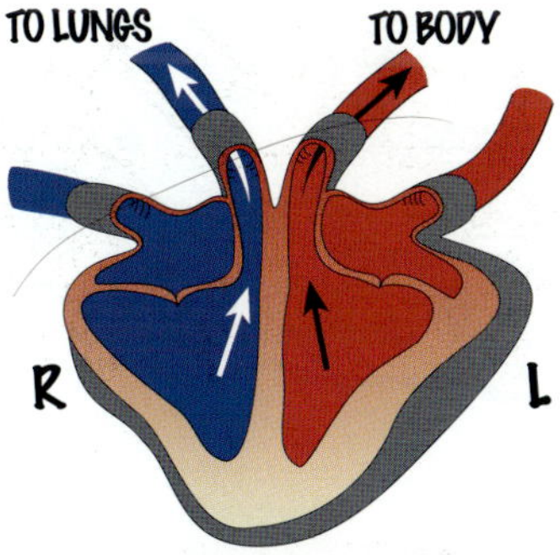

- When the VENTRICLES CONTRACT (squeeze) ...
  ... blood is forced out of the lower chambers into two arteries ...
  ... these carry blood to the body and the lungs.
- The blood can't flow backwards because of VALVES in the heart.
- The heart muscle now relaxes and the whole process starts again.

There are three types of blood vessels ... ARTERIES, VEINS and CAPILLARIES.
They form the 'plumbing' of the circulatory system.

Arteries

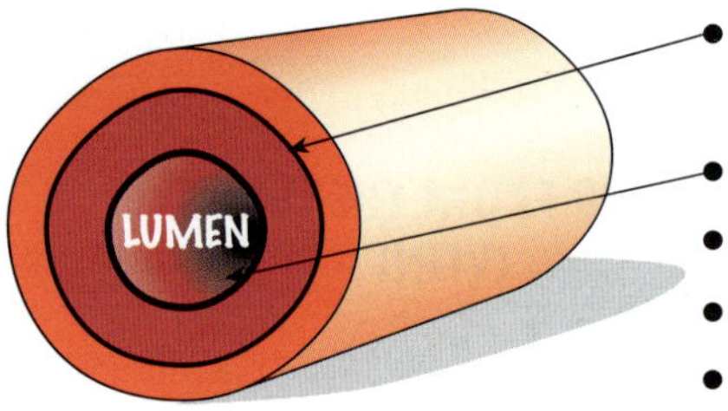

- Thick wall containing ELASTIC and MUSCLE fibres to cope with the much higher pressure in these vessels.
- Much smaller lumen compared to the thickness of the wall.
- No valves.
- Carry blood AWAY from the heart.
- Substances from the blood CANNOT pass through the artery walls.

Veins

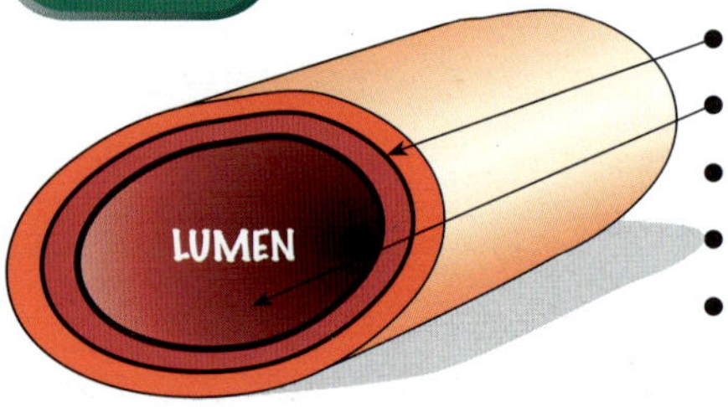

- Thinner wall containing LESS ELASTIC and MUSCLE fibres.
- Much bigger lumen compared to the thickness of the wall.
- Have VALVES to prevent backflow of blood.
- Carry blood TOWARDS the heart.
- Substances CANNOT pass through the veins' walls.

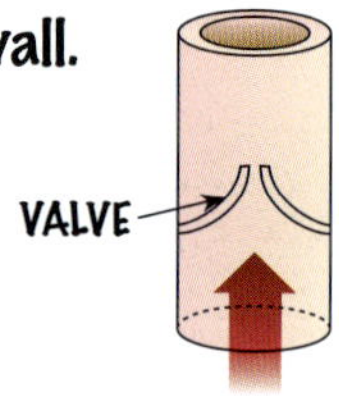

Capillaries

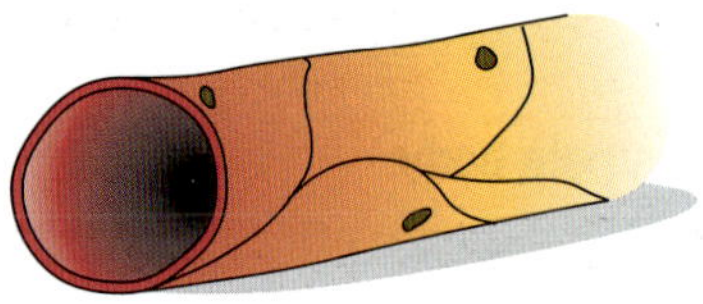

- Narrow, thin-walled vessels, just ONE CELL THICK.
- Microscopic (too small to see without a microscope).
- EXCHANGE OF SUBSTANCES between cells and blood ONLY takes place here.
- Connect arteries to veins.

Exchange Of Substances At The Capillaries

Arteries branch into tiny one cell thick capillaries which pass close to each cell before reuniting to form a vein.

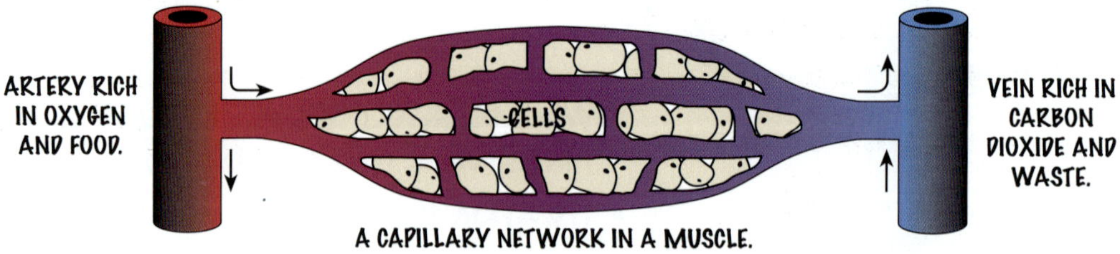

A CAPILLARY NETWORK IN A MUSCLE.

ONLY AT THE CAPILLARIES can SUBSTANCES BE EXCHANGED with the body's cells.
Glucose and oxygen diffuse from the blood to the cells and carbon dioxide and other waste diffuse from the cells to the blood.

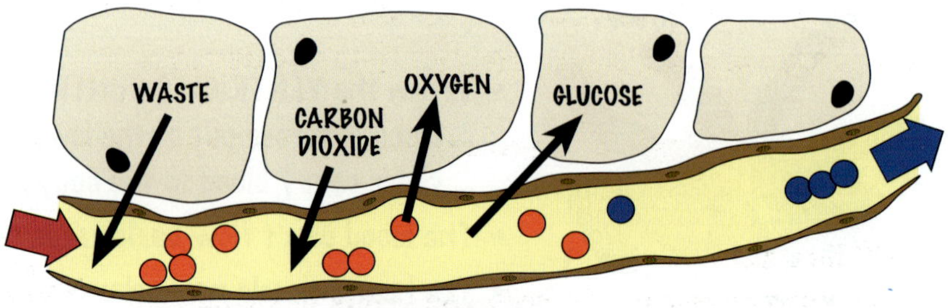

A CAPILLARY VESSEL
(one cell thick)

Bacteria And Viruses

These are the two main types of microbe which may affect health.

A SINGLE BACTERIUM

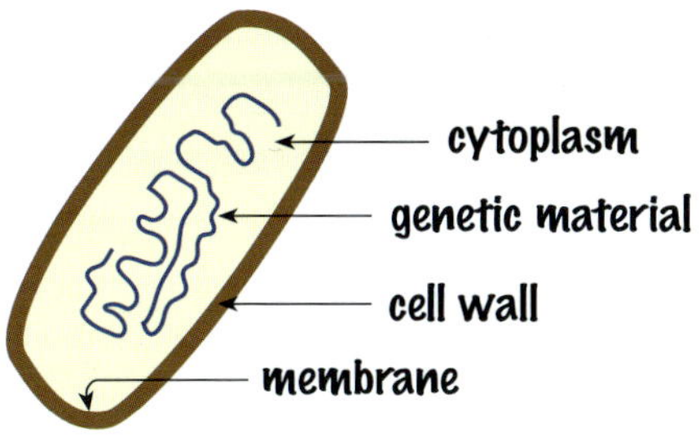

A SINGLE VIRUS

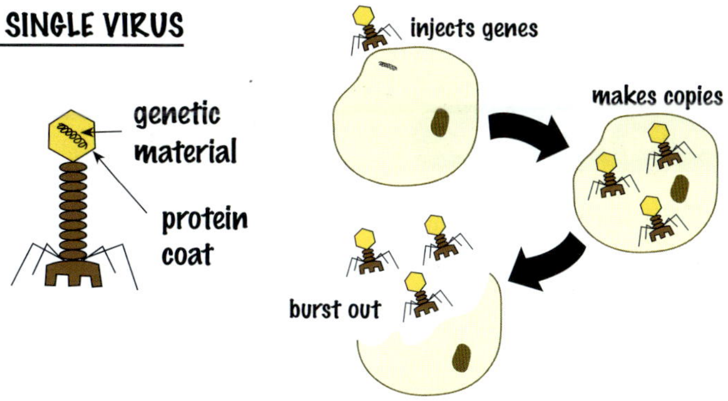

A Comparison Between Bacteria And Viruses

BACTERIA	VIRUSES
Consist of CYTOPLASM and a MEMBRANE surrounded by a CELL WALL.	Have a simple PROTEIN COAT. No membrane or cell wall.
The genetic material is NOT contained within a NUCLEUS.	The genetic material is NOT contained within a NUCLEUS.
Very small.	Even smaller.
Reproduce very quickly.	Reproduce very quickly - BUT ONLY INSIDE LIVING CELLS, WHICH ARE THEN DAMAGED. (see above)
Can produce TOXINS (poisons) which make us feel ill.	Can produce TOXINS (poisons) which make us feel ill.
Responsible for diseases such as TETANUS, CHOLERA, TUBERCULOSIS.	Responsible for diseases such as COLDS, FLU, MEASLES, POLIO.

- Microbes can ENTER THE BODY through NATURAL OPENINGS (eg. the nose or mouth) ...
  ... and through BREAKS IN THE SKIN (cuts, bites).
- If LARGE NUMBERS OF MICROBES enter the body due to UNHYGIENIC CONDITIONS ...
  ... or contact with INFECTED PEOPLE ...
  ... the MICROBES can REPRODUCE RAPIDLY and make the person unwell.

This may form the basis of a data handling question in your TERMINAL EXAMINATION.

Our Defence Against Microbes

1. The blood produces CLOTS that seal cuts.
2. The BREATHING ORGANS produce a STICKY, LIQUID MUCUS, which covers the lining of these organs and traps microbes.
3. The SKIN acts as a barrier to invading microbes.

4. The White Cells
- When a microbe invades the body and starts to multiply ...
- ... the body's WHITE CELLS multiply in response. (see next page).

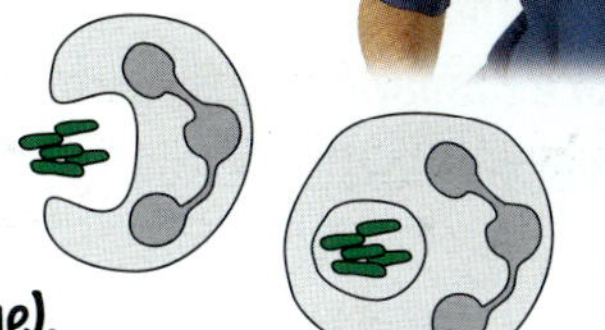

A white cell ingesting (eating) microbes.

THE WHITE CELLS AND IMMUNITY

The **WHITE BLOOD CELLS** form part of the body's **IMMUNE SYSTEM**.
White Blood Cells work by ...

1. **INGESTING MICROBES.**
2. **PRODUCING ANTITOXINS** to **NEUTRALISE TOXINS** produced by the microbes.
3. **PRODUCING ANTIBODIES** to **DESTROY PARTICULAR MICROBES.**

Ingesting Microbes

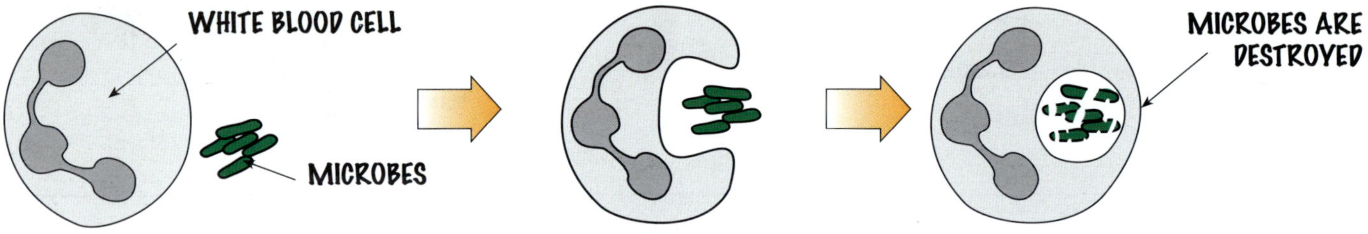

Microbes invade the body ...

... the white blood cell starts to surround the microbes.

The microbes are **INGESTED** by the white blood cell.

Producing Antitoxins

White Blood Cells produce **ANTITOXINS** which **NEUTRALISE HARMFUL TOXINS** (poisons) produced by microbes.

Producing Antibodies

- **WHITE BLOOD CELLS** recognise the microbes as **ANTIGENS** (foreign bodies) ...
  ... and produce **ANTIBODIES** to destroy the **ANTIGENS**. (Often by making them clump together!).
- The reason we feel **ILL** is because it takes **TIME** for the **WHITE BLOOD CELLS** to produce **ANTIBODIES** to the microbes.
- The **PRODUCTION OF ANTIBODIES** is much faster if a person has already had the infectious disease.
  The **WHITE BLOOD CELLS** seem to 'remember' the antigen and in the future can produce **ANTIBODIES** more rapidly providing the person with a **NATURAL IMMUNITY**.

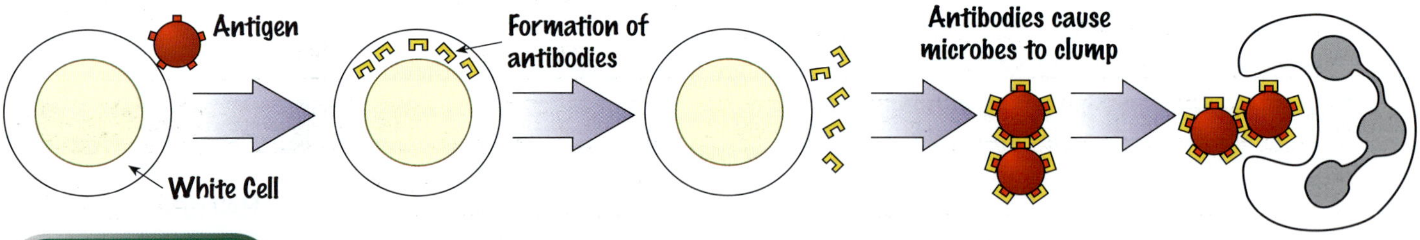

Vaccination

A person can acquire immunity to a particular disease by being vaccinated...

STEP 1: A **WEAKENED** or **DEAD ANTIGEN** is injected into a person.

STEP 2: The body **PRODUCES ANTIBODIES** to fight the antigen.

STEP 3: The body now has an acquired immunity to this particular antigen since the white blood cells are now sensitised to it and will therefore respond to any future infection by producing antibodies very quickly.

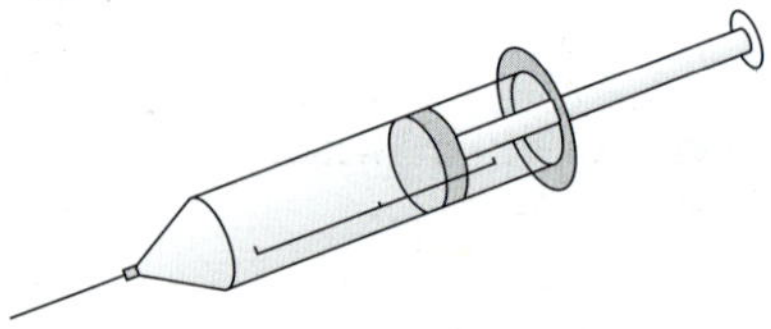

ANIMAL CELLS AND DIFFUSION

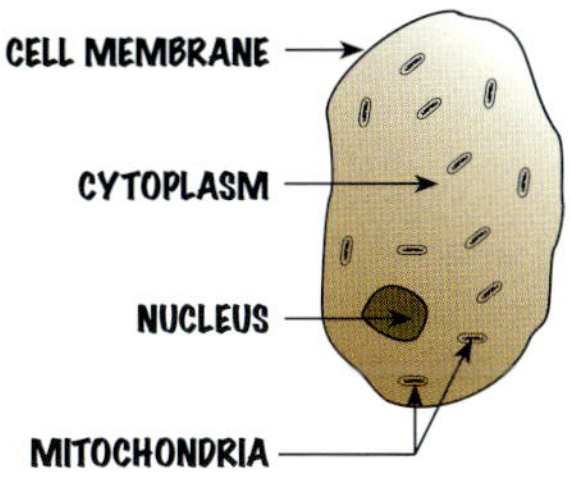

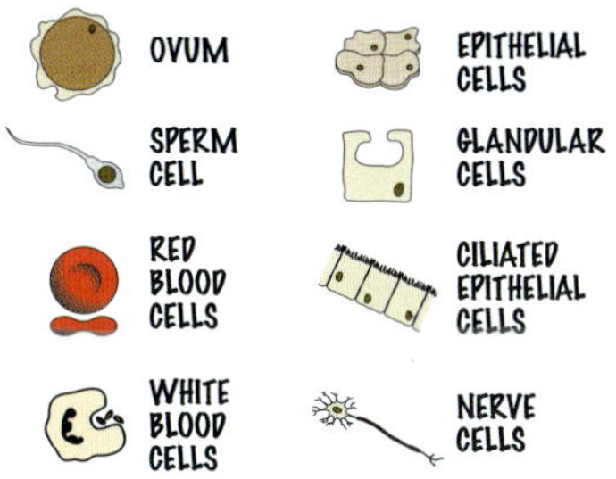

CELLS ⇨ TISSUES ⇨ ORGANS ⇨ ORGAN SYSTEMS ⇨ ORGANISM

'Diffusion is the net movement of a gas or substance in solution from a region of high concentration to a region of lower concentration'.
The greater the difference in concentration, the faster the rate of diffusion.

Examples in humans of specialised exchange surfaces which help to increase surface area ...

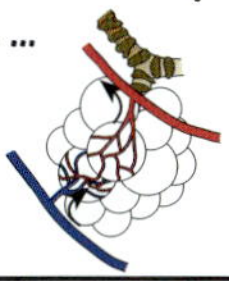
Alveoli in the lungs.

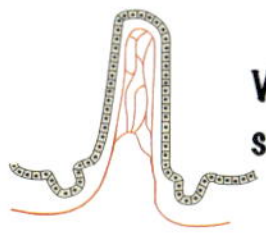
Villi in the small intestine.

DIGESTIVE SYSTEM, ENZYMES AND ABSORPTION

Enzymes break down large molecules into smaller soluble molecules.

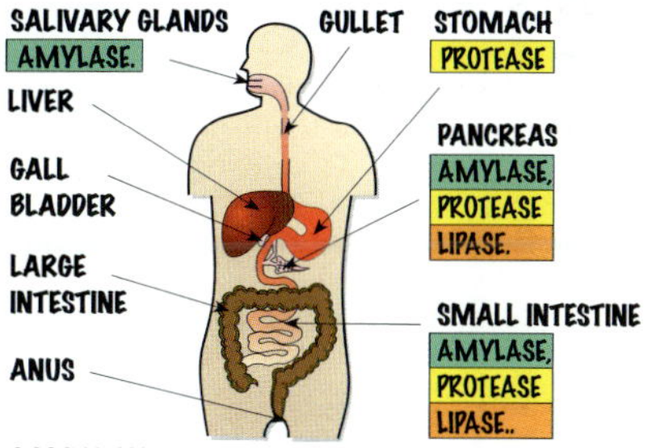

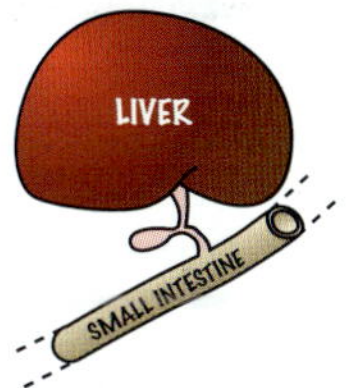

Bile produced in the liver, neutralises acid and emulsifies fats.

Organ	Enzyme	Substrate	Product
SALIVARY GLANDS	AMYLASE	CARBOHYDRATES	SUGARS
STOMACH	PROTEASE	PROTEINS	AMINO ACIDS
PANCREAS	AMYLASE	CARBOHYDRATES	SUGARS
	PROTEASE	PROTEINS	AMINO ACIDS
	LIPASE	LIPIDS	FATTY ACIDS + GLYCEROL
SMALL INTESTINE	AMYLASE	CARBOHYDRATES	SUGARS
	PROTEASE	PROTEINS	AMINO ACIDS
	LIPASE	LIPIDS	FATTY ACIDS + GLYCEROL

The products of digestion are absorbed into the bloodstream in the small intestine.

BREATHING SYSTEM AND GAS EXCHANGE

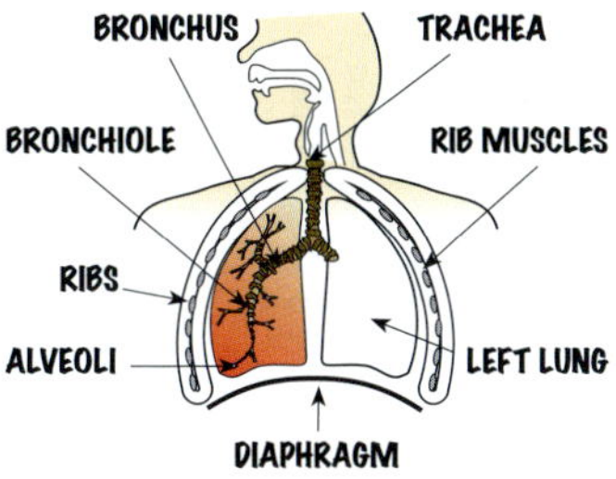

INHALING
Rib muscles and diaphragm contract causing an increase in the volume of the thorax. This causes a decrease in pressure inside the thorax and atmospheric air enters.

EXHALING
Rib muscles and diaphragm relax causing a decrease in the volume of the thorax. This causes an increase in pressure inside the thorax and air is forced out.

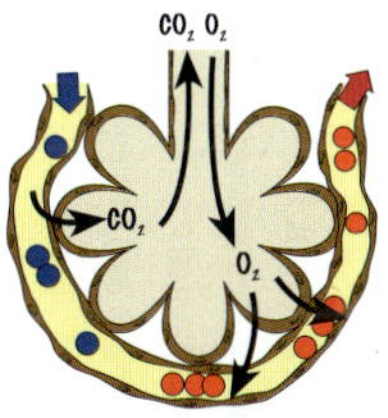

The lungs are an excellent exchange surface because they have ...

- A LARGE, MOIST SURFACE AREA.
- AN EXCELLENT BLOOD SUPPLY.

In the alveoli, CO_2 diffuses from the blood into the lungs and O_2 diffuses from the lungs into the blood. The blood becomes oxygenated.

AEROBIC AND ANAEROBIC RESPIRATION

AEROBIC RESPIRATION

GLUCOSE + OXYGEN ⟶ CARBON DIOXIDE + WATER + ENERGY

Occurs most of the time (in the mitochondria) and provides LOTS of energy efficiently, though slowly.

ANAEROBIC RESPIRATION

GLUCOSE ⟶ LACTIC ACID + A BIT OF ENERGY

Occurs when muscles are working very hard and can operate only for a short time due to build up of lactic acid as a waste product. This results in acute fatigue and 'oxygen debt' which must be repaid by continued deep breathing after exercise.

Not much energy but produced very quickly and therefore ideal in explosive activity.

- Cells use energy ...
  ... to build large MOLECULES
  ... for MUSCLE contraction
  ... to MAINTAIN temperature
  ... to move materials across MEMBRANES

'The 4M's'

THE CIRCULATORY SYSTEM

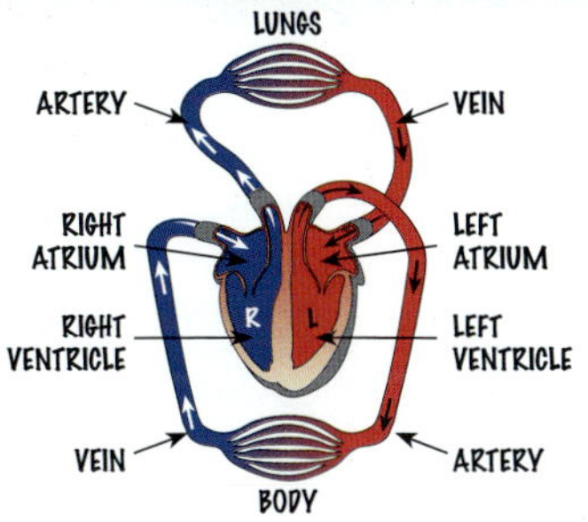

This is a 'double' circulatory system which has 2 loops.

- The Atria contract to squeeze blood into the ventricles ...
- ... which then contract to squeeze blood into the two main arteries.

ARTERIES
Thick wall, no valves, carry blood away from heart.

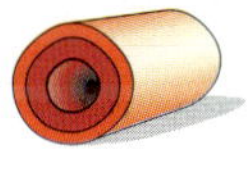

PLASMA
carries CO_2, glucose and waste.

WHITE CELLS
Defence system.

PLATELETS
Clotting mechanism.

RED CELLS
Haemoglobin carries oxygen, no nucleus.

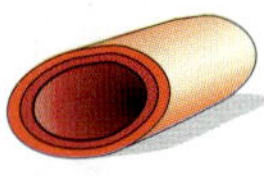

VEINS
Thinner walls, valves, carry blood back to heart.

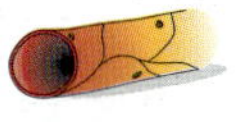

CAPILLARIES
One cell thick so exchange can occur.

DISEASE AND THE WHITE CELLS

Clotting, mucus, skin and white cells are our basic defence against microbes.

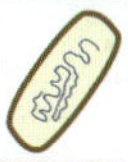
BACTERIUM

VIRUS

BACTERIA	VIRUSES
Consist of CYTOPLASM and a MEMBRANE surrounded by a CELL WALL.	Have a simple PROTEIN COAT. No membrane or cell wall.
The genetic material is NOT contained within a NUCLEUS.	The genetic material is NOT contained within a NUCLEUS.
Very small.	Even smaller.
Reproduce very quickly.	Reproduce very quickly - BUT ONLY INSIDE LIVING CELLS, WHICH ARE THEN DAMAGED.
Can produce TOXINS (poisons) which make us feel ill.	Can produce TOXINS (poisons) which make us feel ill.
Responsible for diseases such as TETANUS, CHOLERA, TUBERCULOSIS.	Responsible for diseases such as COLDS, FLU, MEASLES, POLIO.

WHITE CELLS can ...
INGEST microbes,
produce ANTITOXINS,
produce ANTIBODIES!

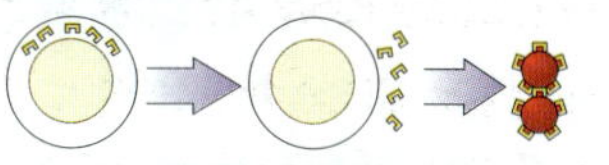
ANTIBODY PRODUCTION

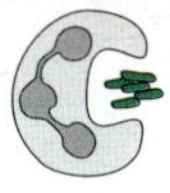
INGESTION

After being exposed to certain microbes, our bodies can produce antibodies quicker next time. We have developed NATURAL IMMUNITY. ACQUIRED IMMUNITY can be developed by being injected with a dead or weakened version of the microbe.

1. The table below is about the digestive system. Match words from the list with each of the numbers 1-4 in the table.
   A. LARGE INTESTINE.
   B. SMALL INTESTINE.
   C. MOUTH.
   D. STOMACH.

1.	Produces only one enzyme, amylase.
2.	Produces only one enzyme, protease.
3.	Produces no enzymes but reabsorbs excess water.
4.	Produces three enzymes, amylase, protease and lipase.

2. These sentences are about the functions of parts of the blood. Match words from the list with each of the spaces 1-4 in the sentences.
   A. PLATELETS.
   B. WHITE CELLS.
   C. RED CELLS.
   D. PLASMA.

   The watery substance which contains the other blood components is called the ____1____. The component which forms part of the body's defence mechanism are the ____2____, whereas the ____3____ transport oxygen from the lungs to the rest of the body. The ____4____ form part of the clotting mechanism of the blood.

3. Mitochondria are found in most animal cells. Which TWO of the following statements are correct about mitochondria?
   A. Anaerobic respiration takes place in them.
   B. They absorb carbon dioxide and water in order to provide energy.
   C. Aerobic respiration takes place in them.
   D. They produce lactic acid when respiration takes place in them.
   E. They absorb glucose and oxygen in order to provide energy.

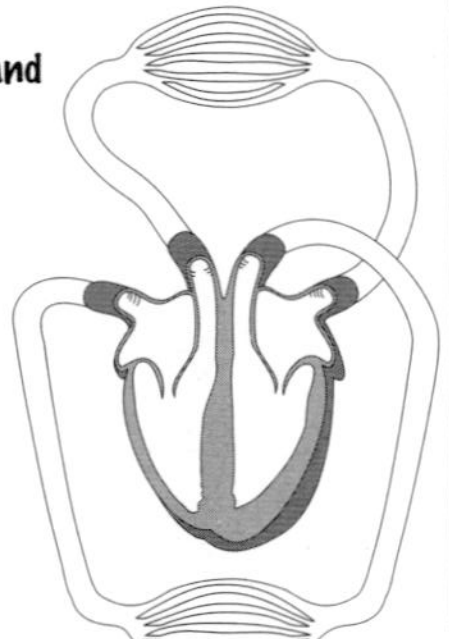

4. Blood is pumped through the blood vessels by the heart. This is our transport system.

4.1 Which of the following substances is NOT transported by the blood?
   A. HORMONES.
   B. OXYGEN.
   C. URINE.
   D. HEAT.

4.2 Veins ...
   A. Have thick muscular walls which contain elastic fibres.
   B. Only carry oxygenated blood.
   C. Carry blood away from the heart.
   D. Contain valves to prevent backflow.

4.3 The left ventricle is ...
   A. A small chamber carrying oxygenated blood.
   B. A small chamber carrying deoxygenated blood.
   C. A large chamber carrying oxygenated blood.
   D. A large chamber carrying deoxygenated blood.

4.4 The correct pathway of the circulation is ...
   A. Heart ⟶ Capillaries ⟶ Veins ⟶ Arteries.
   B. Heart ⟶ Arteries ⟶ Capillaries ⟶ Veins.
   C. Heart ⟶ Veins ⟶ Capillaries ⟶ Arteries.
   D. Heart ⟶ Arteries ⟶ Veins ⟶ Capillaries.

5. The lungs are designed to enable gases to be efficiently exchanged.

5.1 The smaller branches of the bronchi are called ...
   A. The ALVEOLI.
   B. The TRACHEA.
   C. The BRONCHIOLES.
   D. The AIR PIPES.

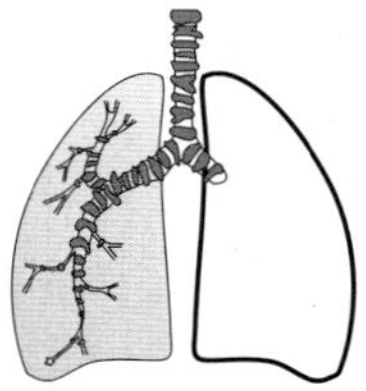

5.2 The gases exchanged in the lungs are ...
   A. Carbon dioxide and nitrogen.
   B. Carbon dioxide and water vapour.
   C. Carbon dioxide and oxygen.
   D. Carbon dioxide, oxygen and nitrogen.

5.3 To exhale (breathe out) ...
   A. The intercostals contract and the diaphragm contracts.
   B. The intercostals relax and the diaphragm contracts.
   C. The intercostals relax and the diaphragm relaxes.
   D. The intercostals contract and the diaphragm relaxes.

5.4 Which of the following is NOT a key feature of a good gas exchange surface?
   A. MOIST LINING.
   B. HUGE SURFACE AREA.
   C. EXCELLENT BLOOD SUPPLY.
   D. THICK CELL WALLS.

6. Respiration is the process by which cells release energy. It can occur aerobically or anaerobically.

6.1 Aerobic respiration produces ...
   A. Carbon dioxide, water and energy.
   B. Carbon dioxide, glucose and energy.
   C. Carbon dioxide, oxygen and energy.
   D. Carbon dioxide, oxygen and glucose.

6.2 The waste product produced during anaerobic respiration is ...
   A. CARBON DIOXIDE.
   B. UREA.
   C. LACTIC ACID.
   D. GLUCOSE.

6.3 Oxygen debt is caused by ...
   A. Too slow a breathing rate.
   B. Accumulation of lactic acid in the tissues.
   C. Accumulation of carbon dioxide in the blood.
   D. Accumulation of lactic acid in the liver.

6.4 The energy released in respiration comes originally from ...
   A. The sun's energy trapped inside glucose molecules.
   B. The molecules of oxygen which combine with glucose.
   C. Oxygen alone.
   D. The blood.

7. The body needs to be able to defend itself against disease in order to remain healthy.

7.1 Which of the following is NOT true of bacteria?
   A. They have cytoplasm.
   B. They have a cell wall.
   C. Can only reproduce inside living cells.
   D. They have no distinct nucleus.

7.2 Which of the following is NOT true of viruses?
   A. Consist of a protein coat surrounding a few genes.
   B. Can only reproduce inside living cells.
   C. They are bigger than bacteria.
   D. They may produce toxins (poisons).

7.3 Which of the following is NOT an effective defence against invading microbes?
   A. The blood clotting mechanism.
   B. Sweat glands.
   C. Mucus along the lining of the respiratory system.
   D. Unbroken skin.

7.4 Which of the following does NOT form part of the white cells' defence against microbes?
   A. Ingestion (eating) of microbes.
   B. Production of antibodies.
   C. Clotting of the blood.
   D. Production of antitoxins.

Plant Cell Structure

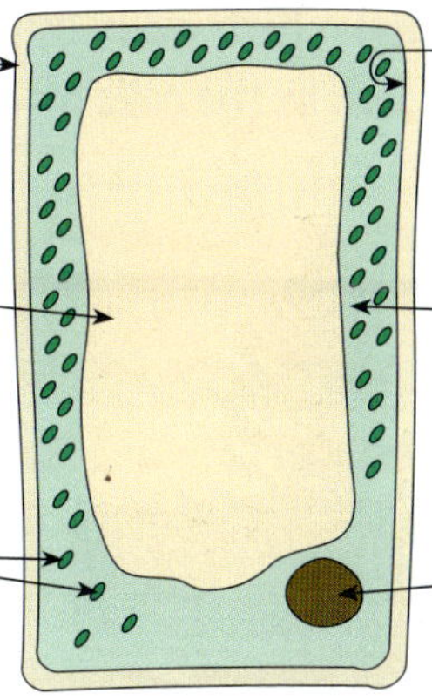

CELL WALL
Made of cellulose, this strengthens the cell.

PERMANENT VACUOLE
Filled with cell sap, it helps to support the cell.

CHLOROPLASTS
Contain chlorophyll which absorbs light energy to make food.

CELL MEMBRANE
Controls movement into and out of the cell.

CYTOPLASM
Most chemical reactions take place here.

NUCLEUS
Controls what the cell does and contains the genetic information.

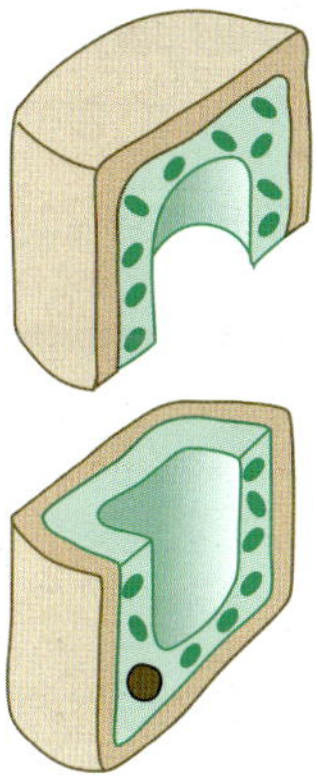

Most cells are made up mainly of water containing dissolved substances in which chemical reactions are constantly occurring. These reactions are controlled by ENZYMES.

Comparing Plant And Animal Cells

PLANT CELLS	FEATURE	ANIMAL CELLS
YES	NUCLEUS	YES
YES	CYTOPLASM	YES
YES	CELL MEMBRANE	YES
YES	CELL WALL	NO
ALMOST ALWAYS	VACUOLE	NO
THOSE WHICH ARE EXPOSED TO LIGHT	CHLOROPLASTS	NO
YES	MITOCHONDRIA	YES

Types Of Plant Cell

Some plant cells are highly SPECIALISED to do a particular job ...

ROOT HAIR CELL
Thin hair-like projections give a big surface area for efficient absorption of water and minerals.

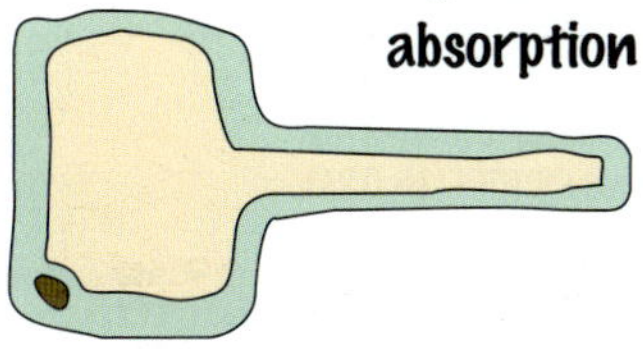

GUARD CELLS
Specialised for regulating water loss from the leaf by opening or closing.

PALISADE CELL
Column-shaped cells on upper surface of leaf. Packed with chloroplasts for photosynthesis.

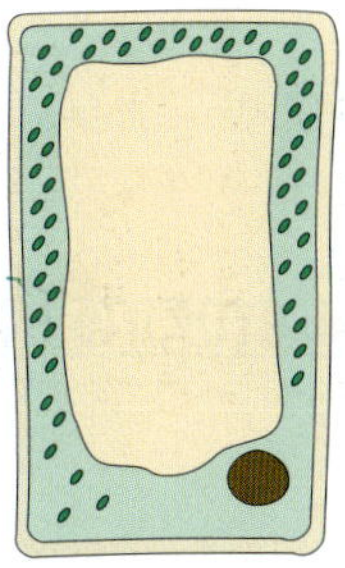

XYLEM
Long cylinder-like cells for transporting water through the stem and root.

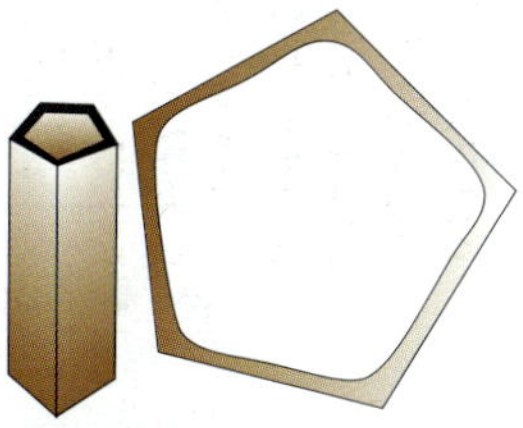

Making Food Using Energy From The Sun

Green plants don't absorb food from the soil. They make their own, using sunlight. This is called PHOTOSYNTHESIS, which actually means 'making through light'. It occurs in the cells of green plants, which are exposed to light.

FOUR THINGS ARE NEEDED ... ... AND TWO THINGS ARE PRODUCED ...

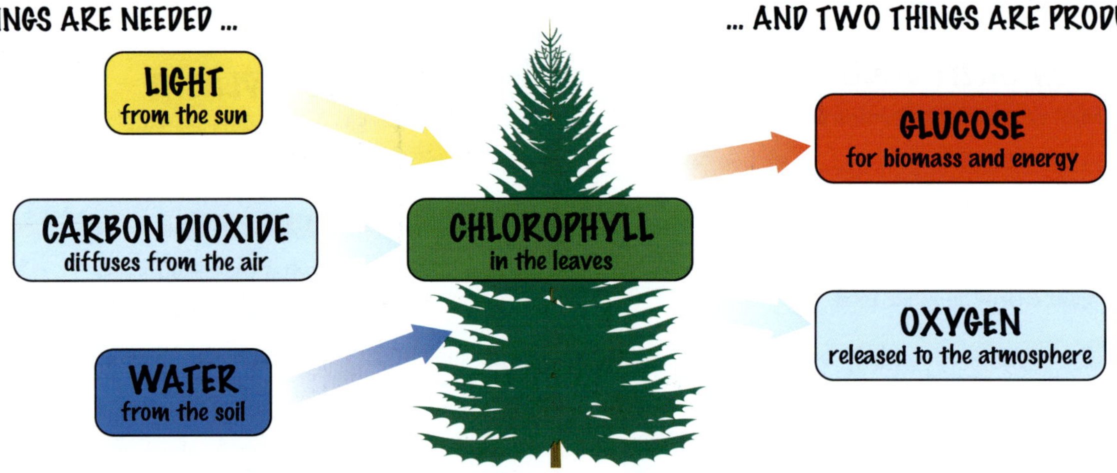

The Word Equation For Photosynthesis

CARBON DIOXIDE + WATER —(LIGHT / CHLOROPHYLL)→ GLUCOSE + OXYGEN

The glucose produced in photosynthesis can be used immediately by the plant to provide energy via RESPIRATION.

Energy Use In Plants

Some of this energy is used to build up SMALLER MOLECULES INTO LARGER MOLECULES.

1. CONVERSION OF SUGARS INTO STARCH. The plant does this because starch is an insoluble carbohydrate and therefore can be stored in cells without causing large amounts of water to accumulate as a result of OSMOSIS.

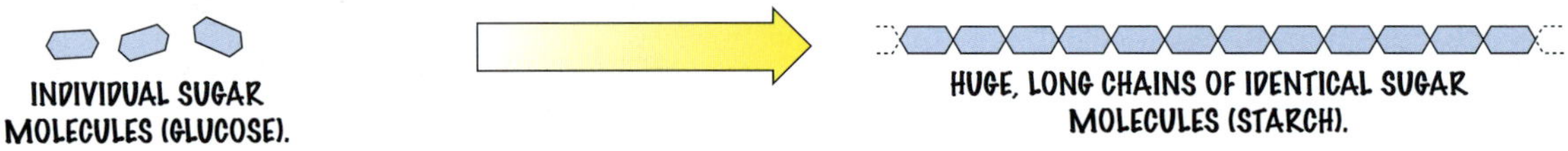

2. CONVERSION OF SUGARS INTO CELLULOSE. Cellulose is needed by the plant for cell walls. It is very similar to the structure of starch, but the long chains are cross-linked to form a meshwork. (You don't need to know the structure for your exam).

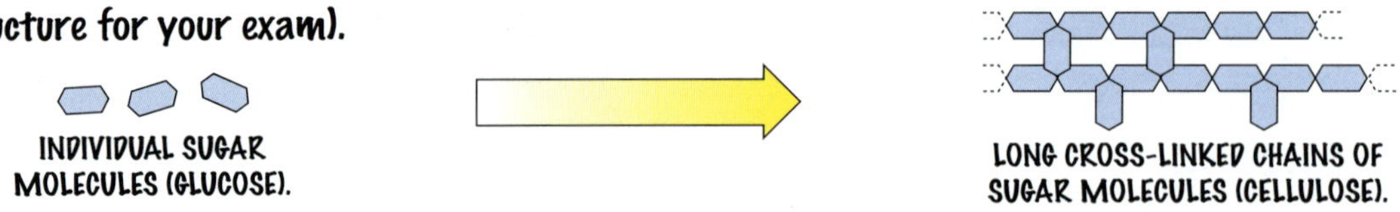

3. CONVERSION OF SUGARS, NITRATES AND OTHER NUTRIENTS INTO PROTEINS. The plant needs protein for growth and also to make enzymes.

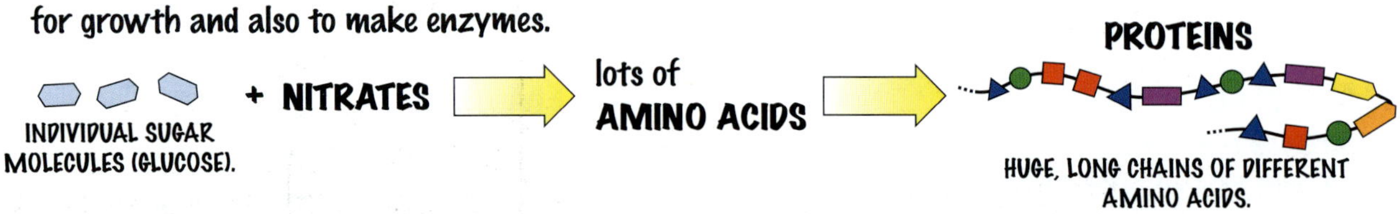

4. CONVERSION OF SUGARS INTO LIPIDS (FATS OR OILS) FOR STORING IN SEEDS.

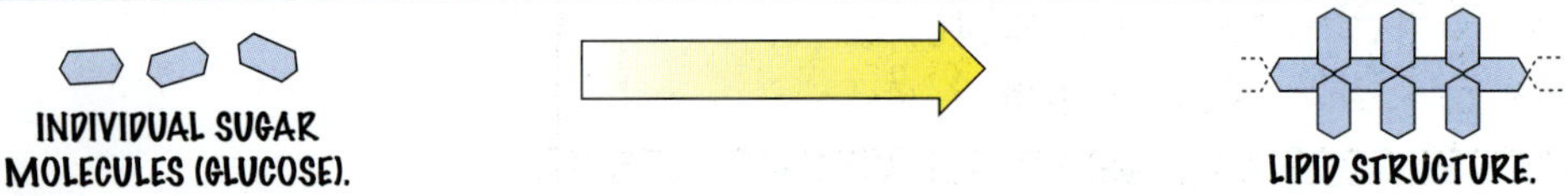

Factors Affecting Photosynthesis

In practice, TEMPERATURE, CARBON DIOXIDE CONCENTRATION and LIGHT INTENSITY can interact to limit the rate of photosynthesis. Any one of them, at a particular time, may be the limiting factor.

EFFECT OF TEMPERATURE

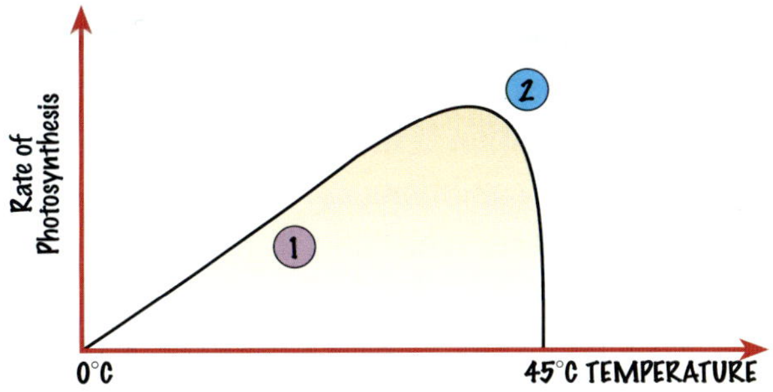

1. As the temperature rises so does the rate of photosynthesis. This means temperature is limiting the rate of photosynthesis.
2. As the temperature approaches 45°C the enzymes controlling photosynthesis start to be destroyed and the rate of photosynthesis eventually declines to zero.

EFFECT OF CARBON DIOXIDE CONCENTRATION

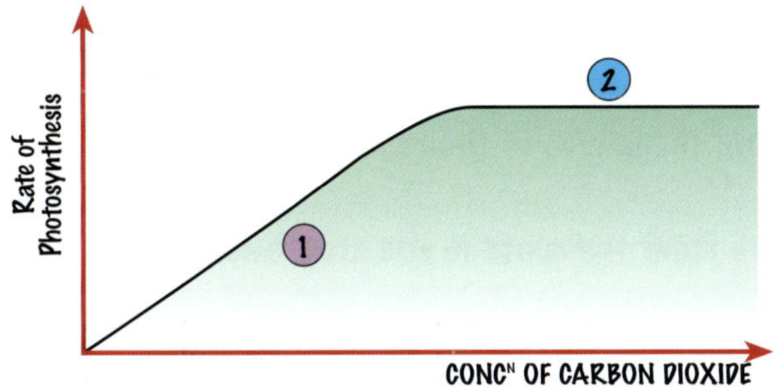

1. As the carbon dioxide concentration rises so does the rate of photosynthesis. This means carbon dioxide is limiting the rate of photosynthesis.
2. Rise in carbon dioxide now has no effect. Carbon dioxide is no longer the limiting factor. This means SUNLIGHT or TEMPERATURE must be the limiting factor.

EFFECT OF LIGHT INTENSITY

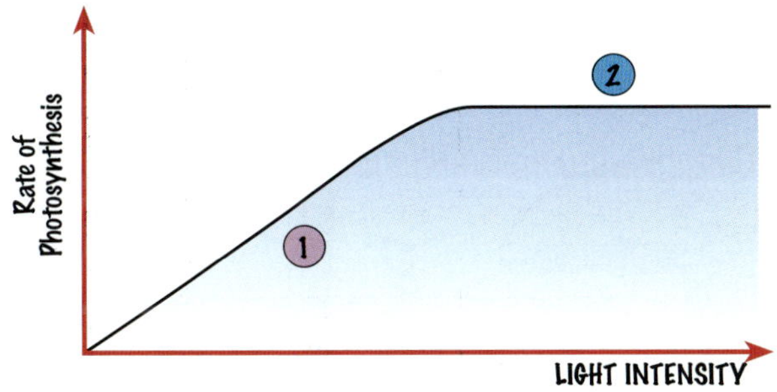

1. As the light intensity increases so does the rate of photosynthesis. This means light intensity is limiting the rate of photosynthesis.
2. Rise in light intensity now has no effect. Light intensity is no longer the limiting factor.
   This means CARBON DIOXIDE or TEMPERATURE must be the limiting factor.

Plant Mineral Requirements

For healthy growth plants need mineral ions which they absorb through their roots ...
... particularly • NITRATES • POTASSIUM and • PHOSPHATES .

NITRATES

- Needed to make proteins ...
- ... if there's a shortage, it leads to ...
- ... STUNTED GROWTH and YELLOW OLDER LEAVES.

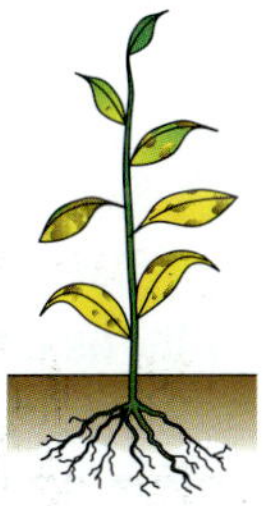

POTASSIUM

- Needed to help ENZYMES involved in photosynthesis and respiration ...
- ... if there's a shortage, it leads to ...
- ... YELLOW LEAVES WITH DEAD SPOTS.

PHOSPHATES

- Needed in photosynthesis and respiration ...
- ... if there's a shortage, it leads to ...
- ... POOR ROOT GROWTH and PURPLE YOUNGER LEAVES.

TRANSPIRATION

The Leaf

Leaves are BROAD, THIN and FLAT with lots of INTERNAL AIR SPACES in order to make them efficient at photosynthesis by providing a large surface area. They also have STOMATA on their undersurface to allow CARBON DIOXIDE in and OXYGEN out. This however leads to loss of water vapour in a process called TRANSPIRATION.

THIS IS A CROSS-SECTION OF A LEAF.

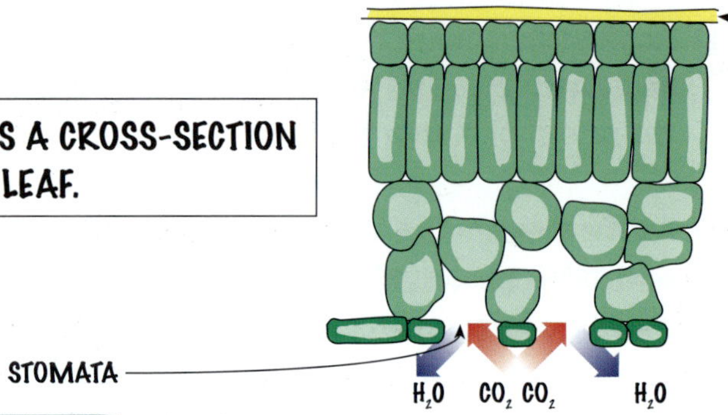

- This WAXY LAYER stops too much water from just evaporating away from the leaf.
- Transpiration is more rapid in HOT, DRY or WINDY conditions, ...
  ... so plants which live in these conditions have a THICKER LAYER OF WAX.
- Water lost by transpiration must be replaced by water from the soil.

The Stem

Flowering plants have separate transport systems for water and nutrients...

- **PHLOEM TISSUE** ... transports nutrients, such as sugars, from the leaves to the rest of the plant, including the storage organs and growing regions.
- **XYLEM TISSUE** ... transports water and soluble mineral salts from the roots to the stem and leaves, to replace the water lost in transpiration and photosynthesis.

1. Water EVAPORATES from the internal leaf cells through the STOMATA.
2. Water passes from the XYLEM vessels to leaf cells due to OSMOSIS ...
3. ... which 'pulls' the entire 'thread' of water in that vessel upwards by a very small amount.
4. Water enters XYLEM from root tissue to replace water which has moved upwards.
5. Water enters ROOT HAIR CELLS by OSMOSIS to replace water which has entered the XYLEM.

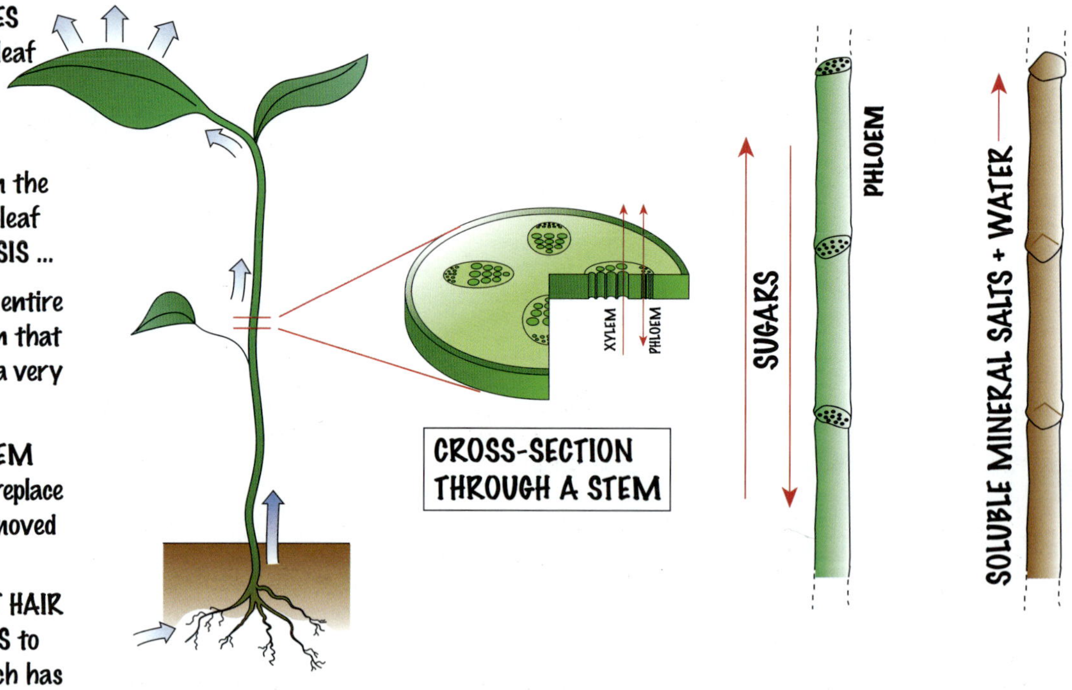

The transpiration stream is powered by evaporation of water from the leaf.

The Root

WATER enters the plant via the roots.

Most of it is absorbed by the ROOT HAIR CELLS by osmosis. This water passes into the xylem vessels to replace water which is continually moving up the stem.

The surface area of the roots is increased by the presence of root hairs. This increases the rate at which they can absorb water and minerals and is another typical example of how exchange surfaces are adapted to their function.

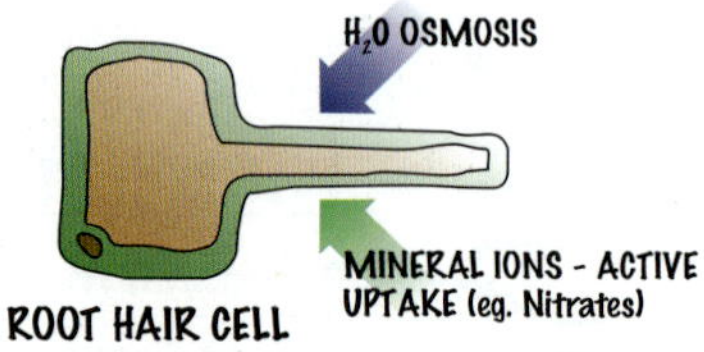

Osmosis

OSMOSIS is ... the **DIFFUSION OF WATER** ...

... from a **DILUTE SOLUTION** ...

... to a **MORE CONCENTRATED SOLUTION** ...

... through a **PARTIALLY PERMEABLE MEMBRANE** that ...

... **ALLOWS THE PASSAGE OF WATER MOLECULES BUT NOT SOLUTE MOLECULES.**

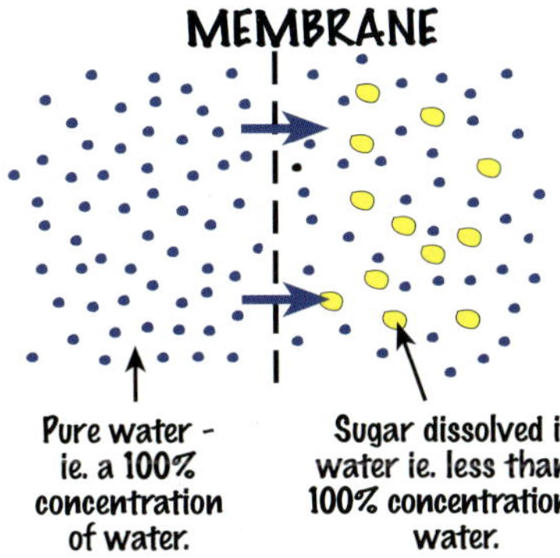

HIGH CONC^N OF WATER → LOW CONC^N OF WATER

- In other words water diffuses from where it's in a HIGH CONCENTRATION to where it's in a LOW CONCENTRATION.
- The only thing that matters is the CONCENTRATION of the water. The solute molecules (eg. sugar) can't pass through the membrane.
- The effect of all this is to gradually dilute the sugar solution.

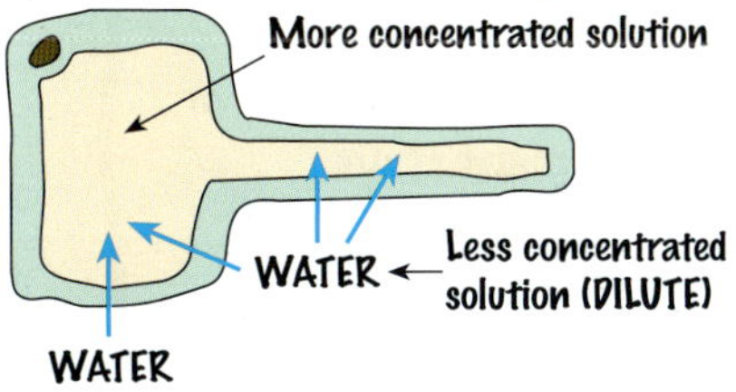

This is what happens at root hair cells, where water moves from the soil into the cell by OSMOSIS, along a CONCENTRATION GRADIENT.

Demonstrating Osmosis

CLASSIC EXPERIMENT No.1

Placed in pure water ⇐ dialysis tubing containing sugar solution ⇒ Placed in CONC^N sugar solution

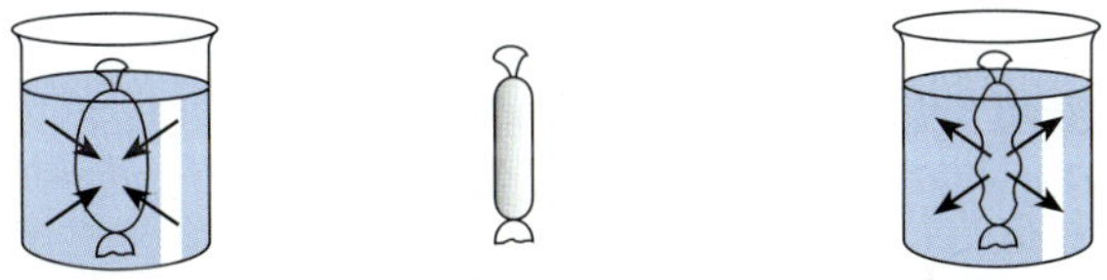

Water enters by OSMOSIS ∴ swells up

Water leaves by OSMOSIS ∴ shrivels up

CLASSIC EXPERIMENT No.2

Placed in pure water ⇐ weighed potato chip ⇒ Placed in CONC^N sugar solution

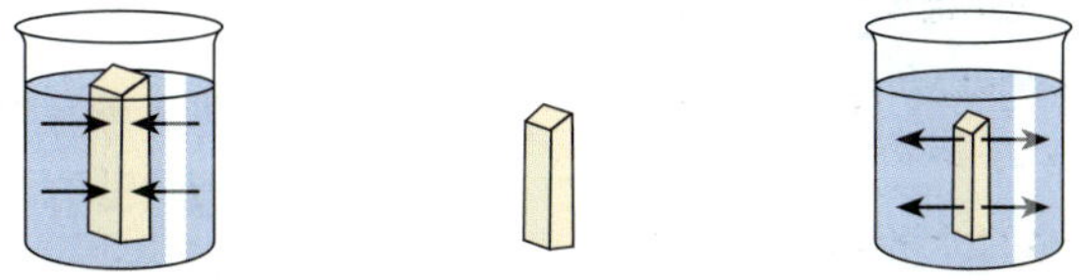

Water enters by OSMOSIS ∴ weighs more after removal

Water leaves by OSMOSIS ∴ weighs less after removal

In each case, water moves from where it's in HIGH CONCENTRATION, to where it's in LOW CONCENTRATION along a CONCENTRATION GRADIENT (a bit like a ball rolling from a high position to a low position).

Active Transport

- Substances are sometimes absorbed AGAINST A CONCENTRATION GRADIENT.
- Plants absorb ions from very dilute solutions in this way ie. ACTIVELY (see diagram below).
- This takes place in the opposite direction to which normal diffusion would occur.
- This process of ACTIVE TRANSPORT requires the use of ENERGY FROM RESPIRATION ... ... just in the same way that pushing a ball up a hill would take energy.

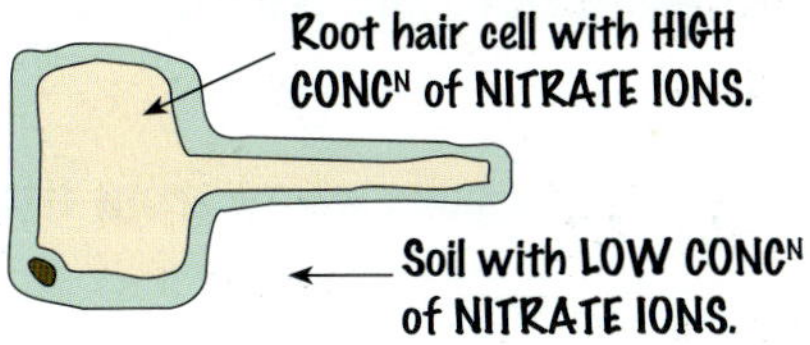

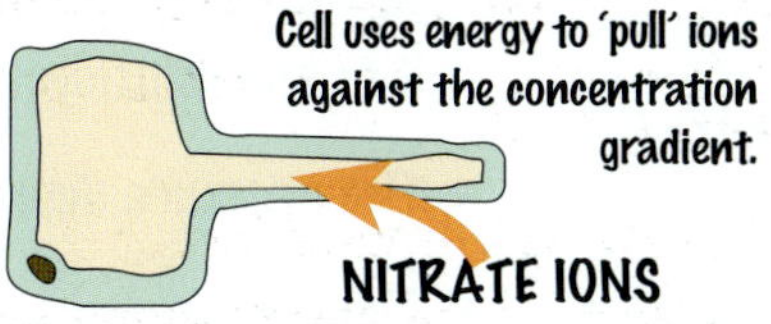

In humans sugar may be absorbed from the intestine and from the kidney tubules by ACTIVE TRANSPORT.

Controlling Water Loss

Plants have STOMATA (small pores) through which carbon dioxide diffuses in order for the plant to photosynthesise. Water is also lost by evaporation through these openings. Guard cells control the size of the stomata, and if plants lose water faster than it is replaced by the roots, then the stomata close to prevent wilting and eventual dehydration.

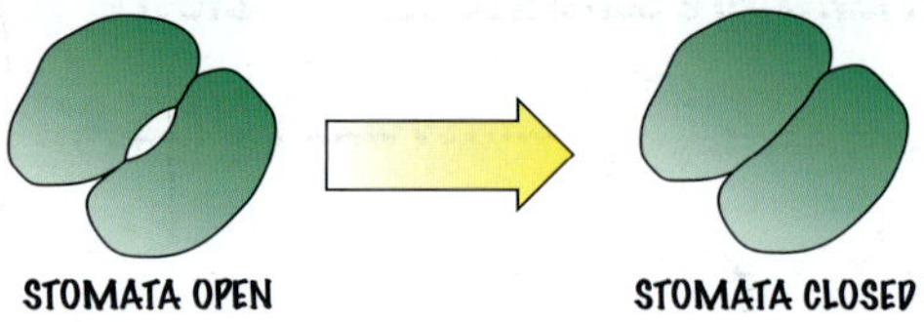

Maintaining Support

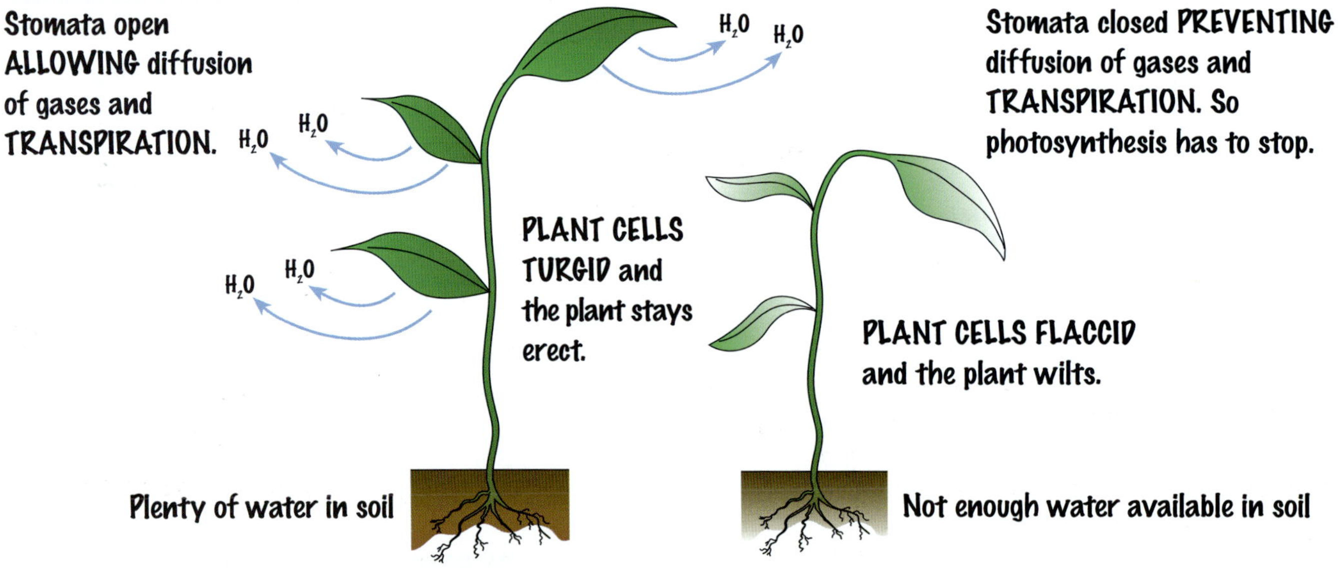

When the plant has plenty of water, the cell contents 'swell up' and press against the cell wall. This increases the rigidity of the plant tissue and provides the main method of support in young, non-woody stems.

Turgor Pressure

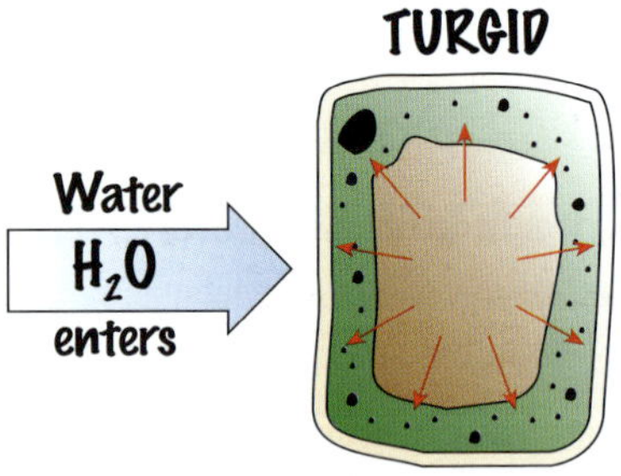

- If a cell is in a less concentrated solution, water passes in by OSMOSIS.
- Water flows through the cell wall and cell membrane into the cytoplasm and into the vacuole.
- The increased pressure of water in the vacuole presses the cytoplasm against the cell wall, which fortunately is strong enough to withstand it.
- When the cell can take no more water we say it is fully TURGID. It is this turgor pressure which keeps the cells rigid and therefore provides support for the plant (a bit like a balloon inside a shoe box).
- This is particularly important for the support of young stems.

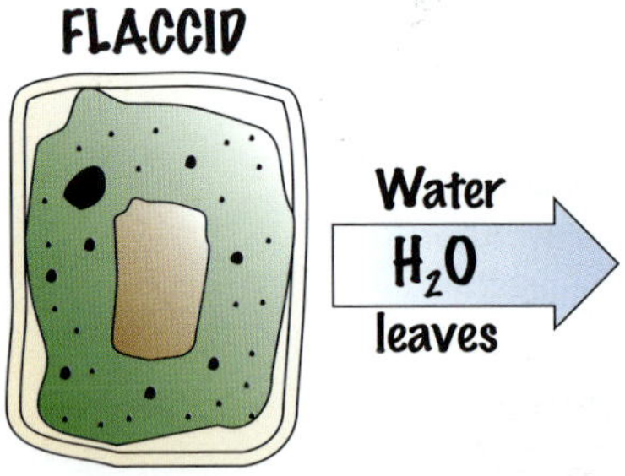

- If a cell is in a more concentrated solution, then water passes out of the cytoplasm through the cell membrane and cell wall and into the solution outside the cell.
- The pressure decreases and the cytoplasm pulls away from the cell wall.
- The cell becomes FLACCID.

PLANT HORMONES

Plant Responses

Plants are sensitive to: • **LIGHT** • **MOISTURE** • **GRAVITY**

- SHOOTS grow TOWARDS LIGHT and AGAINST THE FORCE OF GRAVITY.
- ROOTS grow TOWARDS MOISTURE and in the DIRECTION OF GRAVITY.

These responses are controlled by HORMONES which coordinate and control growth.

Hormones are produced in the growing tips of shoots and roots but can then collect unevenly ...
... causing unequal growth rates in different parts of the plant.

Gravity

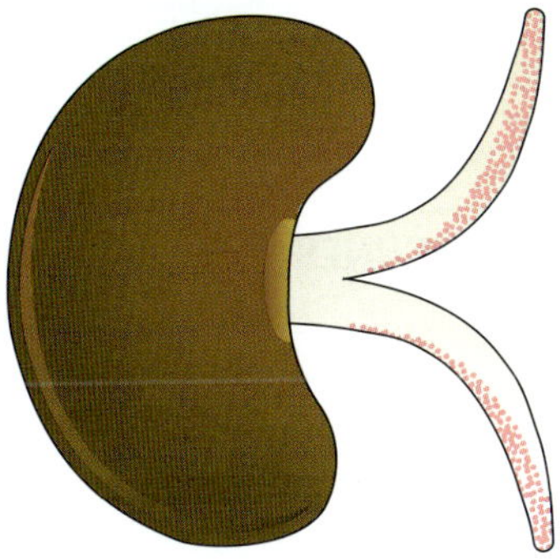

GERMINATING SEEDLING

In the Shoot ...

- ... hormone collects on the lower side ...
- ... and stimulates the growth of the cells on this side.
- Therefore the shoot grows upwards ...
- ... away from the force of gravity.

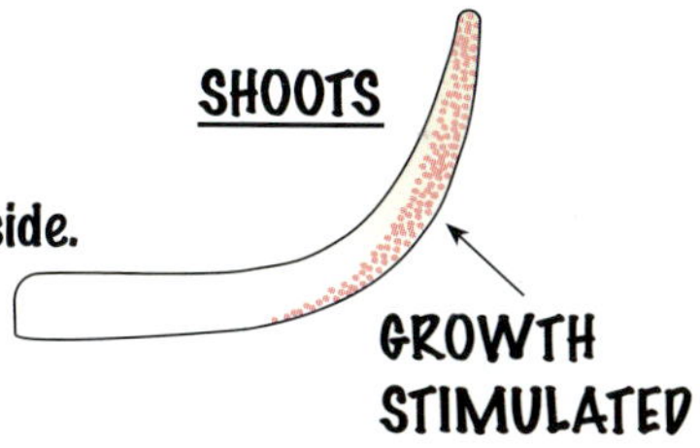

In the Root ...

- ... hormone also collects on the lower side ...
- ... but slows down the growth of the cells on this side.
- Therefore the root grows downwards ...
- ... towards the force of gravity.

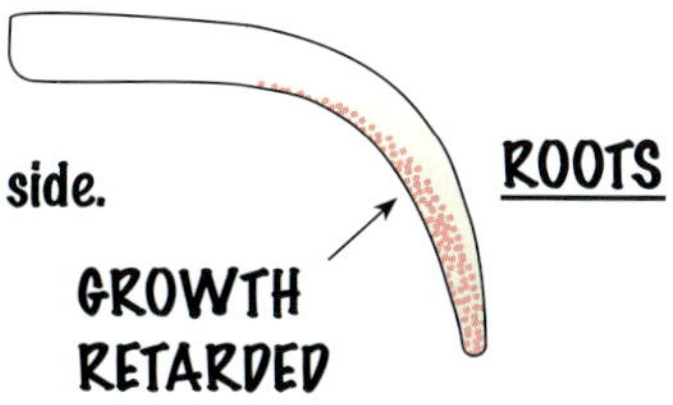

The key thing to remember here is that the hormone produced in the growing tips has the OPPOSITE EFFECT in roots and shoots.

- The hormone STIMULATES cell growth in SHOOTS, and ...
- ... RETARDS cell growth in ROOTS.

Light

- In shoots, LIGHT causes HORMONES ...
  - ... to accumulate on the shaded part of the stem ...
    - ... which causes growth on that side ...
      - ... and the plant grows towards the sun.

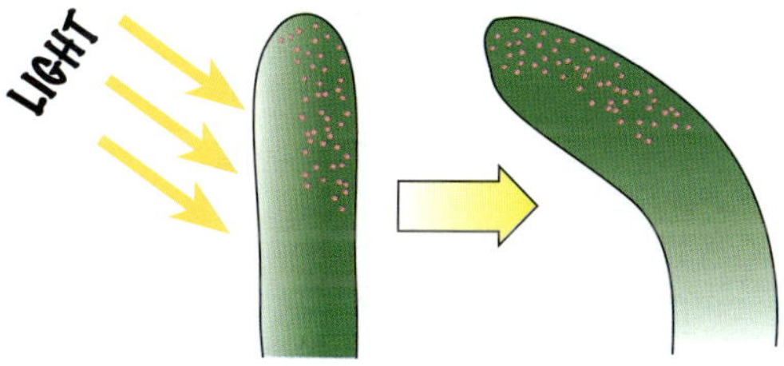

Artificial Use Of Hormones

Farmers do this to increase their yield and to organise ripening times to suit their own convenience.
It's quite unnatural really isn't it?

- ROOTING COMPOUND - Consists of a hormone which encourages ...
  ... the GROWTH OF ROOTS ...
  ... in STEM CUTTINGS ...
  ... so lots of plants can be obtained from only one.

- RIPENING HORMONE - Causes plants to ripen at set time ...
  ... sometimes during transport.
  Achieved by spraying.

- SELECTIVE WEEDKILLERS - Disrupt the normal growth patterns ...
  ... of their target plants ...
  ... leaving other plants untouched.

Components Of The Nervous System

- The nervous system consists of the BRAIN, the SPINAL CORD, the SPINAL NERVES and RECEPTORS.
- It allows organisms to REACT TO THEIR SURROUNDINGS and ...
  ... to COORDINATE THEIR BEHAVIOUR.
- The FIVE SENSES, namely SEEING, HEARING, TASTING, SMELLING and TOUCHING play a very important part in these processes, in which information from receptors passes along neurones to the brain which coordinates the response.

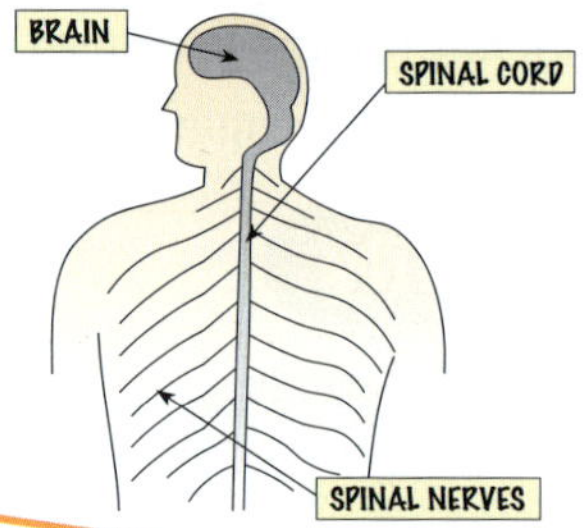

NERVOUS SYSTEM

BRAIN | SPINAL CORD | RELAY NEURONES | SENSORY NEURONES | MOTOR NEURONES | RECEPTORS

BRAIN, SPINAL CORD, RELAY NEURONES: The Central Nervous System (C.N.S)

SENSORY NEURONES, MOTOR NEURONES: These make up the spinal nerves.

RECEPTORS: Respond to stimuli.

The Three Types Of Nerve Cell (Neurone)

1 MOTOR NEURONE

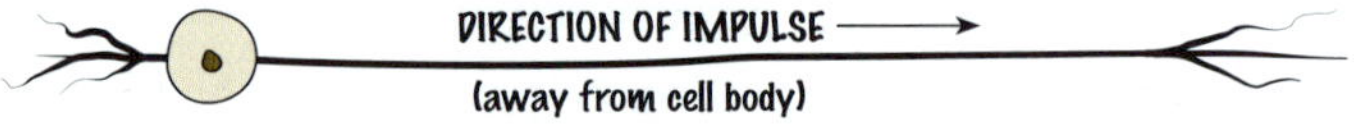

2 SENSORY NEURONE

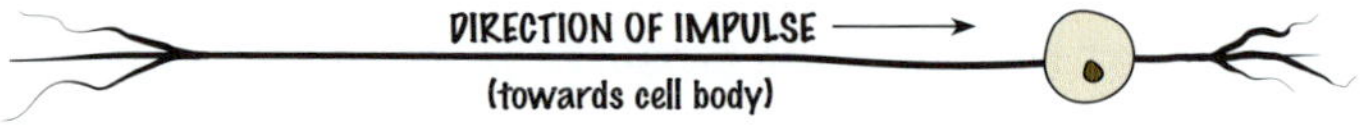

3 RELAY NEURONE

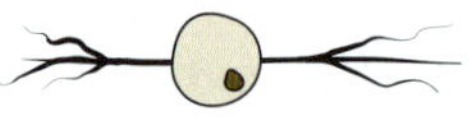

NEURONES are SPECIALLY ADAPTED CELLS that can carry an ELECTRICAL SIGNAL. eg. a NERVE IMPULSE.

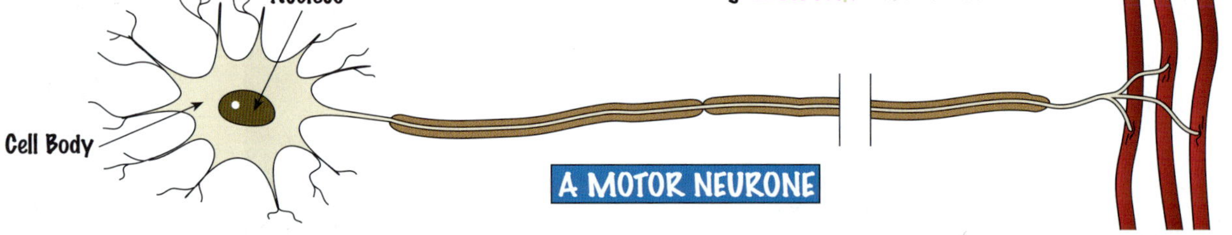

They are ELONGATED (long) to MAKE CONNECTIONS from one part of the body to another.
They have BRANCHED ENDINGS which allow a SINGLE NEURONE to act on MANY MUSCLE FIBRES.
The cell body has many connections to allow communication with other neurones.

Connections Between Neurones

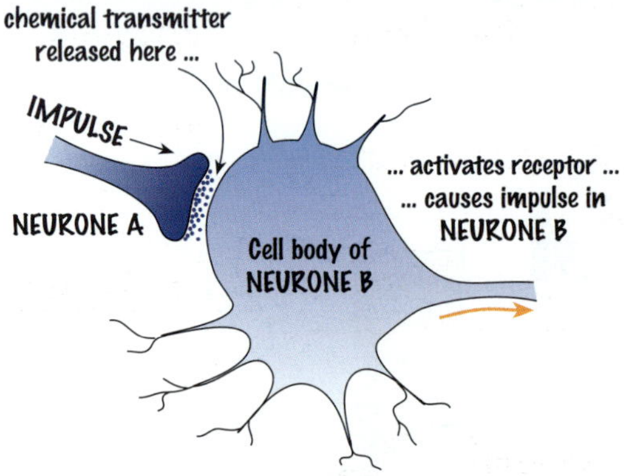

- Neurones do NOT TOUCH EACH OTHER ...
- ... there is a very small gap between them ...
- ... called a SYNAPSE.
- When an electrical impulse reaches this gap via neurone A, a CHEMICAL TRANSMITTER ...
- ... is released and activates receptors on NEURONE B ...
- ... which causes an electrical IMPULSE to be generated in NEURONE B.
- The CHEMICAL TRANSMITTER is then IMMEDIATELY DESTROYED.

RESPONSE TO STIMULI

Types Of Receptor

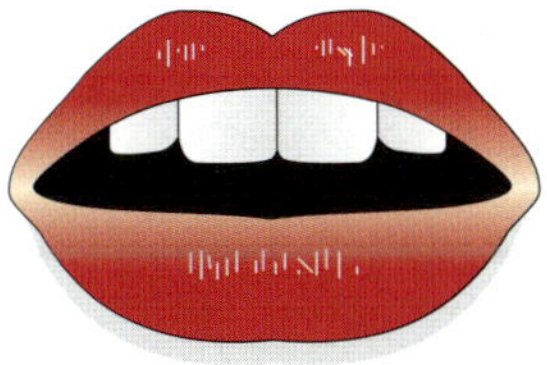

- LIGHT RECEPTORS IN THE EYES.
- SOUND RECEPTORS IN THE EARS.
- CHANGES OF POSITION RECEPTORS IN THE EARS (for balance).
- TASTE RECEPTORS ON THE TONGUE.
- SMELL RECEPTORS IN THE NOSE.
- TOUCH, PRESSURE AND TEMPERATURE RECEPTORS IN THE SKIN.

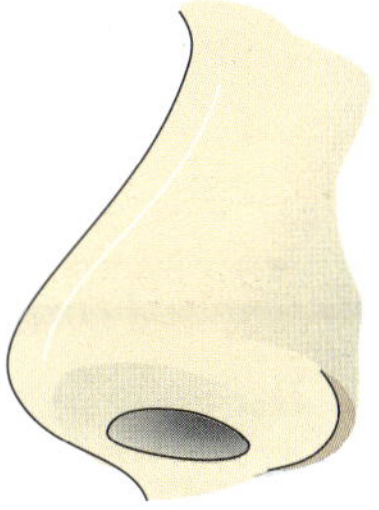

The pathway for receiving information and then acting upon it is:

STIMULUS → RECEPTOR → COORDINATOR (ANALYSER) → EFFECTOR → RESPONSE

The coordinator is the central nervous system, to which impulses are transmitted via the spinal nerves.

Examples Of Responses To Stimuli

STIMULUS - Change in the environment	RECEPTORS - Detect stimuli				EFFECTORS - Muscles or glands	RESPONSE Action taken
BRIGHT LIGHT	Light sensitive receptors in the eye	SENSORY NEURONE	CENTRAL NERVOUS SYSTEM	MOTOR NEURONE	Muscles in the eyelids	Eyelids close
LOUD MUSIC	Sound sensitive receptors in the ear				Muscles in arms and fingers	Turn music down
LOSING BALANCE	Receptors in the ear detect changes in position				Muscles in arms and legs	Move to regain balance
SMELL OF FOOD	Chemical sensitive receptors in nose				Salivary glands	Begin to salivate
SOUR TASTE	Chemical receptors on the tongue				Muscles in face	Cheeks sucked in
HOT PAN	Temperature receptors in the skin				Muscles in arms	Hand pulled away
SIT ON A DRAWING PIN	Pain receptors in the skin				Muscles in legs, tear glands	Jump up, eyes water
HAND BEING SQUEEZED HARD	Pressure receptors in the skin				Muscles in arms	Hand pulled away

The EFFECTORS are either MUSCLES or GLANDS.

These responses can be either ...

... CONSCIOUS RESPONSES, or ...

... REFLEX RESPONSES (see next page).

CONSCIOUS AND REFLEX ACTION

Conscious Action

After receiving a stimulus the body can make a considered response, ie. it acts consciously in making its response

1. RECEPTORS in the skin of your thigh detect an insect crawling on you ...
2. ... these cause an impulse to travel along a SENSORY NEURONE to the ...
3. ... spinal cord (part of the Central Nervous System). Here, another SENSORY NEURONE carries the impulse to the brain.
4. The brain (part of the Central Nervous System) thinks about this and decides to flick the insect away with the left hand ...
5. An impulse is sent down a MOTOR NEURONE in the spinal cord ...
6. ... and causes an impulse to be sent out of the spinal cord via another MOTOR NEURONE ...
7. ... to a muscle (an EFFECTOR) in the hand. This causes the hand to move and flick away the insect (a RESPONSE).

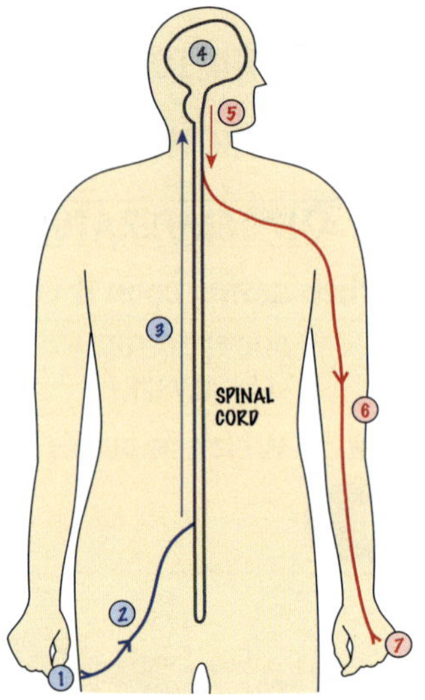

This pathway for receiving information and then acting upon it is:

STIMULUS	RECEPTOR	SENSORY NEURONE	COORDINATOR (ANALYSER)	MOTOR NEURONE	EFFECTOR	RESPONSE
Insect crawling on skin	Pressure receptor in skin	Nerve from skin receptor	Brain via spinal cord	Nerve to muscle	Muscle in hand	Flick insect away

Reflex Action

Sometimes 'Conscious Action' would be too slow to prevent harm to the body eg. putting your hand on a hot plate! 'Reflex Action' speeds up the response time by missing out the brain (steps (3) ⇨ (5) in the diagram above) completely. The spinal cord acts as the coordinator and passes impulses directly from a sensory neurone to a motor neurone via a RELAY NEURONE which 'short-circuits' the brain.

THIS HAPPENS AUTOMATICALLY - WITHOUT CONSCIOUS THOUGHT.

<u>STAGES OF REFLEX ACTION</u>

1. A RECEPTOR is stimulated by the drawing pin (stimulus) ...
2. ... causing impulses to pass along a SENSORY neurone into the spinal cord.
3. The sensory neurone synapses with a RELAY neurone, 'short-circuiting' the BRAIN.
4. The relay neurone synapses with a MOTOR neurone, sending impulses down it ...
5. ... to the MUSCLES (effectors) causing them to CONTRACT in RESPONSE to the sharp drawing pin.

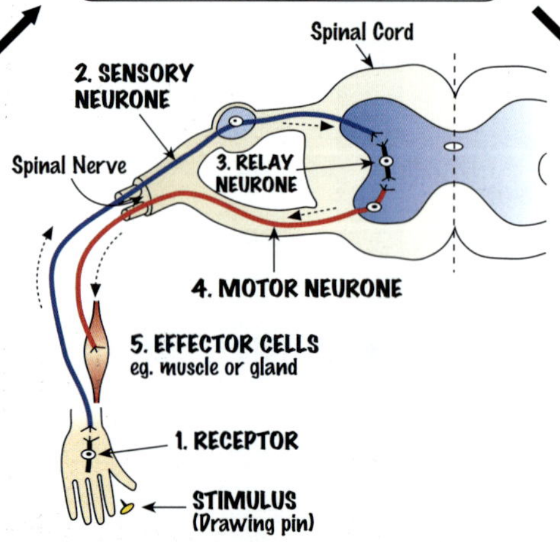

This pathway can be analysed in the following way:

STIMULUS	RECEPTOR	SENSORY NEURONE	COORDINATOR (ANALYSER)	MOTOR NEURONE	EFFECTOR	RESPONSE
Drawing pin	Pain receptor	Nerve from receptor	Relay neurone in spinal cord	Nerve to muscle	Muscle in hand	Withdraw hand

The Structure Of The Eye

The Eye is quite a complicated sense organ which focuses light onto light-sensitive receptor cells in the retina. These are then stimulated and cause nerve impulses to pass along sensory neurones to the brain.

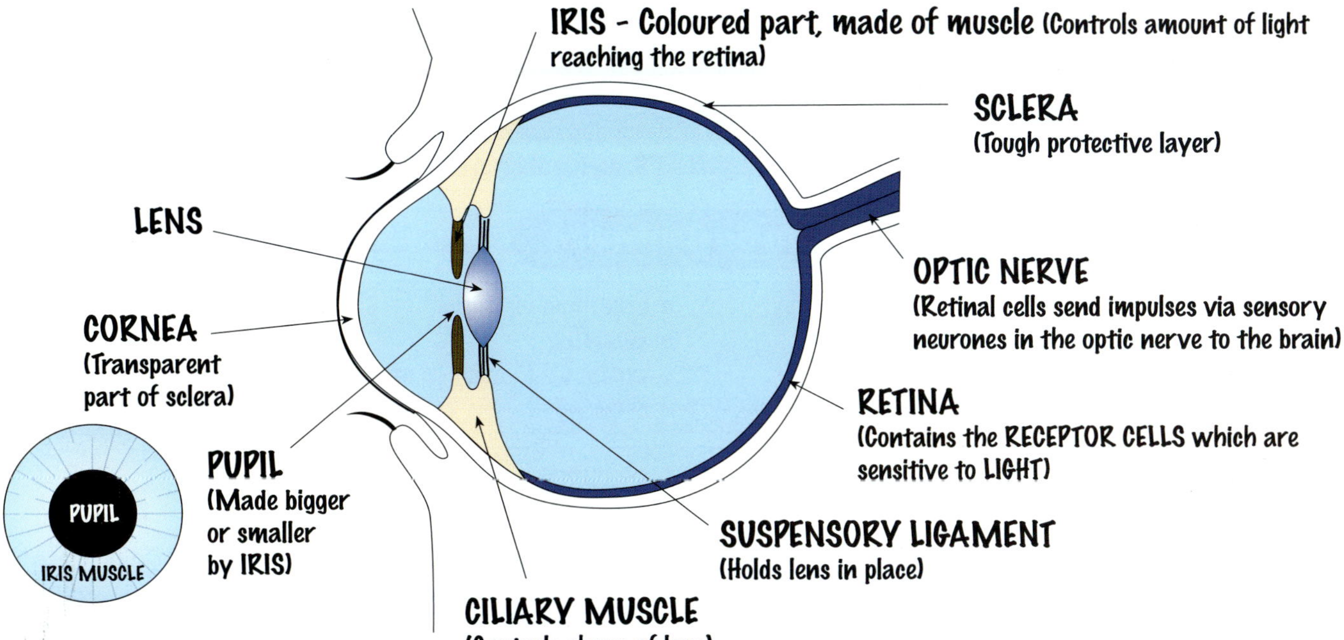

The CORNEA and the LENS focus rays of light ...
... so that an IMAGE is formed on the RETINA.

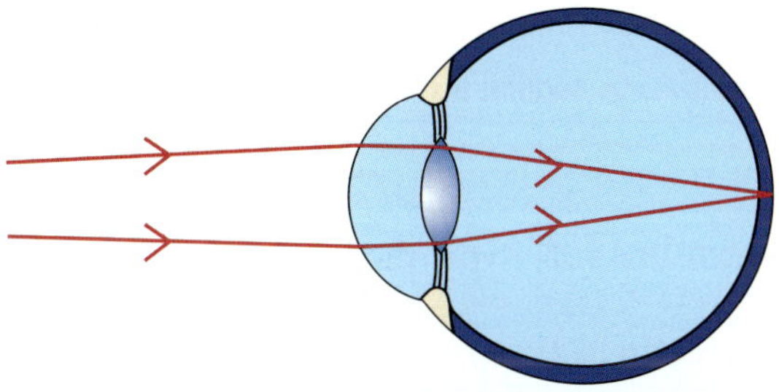

Rays of light are BENT (REFRACTED) BY THE CORNEA.
The rays of light are then ...
... further BENT (REFRACTED) BY THE LENS ...
... to produce a CLEAR IMAGE ...
... on the RETINA.

Focusing On Objects At Different Distances

DISTANT OBJECT

- CILIARY MUSCLES RELAX.
- SUSPENSORY LIGAMENTS PULL TIGHT.
- LENS IS PULLED 'THINNER', and ...
- ... LIGHT ISN'T BENT AS MUCH.

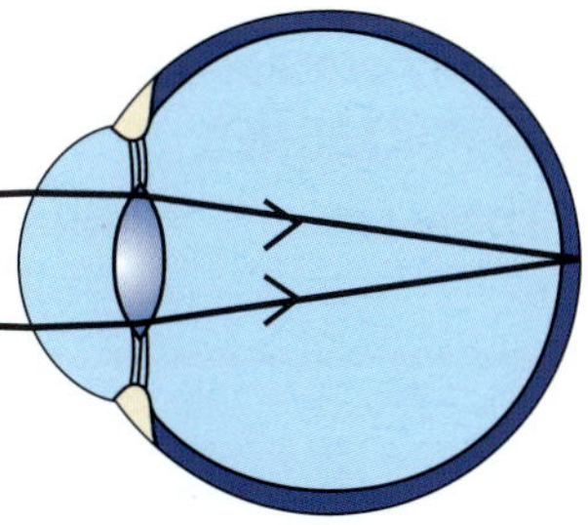

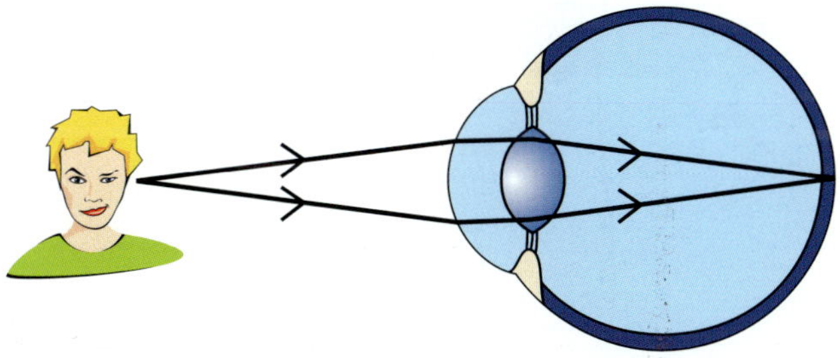

NEAR OBJECT

- CILIARY MUSCLES CONTRACT.
- SUSPENSORY LIGAMENTS GO SLACK ...
- ... ALLOWING LENS TO BECOME 'FATTER', ...
- ... BENDING LIGHT MUCH MORE.

It's important to understand that the FLUID in the eye retains the shape of the eye and keeps the SUSPENSORY LIGAMENTS TIGHT. The CILIARY MUSCLES have to work to overcome this tension which is why eyes get tired after lots of focusing on near objects, eg. reading.

Humans need to remove waste products from their body to keep their INTERNAL ENVIRONMENT relatively CONSTANT. Humans need to be at just the right temperature and have just the right amount of water and sugar in the bloodstream.

Waste Products Which Have To Be Removed

CARBON DIOXIDE	• Produced by RESPIRATION. Removed via the LUNGS when we breathe out.
UREA	• Produced by LIVER breaking down excess amino acids. • Removed by KIDNEYS, and transferred to the bladder before being released.

Internal Conditions Which Have To Be Controlled

WATER CONTENT	Water lost by:- • breathing via lungs • sweating • excess via kidneys in urine Water gained by:- • drinking
ION CONTENT (Sodium, Potassium etc.)	Ions are lost by:- • sweating • excess via kidneys in urine Ions are gained by:- • eating • drinking
TEMPERATURE (Ideally at 37°C) - because this is the temperature at which ENZYMES work best!	Temperature increased by:- • shivering • 'shutting down' skin capillaries Temperature decreased by:- • sweating • 'opening up' skin capillaries
BLOOD GLUCOSE	Blood glucose increased by:- • hormone GLUCAGON (from the PANCREAS) Blood glucose decreased by:- • hormone INSULIN (from the PANCREAS)

The Mechanisms And Organs Involved In These Processes

Many processes within the body (including control of some of the above internal conditions) are coordinated by HORMONES.

These are ...
- CHEMICAL SUBSTANCES, produced by GLANDS ...
- ... which are transported to their TARGET ORGANS by the BLOODSTREAM.

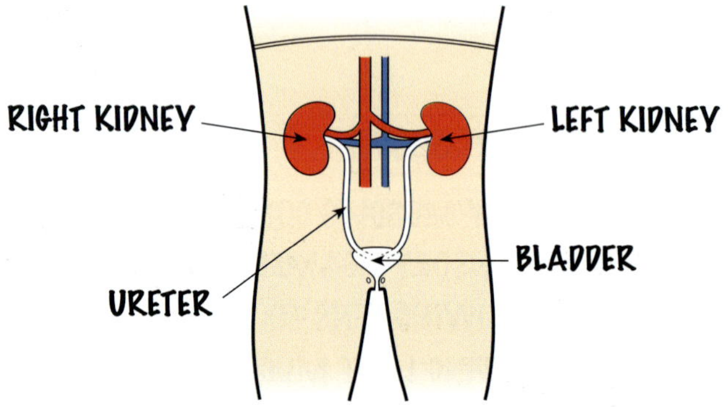

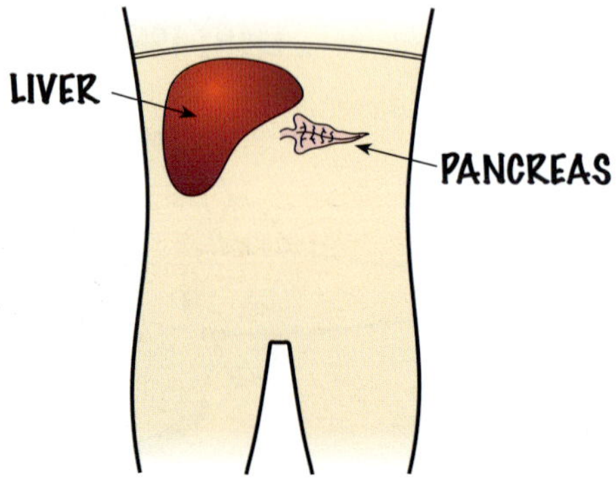

Some of the key organs involved in the control of internal conditions are the KIDNEYS, the LIVER, the PANCREAS, and the SKIN. We've shown the positions of these (except skin!) in the diagrams above and we'll look more closely at them on the next two pages.

Control Of Ion Content And Excretion Of Urea

You don't need to understand the structure of the kidney but you do need to know how it works.

- Firstly, it is made up of two important tissues, BLOOD VESSELS and TUBULES.
- BLOOD VESSELS take the blood through the kidney where unwanted substances ...
- ... end up in millions of tiny TUBULES which eventually join together to form one tube ...
- ... the URETER which leaves the kidney and ends up at the BLADDER.

THE KIDNEY REGULATES THE AMOUNT OF WATER AND IONS IN THE BLOOD AND REMOVES ALL UREA.

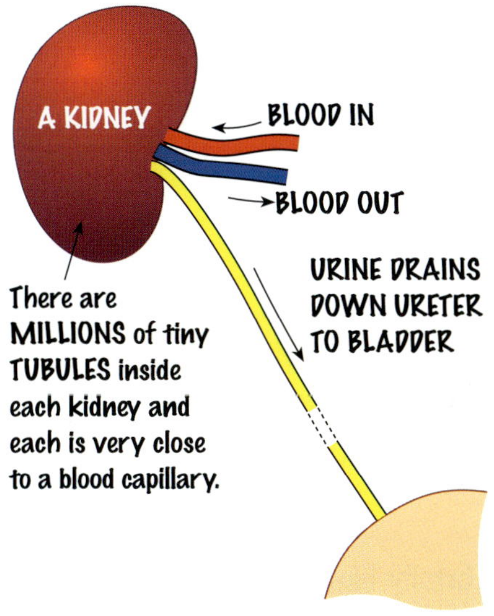

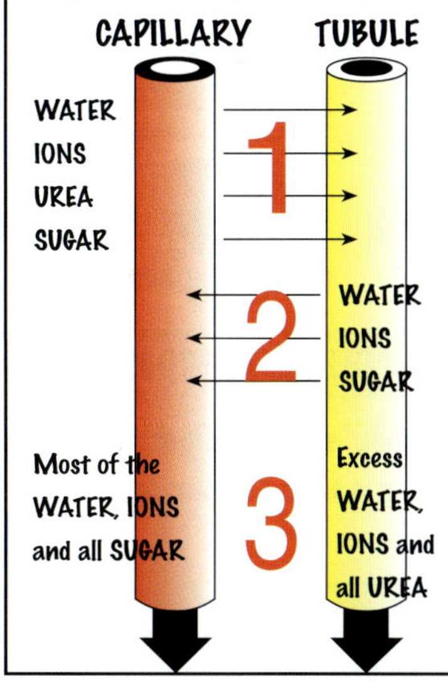

ULTRAFILTRATION
Lots of water plus all the small molecules are squeezed out of the blood, under pressure, into the tubules.

SELECTIVE REABSORPTION
The useful substances are reabsorbed into the blood from the tubules. Sugar and ions may have to be ACTIVELY ABSORBED against a concentration gradient using energy.

EXCRETION OF WASTE
Excess water, ions and all the urea now pass to the bladder in the form of urine and are eventually released from the body.

So, ... in principle there are THREE STAGES to learn ...

1. ... nearly everything is SQUEEZED OUT of the blood into the TUBULES ...
2. ... the substances we want to keep are REABSORBED back into the blood ...
3. ... unwanted substances are RELEASED as URINE.

Control Of Water Content – Effect Of A.D.H. On The Kidney

The amount of water reabsorbed in stage 2 above, is controlled by a hormone, A.D.H., which is produced by the PITUITARY GLAND in the brain. Everything you need to know is in this little flow diagram:-

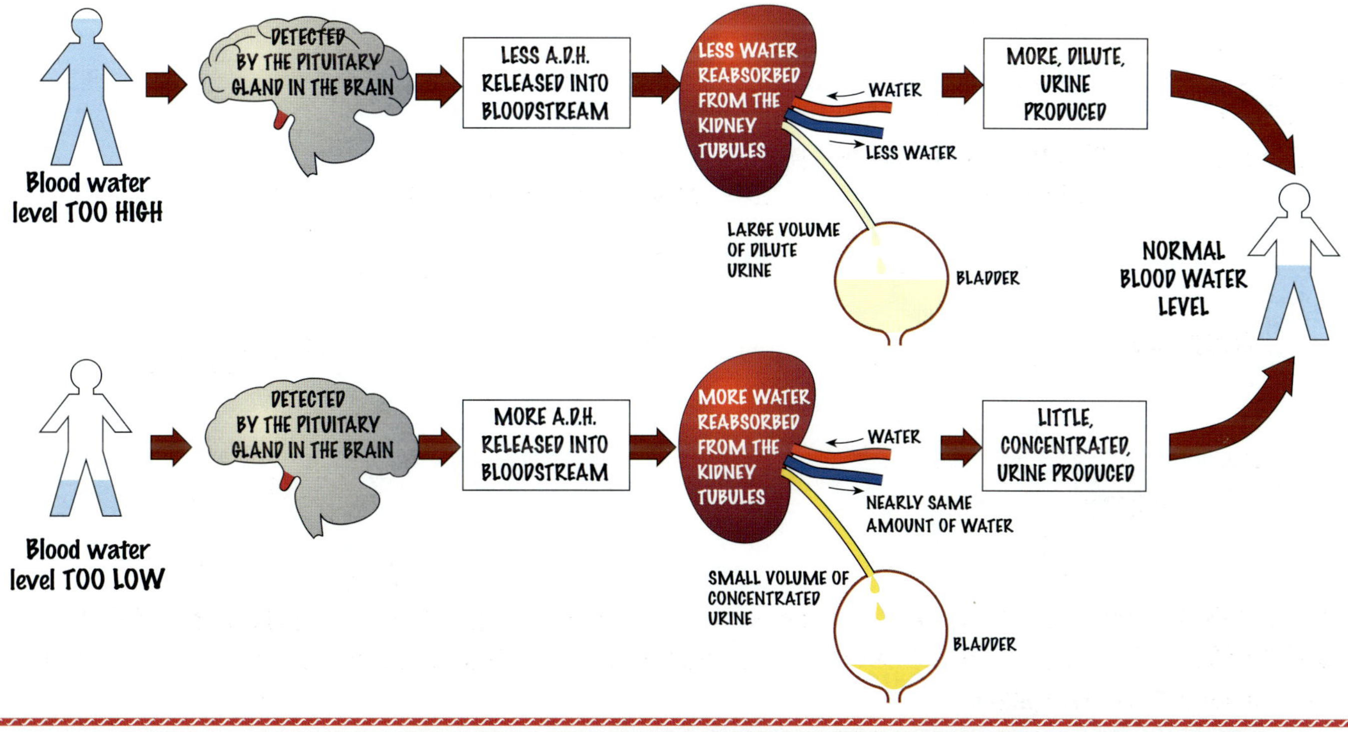

Control Of Blood Glucose Concentration

Blood glucose concentration is monitored and controlled by the PANCREAS which secretes two hormones, INSULIN and GLUCAGON, which act on the liver in the following ways ...

GLUCAGON converts INSOLUBLE GLYCOGEN into GLUCOSE and RAISES BLOOD GLUCOSE

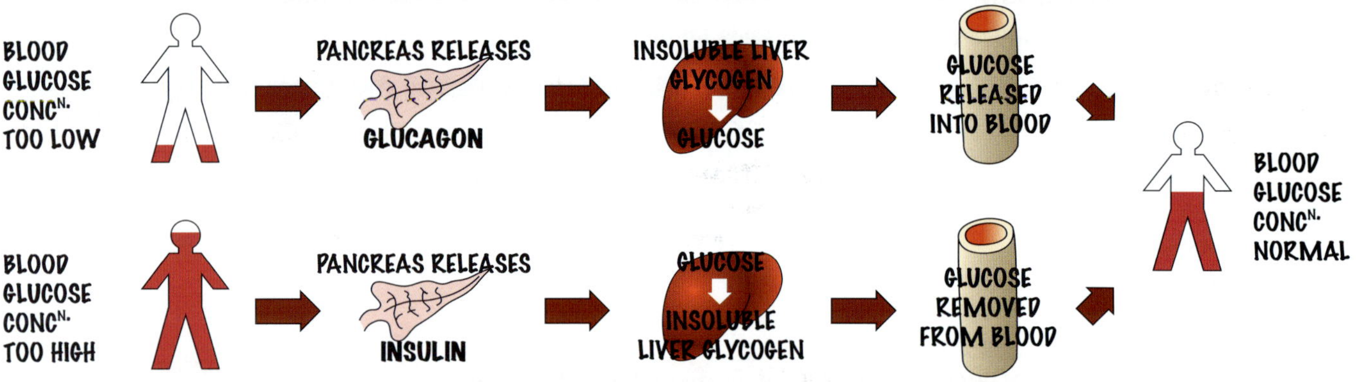

INSULIN converts GLUCOSE into INSOLUBLE GLYCOGEN and LOWERS BLOOD GLUCOSE

The PANCREAS CONTINUALLY MONITORS the body's blood sugar levels and ADJUSTS THE AMOUNT of INSULIN and GLUCAGON released to keep the body's blood sugar levels AS CLOSE TO NORMAL as possible.

Diabetes

This is a disease in which a person's blood glucose concentration may rise to a fatally high level because the pancreas does not produce enough insulin. This means that the liver doesn't convert glucose in the blood into insoluble glycogen for storage. Diabetes may be treated by careful attention to diet or by injecting insulin into the blood at appropriate times.

For people with DIABETES to properly control their blood sugar level they must TEST THE AMOUNT of sugar in their blood and ADJUST THE DOSE OF INSULIN which they inject.

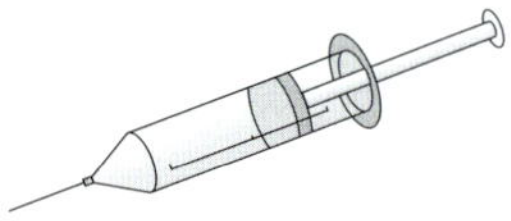

Control Of Body Temperature

This is controlled by the NERVOUS SYSTEM.

- The CORE TEMPERATURE of the body should be kept at around 37°C (best for enzymes!).
- MONITORING AND CONTROL is done by the THERMO-REGULATORY CENTRE in the BRAIN ...
  ... which has receptors which are sensitive to the temperature of the blood flowing through it.
- There are also temperature receptors in the skin which provide information about skin temperature.

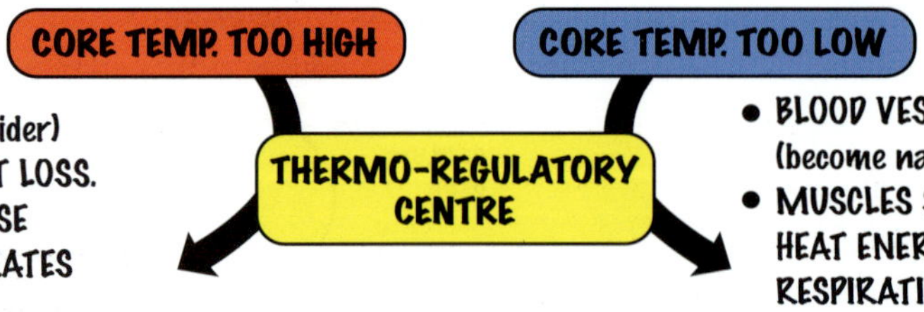

CORE TEMP. TOO HIGH:
- BLOOD VESSELS IN SKIN DILATE (become wider) CAUSING GREATER HEAT LOSS.
- SWEAT GLANDS RELEASE SWEAT WHICH EVAPORATES CAUSING COOLING.

CORE TEMP. TOO LOW:
- BLOOD VESSELS IN SKIN CONSTRICT (become narrower) REDUCING HEAT LOSS.
- MUSCLES START TO 'SHIVER' CAUSING HEAT ENERGY TO BE RELEASED VIA RESPIRATION IN CELLS.

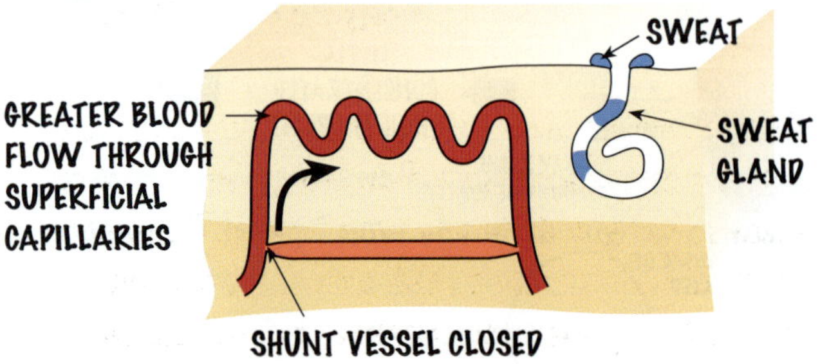

IN HOT CONDITIONS

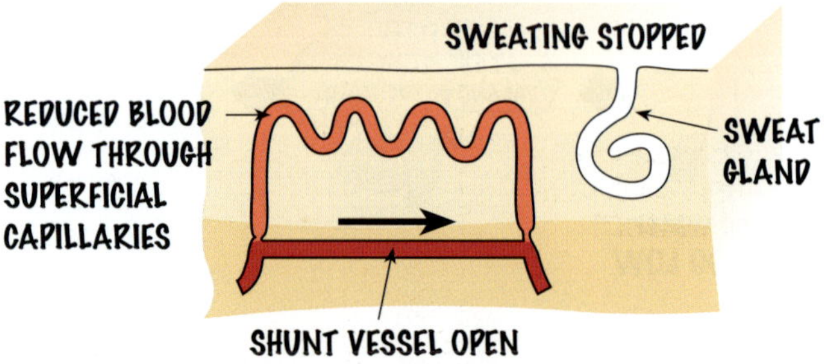

IN COLD CONDITIONS

DRUGS

DRUGS are chemical substances which **ALTER THE WAY THE BODY WORKS.**
Some drugs can be obtained from **LIVING THINGS**, others are **SYNTHETIC (MAN-MADE).**
Some drugs are called **MEDICINES** and these are taken to **CURE ILLNESSES** or **EASE THE SYMPTOMS** produced during an illness. Examples include **PAIN-KILLERS** and **ANTIBIOTICS** (which destroy bacteria and some other microbes).

Alcohol, Tobacco And Solvents

NAME OF DRUG	FURTHER NOTES
ALCOHOL Contains the chemical ethanol. 	• ALCOHOL is a DEPRESSANT and causes SLOW REACTIONS. • ALCOHOL can lead to a LACK OF SELF CONTROL. • EXCESS can lead to UNCONSCIOUSNESS and even COMA or DEATH. • The LONG TERM effects of ALCOHOL can be LIVER DAMAGE (due to the liver removing the toxic alcohol from the body) or BRAIN DAMAGE.
TOBACCO Contains the chemicals Tar Carbon Monoxide Nicotine (which is addictive) 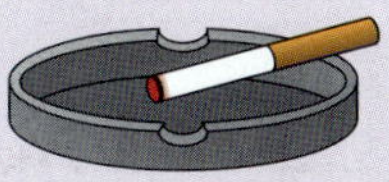	TOBACCO is a MAJOR CAUSE of HEALTH PROBLEMS: • EMPHYSEMA - alveoli damage due to excessive coughing. • BRONCHITIS - increased infection due to INCREASED mucus production. • PROBLEMS IN PREGNANCY - Tobacco smoke contains carbon monoxide which combines irreversibly with the haemoglobin in red blood cells, reducing the oxygen-carrying capacity of the blood. In pregnant women this can deprive a foetus of oxygen and lead to a low birth mass. • ARTERIAL and HEART DISEASE - damage to blood vessels which can lead to HEART ATTACKS, STROKES and even AMPUTATIONS.
SOLVENTS Different kinds of vapours are given off by solvents. 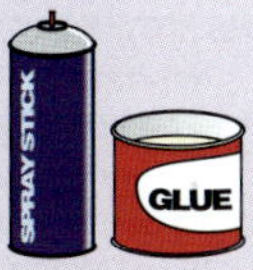	• SOLVENTS lead to SLOWED REACTIONS and HALLUCINATIONS. • SOLVENTS can affect a person's BEHAVIOUR and cause CHARACTER CHANGES. • SOLVENTS may cause PERMANENT DAMAGE to the LUNGS, LIVER, BRAIN or KIDNEYS.

People may become dependent or **ADDICTED** to certain drugs and may therefore suffer **WITHDRAWAL SYMPTOMS** without them. These may be psychological or physical (such as sweating, shaking, feeling sick or vomiting.)

The Link Between Lung Cancer And Smoking

The marked increase in deaths from lung cancer during the 1940's and 1950's prompted scientists to investigate the cause by monitoring a group of smokers and a group of non-smokers over a long period of time.
This study showed that smokers were more likely to get lung cancer than non-smokers, and that the more a person smoked, the greater their chances of getting lung cancer.
The non-smokers in this study are called the control group and as far as possible would be in the same age range and same occupational groups as the smokers. In other words, ideally you want the control group to differ from the smoking group only because they don't smoke.

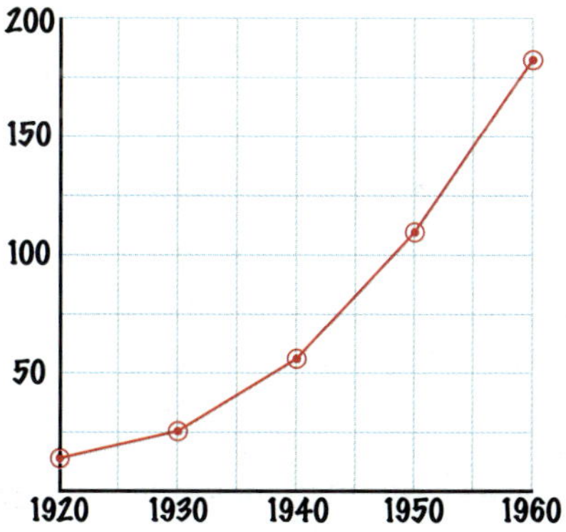

No. OF DEATHS PER 100,000 PEOPLE DUE TO LUNG CANCER

INCREASED RISK OF DYING OF LUNG CANCER

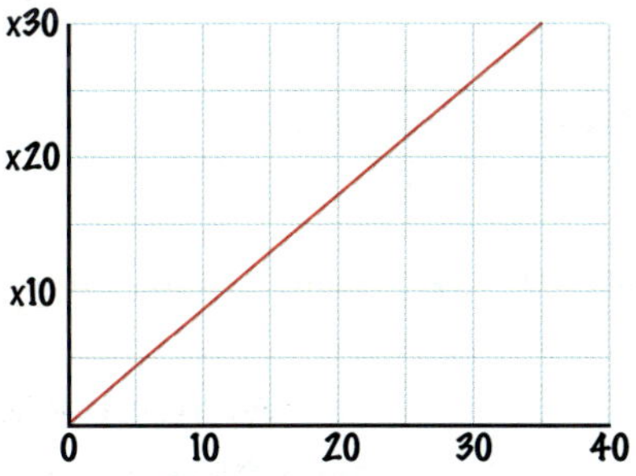

NO OF CIGARETTES SMOKED/DAY

Being a smoker doesn't mean that you will definitely get lung cancer any more than being a non-smoker means that you definitely won't get it. However, your chances are increased, and the more you smoke the greater your chances are increased.

PLANT CELLS AND OSMOSIS

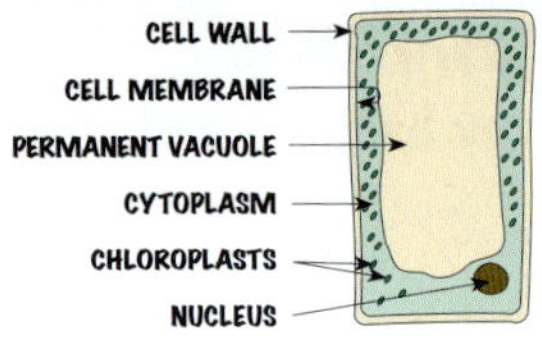

PLANT CELLS	FEATURE	ANIMAL CELLS
YES	NUCLEUS	YES
YES	CYTOPLASM	YES
YES	CELL MEMBRANE	YES
YES	CELL WALL	NO
ALMOST ALWAYS	VACUOLE	NO
THOSE WHICH ARE EXPOSED TO LIGHT	CHLOROPLASTS	NO
YES	MITOCHONDRIA	YES

'**OSMOSIS** is the diffusion of water from a dilute solution to a more concentrated solution through a partially permeable membrane that allows the passage of water molecules but not solute molecules'

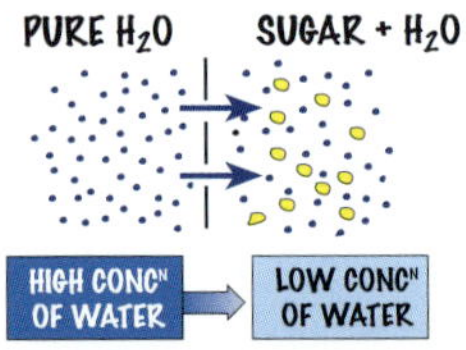

- Remember the two classic experiments with dialysis tubing and 'chips'.

ACTIVE TRANSPORT requires energy to absorb ions against a concentration gradient

PHOTOSYNTHESIS AND PLANT MINERAL REQUIREMENTS

CARBON DIOXIDE + WATER —Light / Chlorophyll→ GLUCOSE + OXYGEN

The glucose provides energy via respiration which is used to ...

CONVERT SUGARS INTO STARCH
CONVERT SUGARS INTO CELLULOSE for cell walls
CONVERT SUGARS AND NITRATES INTO AMINO ACIDS for proteins
CONVERT SUGARS INTO LIPIDS (fats or oils) for storage in seeds

FACTORS AFFECTING PHOTOSYNTHESIS

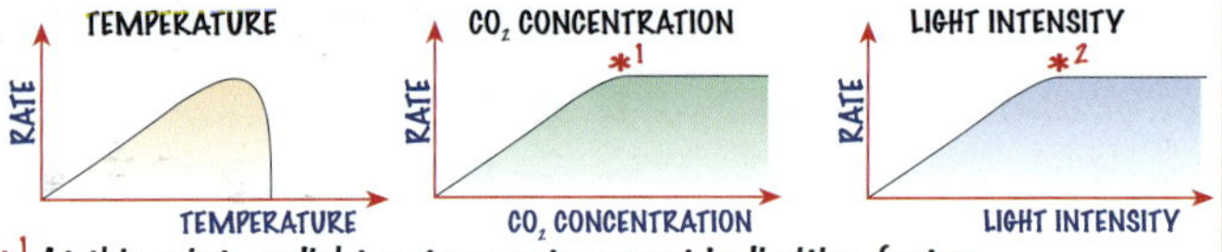

*[1] At this point, sunlight or temperature must be limiting factor.
*[2] At this point, carbon dioxide or temperature must be limiting factor.

MINERAL REQUIREMENTS

Lack of NITRATES, leads to stunted growth and yellow older leaves.

POTASSIUM needed for enzymes ... yellow leaves with dead spots.

PHOSPHATES for respiration and photosynthesis ... poor root growth and purple younger leaves.

TRANSPIRATION, WATER LOSS AND WILTING

1. Evaporation via stomata.
2. Water from the xylem to leaf via osmosis ...
3. 'Thread' of water in xylem pulled upwards.
4. Water enters xylem from roots.
5. Water enters root hair cells via osmosis to replace water which has entered the xylem.

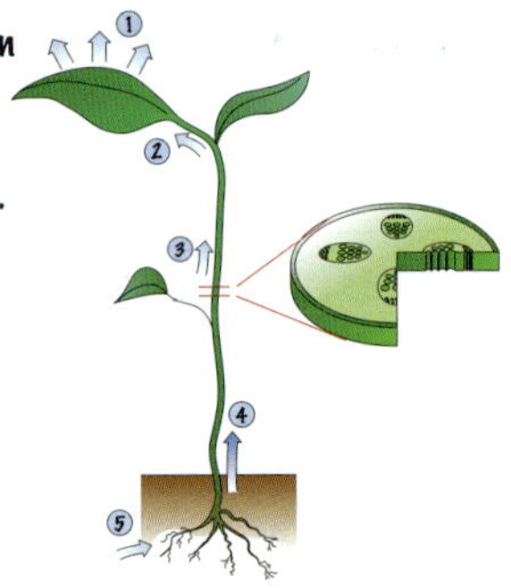

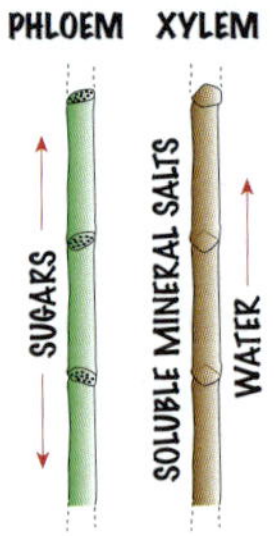

'**CONTROLLING WATER LOSS** ... stomata stay open to allow diffusion of gases in photosynthesis but if there is insufficient water the guard cells become flaccid and the stomata close'.

TURGID

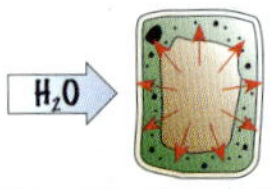

Water passes into the cells by osmosis if they are in a less concentrated solution.

FLACCID

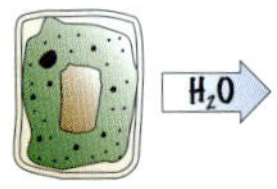

PLANT HORMONES, DRUGS AND THE EYE

HORMONES

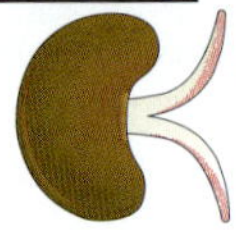

In shoots growth is stimulated.

In roots growth is retarded.

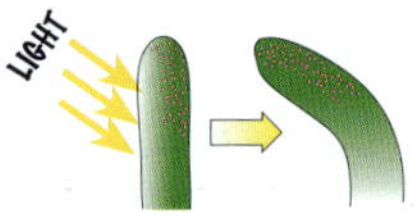

Light causes hormones to accumulate on the shaded part of the stem.

Hormones can be used artificially as ROOTING COMPOUNDS, RIPENING HORMONE and SELECTIVE WEEDKILLERS.

DRUGS: Alcohol affects the nervous system and can cause damage to the liver and brain.

Solvents affect behaviour and can damage the lungs, liver and brain.

Tobacco contains addictive nicotine and can cause lung cancer, bronchitis, emphysema and heart disease. Can lead to 'low birth' weights in infants.

THE EYE

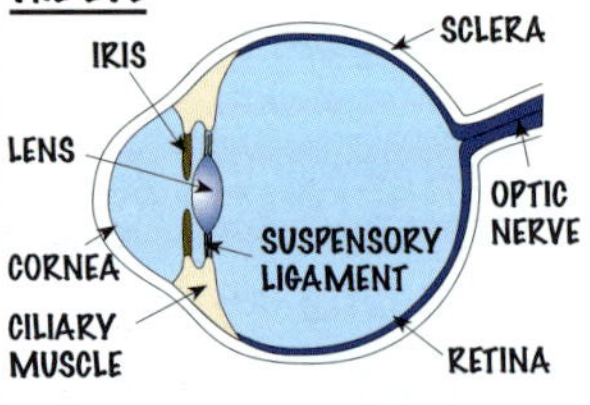

FOR DISTANT OBJECTS
- Ciliary muscles relax
- Suspensory ligaments pull tight
- Lens is pulled thinner
- Light is bent less

FOR NEAR OBJECTS
- Ciliary muscles contract
- Suspensory ligaments go slack.
- Lens becomes 'fatter'.
- Light is bent more.

THE NERVOUS SYSTEM

STIMULUS → RECEPTOR → COORDINATOR → EFFECTOR → RESPONSE

NERVOUS SYSTEM

BRAIN | SPINAL CORD | RELAY NEURONES | SENSORY NEURONES | MOTOR NEURONES | RECEPTORS

Neurones connect with other neurones via synapses.

These are gaps which can be bridged via the production of a chemical transmitter.

REFLEX ACTION

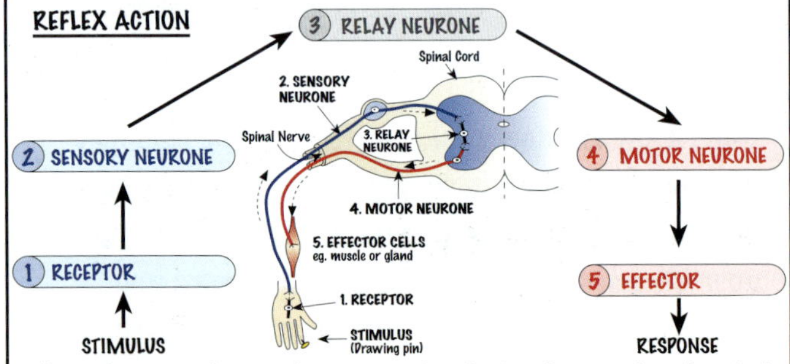

This is for speed of action. In conscious thought, impulses travel up the spinal cord to the brain before a decision is made.

CONTROLLING INTERNAL ENVIRONMENT

CO_2 and urea must be removed, and water content, ion content, temperature and blood glucose must be controlled. Much of this is hormonal.

ION, UREA + WATER CONTENT

Between the vessels and the tubules, the following three processes occur ...

1. ULTRA FILTRATION 2. SELECTIVE REABSORPTION 3. EXCRETION OF WASTE

H_2O TOO HIGH → PITUITARY DETECTS → LESS ADH → LESS REABSORPTION FROM TUBULES → MORE DILUTE URINE → NORMAL BLOOD WATER LEVEL

H_2O TOO LOW → PITUITARY DETECTS → MORE ADH → MORE REABSORPTION FROM TUBULES → LITTLE CONCENTRATED URINE → NORMAL BLOOD WATER LEVEL

BLOOD GLUCOSE CONCENTRATION

GLUCOSE TOO LOW → PANCREAS RELEASES GLUCAGON → LIVER GLYCOGEN ↓ GLUCOSE → GLUCOSE INTO BLOOD → NORMAL GLUCOSE LEVEL

GLUCOSE TOO HIGH → PANCREAS RELEASES INSULIN → GLUCOSE ↓ LIVER GLYCOGEN → GLUCOSE OUT OF BLOOD → NORMAL GLUCOSE LEVEL

BODY TEMPERATURE Thermo-regulatory centre

SKIN CAPILLARY DILATION + SWEATING IF TEMPERATURE TOO HIGH V SKIN CAPILLARY CONSTRICTION + SHIVERING IF TEMPERATURE TOO LOW

1. Choose from the list to match the numbers 1-4 below.
   A. CYTOPLASM.
   B. CHLOROPLAST.
   C. NUCLEUS.
   D. CELL MEMBRANE.

1.	Photosynthesis occurs in this structure.
2.	Controls what the cell does and contains the genetic information.
3.	Most chemical reactions take place in this.
4.	Controls movement into and out of the cell.

2. These sentences are about photosynthesis in green plants. Match words from the list with each of the spaces 1-4 in the sentences.
   A. STOMATA.
   B. XYLEM VESSELS.
   C. LIGHT ENERGY.
   D. GLUCOSE.

   Carbon dioxide diffuses into the leaf through the _____1_____. The chlorophyll molecules inside the chloroplasts absorb_____2_____. Water passes from the roots through the_____3_____ to the leaves. _____4_____ is a sugar which is produced during photosynthesis.

3. The body has to control certain internal conditions. Which TWO of the following are NOT controlled to some extent by the kidney?
   A. WATER CONTENT.
   B. ION CONTENT.
   C. TEMPERATURE LEVEL.
   D. UREA CONTENT.
   E. BLOOD GLUCOSE LEVEL.

4.

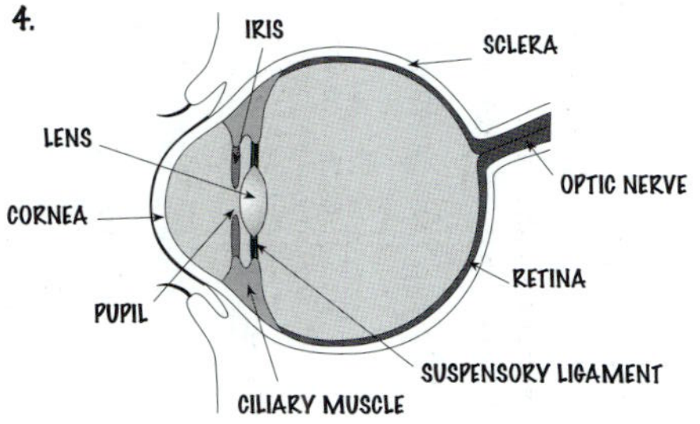

The diagram of the eye shows some of the important structures in it.

4.1 Which one of these structures controls the amount of light entering the eye?
   A. CORNEA.
   B. LENS.
   C. IRIS.
   D. CILIARY MUSCLE.

4.2 Which one of these structures contain the light-sensitive cells which send impulses to the brain?
   A. OPTIC NERVE.
   B. RETINA.
   C. SCLERA.
   D. CORNEA.

4.3 For the eye to focus on a distant object, which one of the following must happen?
   A. Ciliary muscles contract; suspensory ligaments become tight; lens becomes thinner.
   B. Ciliary muscles contract; suspensory ligaments become relaxed; lens becomes fatter.
   C. Ciliary muscles relax; suspensory ligaments become relaxed; lens becomes fatter.
   D. Ciliary muscles relax; suspensory ligaments become tight; lens is pulled thinner.

4.4 Which TWO structures in the eye actually focus the image on the retina?
   A. LENS AND CORNEA.
   B. LENS AND PUPIL.
   C. CORNEA AND PUPIL.
   D. CORNEA AND CILIARY MUSCLE.

5. Plants need to obtain raw materials and move substances to different regions within the plant.

5.1 How do plants obtain water?
   A. It diffuses into root hair cells.
   B. It passes into root hair cells by osmosis.
   C. It passes into stomata in root hair cells.
   D. It diffuses into stomata in leaves.

5.2 How is water transported to the growing regions of the plant?
   A. By osmosis from cell to cell.
   B. Through phloem tissue.
   C. Through xylem tissue.
   D. Through stomata.

5.3 How are the products of photosynthesis transported through the plant?
   A. By osmosis from cell to cell.
   B. Through phloem tissue.
   C. Through xylem tissue.
   D. By diffusion through the stem.

5.4 How does carbon dioxide get to the sites of photosynthesis?
   A. By osmosis through the stomata and then to the chloroplasts.
   B. By diffusion through the stomata and then to the chloroplasts.
   C. By diffusion through the leaf's surface and then to the chloroplasts.
   D. By diffusion through the plant stem and then to the chloroplasts.

6. The diagram opposite shows a young plant developing from a seed.

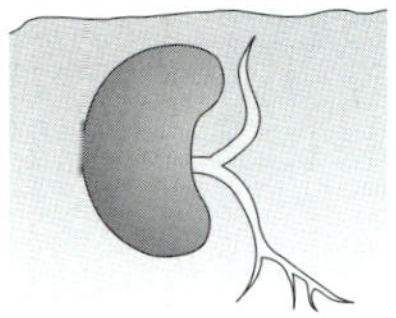

6.1 The root grows out of the seed and ...
   A. Away from the light.
   B. Away from the force of gravity.
   C. Towards water.
   D. Towards the force of gravity.

6.2 The stem (or shoot) grows out of the seed and ...
   A. Towards the light.
   B. Away from the force of gravity.
   C. Away from water.
   D. Towards the air.

6.3 The stem (or shoot) turns upwards due to ...
   A. An equal distribution of plant hormones.
   B. An equal distribution of water.
   C. An unequal distribution of hormones.
   D. An unequal distribution of chloroplasts in the stem.

6.4 Which of the following are plants <u>NOT</u> sensitive to?
   A. Light.
   B. Air pressure.
   C. Moisture.
   D. Gravity.

7. The body needs to maintain the blood glucose level between fairly narrow limits.

7.1 The organs responsible for controlling blood glucose are ...
   A. The small intestine and the pancreas.
   B. The small intestine and the liver.
   C. The pituitary gland and the pancreas.
   D. The pancreas and the liver.

7.2 When the blood glucose level becomes too low ...
   A. The pancreas releases insulin which causes the liver to release glucose into the blood.
   B. The pancreas releases glucagon which causes the liver to remove glucose from the blood.
   C. The pancreas releases glucagon which causes the liver to release glucose into the blood.
   D. The pancreas releases insulin which causes the liver to remove glucose from the blood.

7.3 When the blood sugar level becomes too high ...
   A. The pancreas releases insulin which causes the liver to release glucose into the blood.
   B. The pancreas releases glucagon which causes the liver to remove glucose from the blood.
   C. The pancreas releases glucagon which causes the liver to release glucose into the blood.
   D. The pancreas releases insulin which causes the liver to remove glucose from the blood.

7.4 Diabetes is a disease in which a person ...
   A. Cannot produce enough insulin.
   B. Cannot produce enough glucagon.
   C. Cannot produce enough glycogen.
   D. Cannot produce enough glucose.

The Periodic Table

The chemical elements can be arranged in order of their RELATIVE ATOMIC MASSES. The list can then be arranged in rows so that elements with similar properties are in the same columns, or GROUPS.
This forms the basis of the PERIODIC TABLE ...

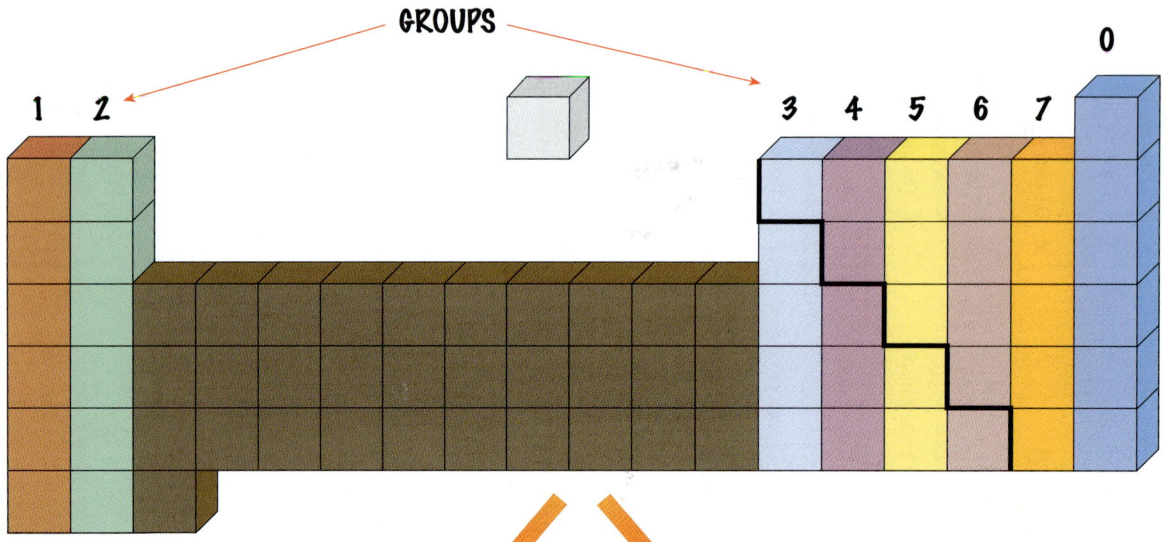

Metals are found mainly in Groups 1 and 2 and in the central block.

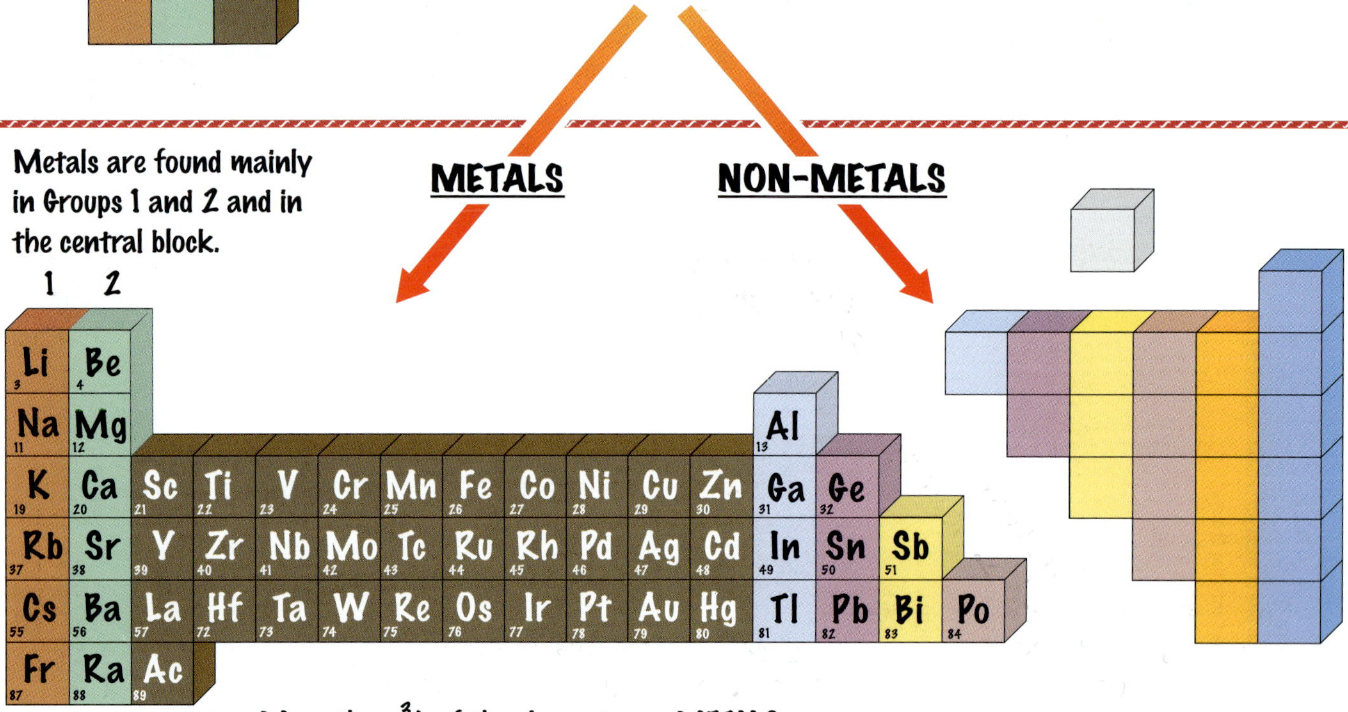

- More than ¾ of the elements are METALS.

In the modern Periodic Table, the elements are arranged in order of proton number since arranging them in order of relative atomic mass results in some oddities such as argon ending up in Group 1 while potassium goes to Group 0!! (instead of the other way round!).

Some Common Metals

The Periodic Table above shows the symbols for all the metallic elements.
The ones you should be familiar with are ...
LITHIUM Li, SODIUM Na, POTASSIUM K, MAGNESIUM Mg, CALCIUM Ca, IRON Fe, COPPER Cu, ZINC Zn, ALUMINIUM Al, GOLD Au, LEAD Pb.

The Alkali Metals

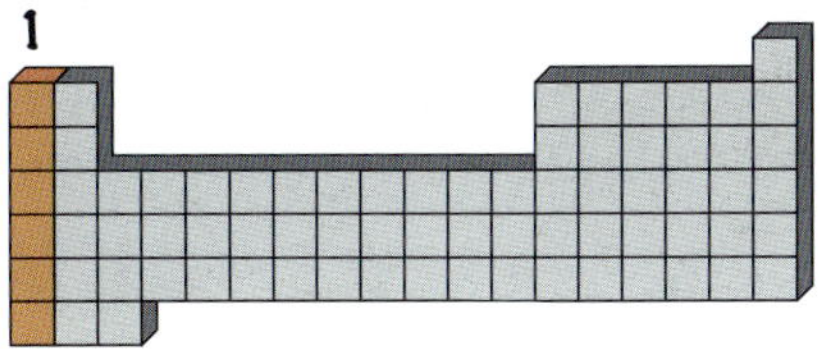

The elements in Group 1 of the Periodic Table are known as the ALKALI METALS.
These include: LITHIUM, SODIUM and POTASSIUM.

- The ALKALI METALS are stored under oil because they REACT VERY VIGOROUSLY with water.
  If lithium, sodium or potassium are put in cold water ...
  ... they FLOAT ON TOP because of their LOW DENSITY and ...
  ... MELT because the heat from the reaction is great enough to turn them into liquids. Alkali metals have LOW MELTING POINTS.

- When alkali metals react with water a METAL HYDROXIDE and HYDROGEN GAS are formed. The metal hydroxide (eg. lithium hydroxide, sodium hydroxide) dissolves in water to form an ALKALINE SOLUTION.
- Alkali metals react with non-metals to form IONIC compounds which are white solids which dissolve in water forming colourless solutions eg. ...

SODIUM + CHLORINE → SODIUM CHLORIDE

Na +

Cl →

NaCl

The Transition Metals

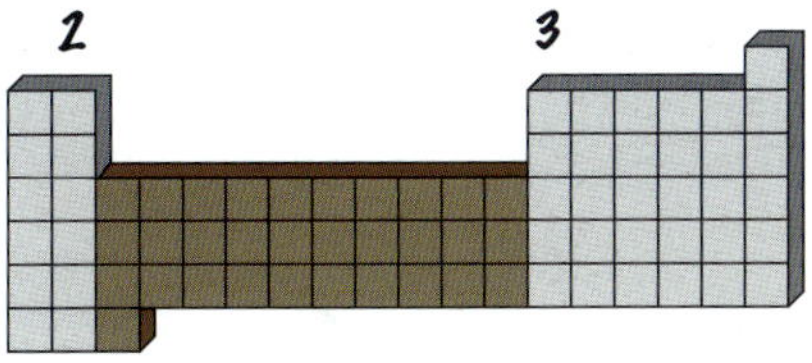

In the centre of the Periodic Table, between Groups 2 and 3, is a block of metallic elements called the TRANSITION METALS.
These include: IRON, COPPER, PLATINUM, MERCURY, CHROMIUM and ZINC.

- These metals are HARD and MECHANICALLY STRONG (except Mercury).
- They have HIGH MELTING POINTS (except Mercury - which is liquid at room temperature).
- They are much LESS REACTIVE than Group 1 metals and do not react as quickly with oxygen or water.
- They form COLOURED COMPOUNDS which can be used as pottery glazes and can be seen in weathered copper which turns green.
- Many transition metals can be used as CATALYSTS in chemical reactions. Iron and platinum are used in this way to speed up certain chemical processes.
- In addition to these qualities, transition metals, like all other metals, are good conductors of heat and electricity, and can also be easily bent or hammered into shape.

These properties make transition metals very useful as structural materials, and as electrical and thermal conductors.

COPPER

- Is used for ELECTRICAL WIRING.

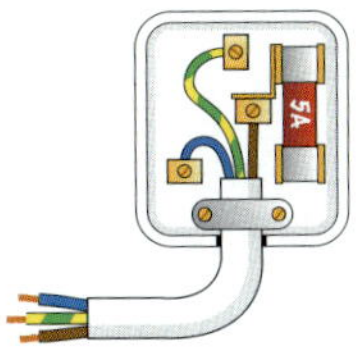

- Is used for PIPES ...
  ... in PLUMBING.

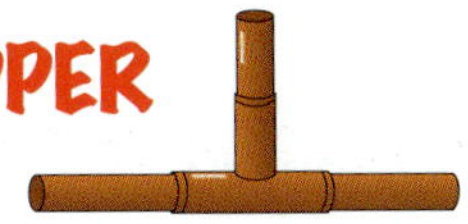

IRON

- Is mixed with CARBON + ...
  ... small quantities of other metals ...
  to make STEEL.

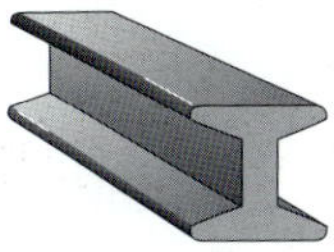

- Is used for CAST IRON SAUCEPANS.

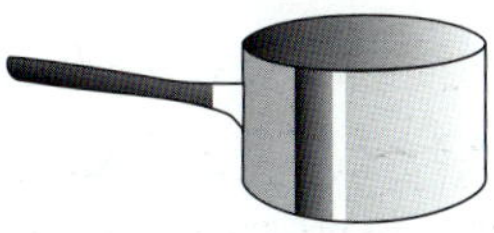

Reaction Of Metals With Oxygen

- Metals which react with OXYGEN from the AIR form METAL OXIDES.

METAL + OXYGEN → METAL OXIDE

- Some metals react more vigorously than others. If we were to heat four different metals in air ...

SODIUM ...

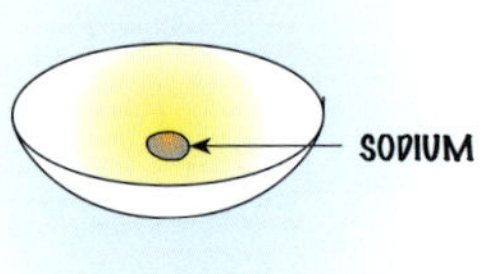

... BURNS VERY EASILY

MAGNESIUM ...

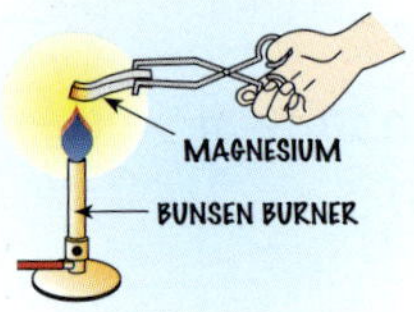

... BURNS BRIGHTLY

COPPER ...

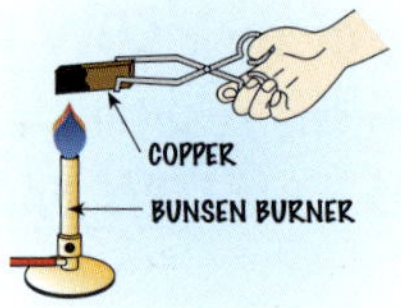

... SLOW REACTION

SILVER ...

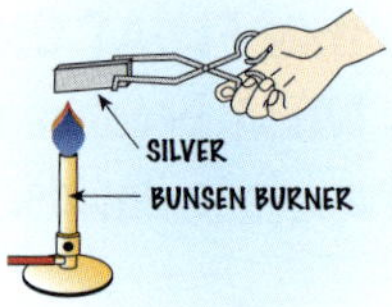

... NO REACTION

Reaction Of Metals With Water

- Metals which react with WATER form either METAL HYDROXIDES or METAL OXIDES and HYDROGEN.

METAL + WATER → METAL HYDROXIDE or METAL OXIDE + HYDROGEN

- Yet again some metals react more vigorously than others. If we were to add four different metals to water ...

SODIUM ...

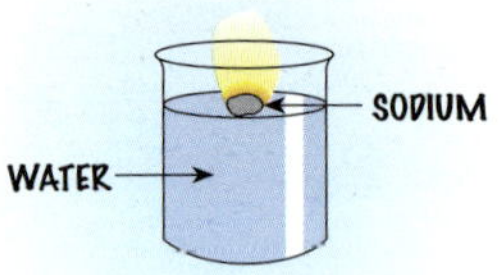

... VERY VIGOROUS REACTION

CALCIUM ...

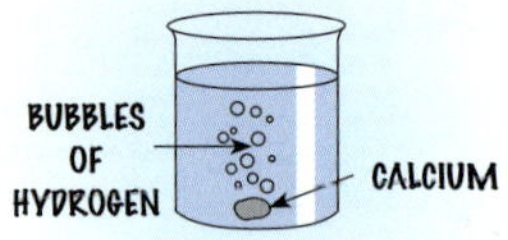

... SLOW REACTION

IRON ...

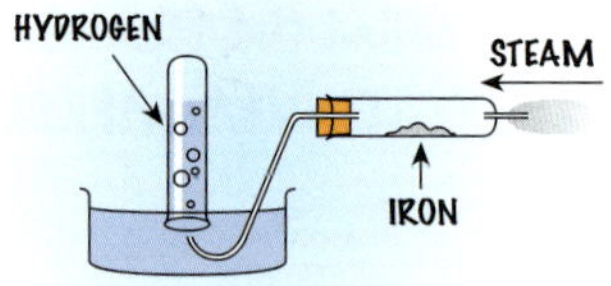

... REACTS WITH STEAM BUT NOT WATER TO FORM OXIDE

COPPER ...

... NO REACTION WITH WATER OR STEAM

Reaction Of Metals With Dilute Acids

- Metals which react with DILUTE ACID form a METAL 'SALT' and HYDROGEN. A 'SALT' is a word used to describe ANY METAL COMPOUND made when a reaction takes place between a metal and an acid.

METAL + ACID → SALT + HYDROGEN

- However some metals react more vigorously than others. If we were to add four different metals to acid ...

POTASSIUM ...

... NOT ATTEMPTED AS THE REACTION IS VIOLENT AND VERY DANGEROUS

MAGNESIUM ...

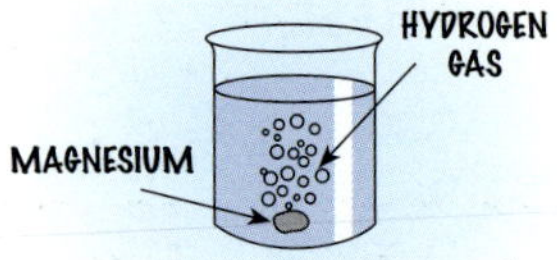

... VIGOROUS REACTION

ZINC ...

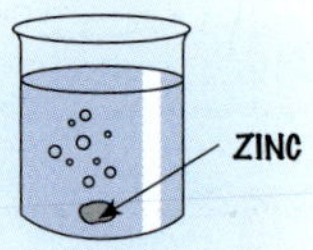

... FAIRLY REASONABLE REACTION

SILVER ...

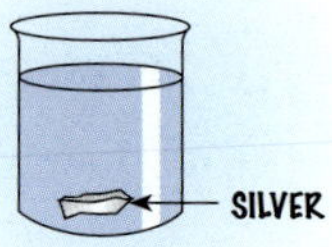

... NO REACTION

The **REACTIVITY SERIES** places metals in order of their reactivity based on how vigorously they react with ...

... ❶ OXYGEN (or AIR)

... ❷ WATER

... ❸ DILUTE ACID

The more vigorously a metal reacts, the higher up the reactivity series it is.

<table>
<tr><th></th><th>ELEMENT</th><th>REACTION WITH OXYGEN (AIR)</th><th>REACTION WITH WATER</th><th>REACTION WITH DILUTE ACID</th></tr>
<tr><td rowspan="3">VERY REACTIVE</td><td>POTASSIUM</td><td rowspan="2">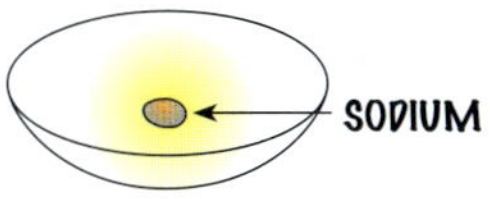
BURN BRIGHTLY WHEN HEATED TO FORM OXIDE</td><td rowspan="2">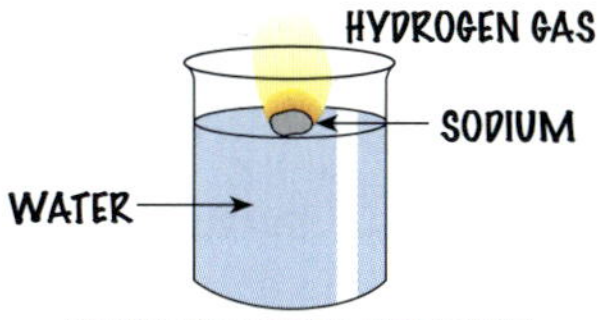
VERY VIGOROUS REACTION IN COLD WATER FORMS HYDROXIDE</td><td rowspan="4">
VIOLENT REACTION AND VERY DANGEROUS</td></tr>
<tr><td>SODIUM</td></tr>
<tr><td>CALCIUM</td><td rowspan="2">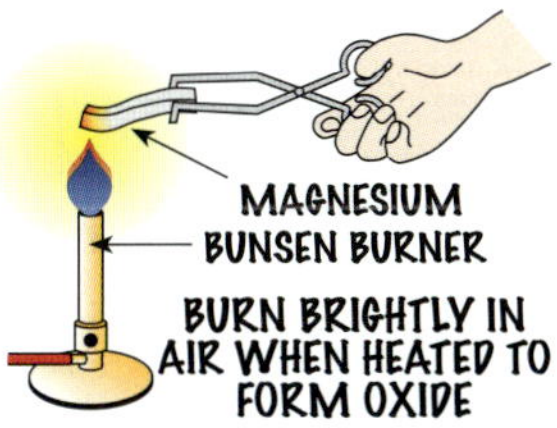
BURN BRIGHTLY IN AIR WHEN HEATED TO FORM OXIDE</td><td rowspan="2">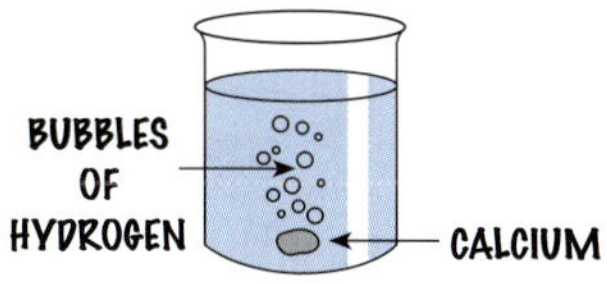
SLOW REACTION IN COLD WATER TO FORM HYDROXIDE</td></tr>
<tr><td rowspan="4">QUITE REACTIVE</td><td>MAGNESIUM</td></tr>
<tr><td>ALUMINIUM</td><td rowspan="8">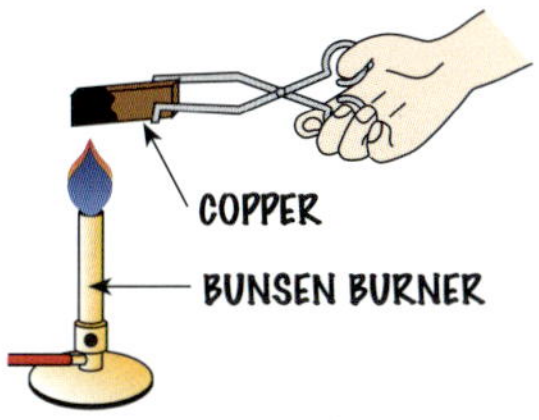
SLOW REACTION WHEN HEATED TO FORM OXIDE</td><td rowspan="4">
REACTION WITH STEAM, BUT NOT WATER, TO FORM OXIDE</td><td rowspan="6">
REASONABLE REACTION WHICH DECREASES AS WE GO DOWN
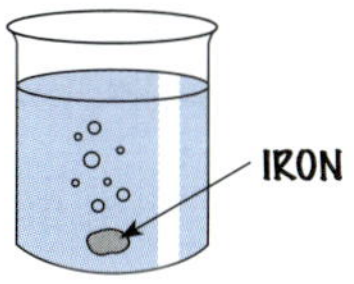</td></tr>
<tr><td>CARBON</td></tr>
<tr><td>ZINC</td></tr>
<tr><td rowspan="5">NOT SO REACTIVE</td><td>IRON</td></tr>
<tr><td>TIN</td><td rowspan="7">
NO REACTION WITH WATER OR STEAM</td></tr>
<tr><td>LEAD</td></tr>
<tr><td>HYDROGEN</td><td rowspan="5">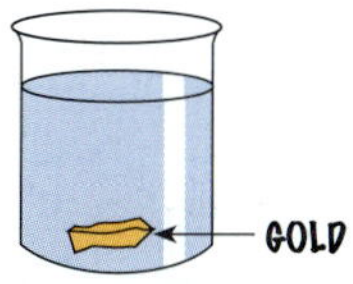
NO REACTION</td></tr>
<tr><td>COPPER</td></tr>
<tr><td rowspan="3">NOT REACTIVE AT ALL</td><td>SILVER</td><td rowspan="3">
NO REACTION</td></tr>
<tr><td>GOLD</td></tr>
<tr><td>PLATINUM</td></tr>
</table>

INCREASING REACTIVITY ↑

Carbon and hydrogen, although non-metals, are often shown in the Reactivity Series because they can displace less reactive metals from their oxides (see P.43).

A **DISPLACEMENT REACTION** is one in which a **MORE REACTIVE METAL DISPLACES** a **LESS REACTIVE METAL** from a compound. In other words a metal higher up in the Reactivity Series will 'push out' a metal lower in the Series.

- If we put an **IRON** nail into a beaker of **COPPER SULPHATE** solution ...

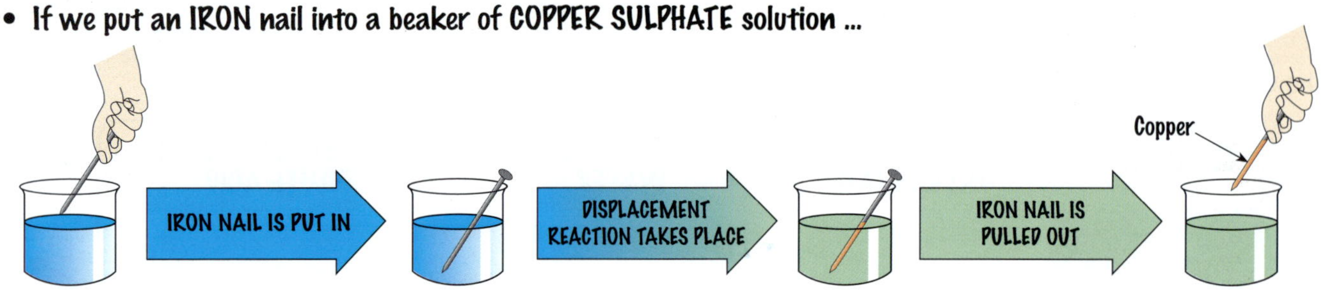

... then a **DISPLACEMENT REACTION OCCURS** because **IRON** is higher ...
... in the **REACTIVITY SERIES** than **COPPER**.

The more REACTIVE iron ... | ... takes the sulphate from the copper ... | ... to form iron sulphate ... | ... and copper.

IRON + COPPER SULPHATE → IRON SULPHATE + COPPER

There is one simple rule to remember:

A METAL HIGHER UP THE REACTIVITY SERIES (MORE REACTIVE) WILL DISPLACE A LESS REACTIVE METAL FROM ITS COMPOUND.

Similarly if a mixture of aluminium powder and iron oxide is heated, an extremely vigorous displacement reaction occurs, because ...

... aluminium is higher in the reactivity series than iron.

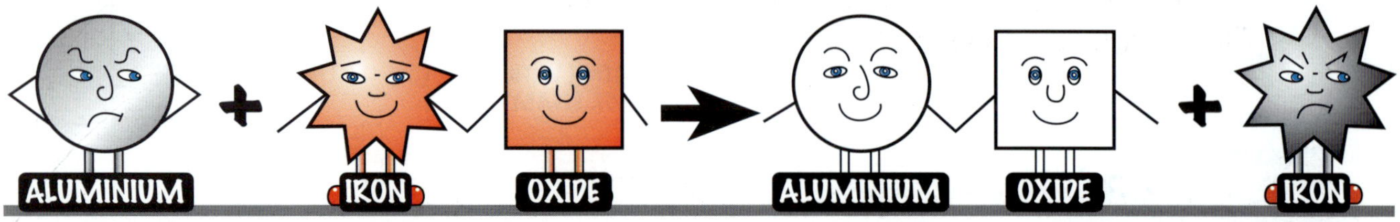

The more REACTIVE aluminium ... | ... takes the oxygen from the iron ... | ... to form aluminium oxide ... | ... and iron.

ALUMINIUM + IRON OXIDE → ALUMINIUM OXIDE + IRON

POTASSIUM
SODIUM
CALCIUM
MAGNESIUM
ALUMINIUM
CARBON
ZINC
IRON
TIN
LEAD
HYDROGEN
COPPER
SILVER
GOLD
PLATINUM

Example No. 1 ZINC + COPPER SULPHATE SOLUTION

ZINC + COPPER SULPHATE ⟶ ZINC SULPHATE + COPPER

Yes! Zinc is higher in the Reactivity Series so it displaces the copper forming zinc sulphate. ✔

POTASSIUM
SODIUM
CALCIUM
MAGNESIUM
ALUMINIUM
CARBON
ZINC
IRON
TIN
LEAD
HYDROGEN
COPPER
SILVER
GOLD
PLATINUM

Example No. 2 COPPER + LEAD NITRATE SOLUTION

COPPER + LEAD NITRATE ⟶ LEAD NITRATE + COPPER

No! Copper is lower in the 'series' than lead so no reaction takes place. ✘

POTASSIUM
SODIUM
CALCIUM
MAGNESIUM
ALUMINIUM
CARBON
ZINC
IRON
TIN
LEAD
HYDROGEN
COPPER
SILVER
GOLD
PLATINUM

Example No. 3 MAGNESIUM + COPPER SULPHATE SOLUTION

MAGNESIUM + COPPER SULPHATE ⟶ MAGNESIUM SULPHATE + COPPER

Yes! Magnesium is higher in the 'series' so it displaces the copper forming magnesium sulphate. ✔

POTASSIUM
SODIUM
CALCIUM
MAGNESIUM
ALUMINIUM
CARBON
ZINC
IRON
TIN
LEAD
HYDROGEN
COPPER
SILVER
GOLD
PLATINUM

Example No. 4 SILVER + IRON SULPHATE SOLUTION

SILVER + IRON SULPHATE ⟶ IRON SULPHATE + SILVER

No! Silver is lower in the 'series' than iron so no reaction takes place. ✘

Displacement Reactions Involving Carbon And Hydrogen

Although they are non-metals, carbon and hydrogen often appear in the Reactivity Series because of their ability to displace less reactive METALS from their OXIDES (See P.41).

POTASSIUM
SODIUM
CALCIUM
MAGNESIUM
ALUMINIUM
CARBON
ZINC
IRON
TIN
LEAD
HYDROGEN
COPPER
SILVER
GOLD
PLATINUM

Example No. 1 CARBON + LEAD OXIDE

CARBON + LEAD OXIDE ⟶ LEAD + CARBON DIOXIDE

Yes! Carbon is higher in the 'series' so it displaces the lead.
This reaction needs heat for it to occur. ✔

POTASSIUM
SODIUM
CALCIUM
MAGNESIUM
ALUMINIUM
CARBON
ZINC
IRON
TIN
LEAD
HYDROGEN
COPPER
SILVER
GOLD
PLATINUM

Example No. 2 HYDROGEN + COPPER OXIDE

HYDROGEN + COPPER OXIDE ⟶ COPPER + WATER

Yes! Hydrogen is higher in the 'series', so it displaces the copper.
This reaction needs heat for it to occur. ✔

Methods Of Extraction

- The Earth's crust contains many naturally occurring elements and compounds called MINERALS.
- A METAL ORE is a mineral or mixture of minerals from which economically viable amounts of pure metal can be extracted.
- Most ores contain either METAL OXIDES or substances which can be easily changed into a METAL OXIDE.
- To extract the metal from a metal oxide the OXYGEN MUST BE REMOVED.
- The removal of OXYGEN is called REDUCTION.
- The METHOD OF EXTRACTION depends on the metals' position in the REACTIVITY SERIES.

POSITION OF METAL	METHOD OF EXTRACTION	EXAMPLES
METALS ABOVE CARBON eg. potassium, sodium calcium, magnesium and aluminium.	Due to the high reactivity of these metals, a large amount of energy is required in a process called ELECTROLYSIS.	Electrolysis of aluminium oxide. 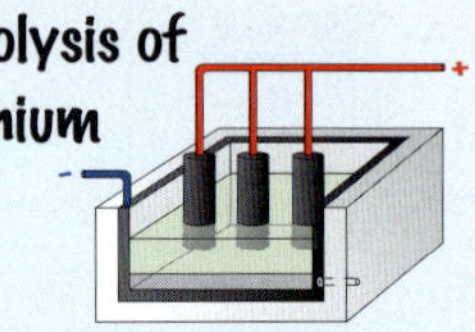
METALS BELOW CARBON eg. zinc, iron, tin, lead and copper.	These metals can be extracted by HEATING WITH CARBON since carbon is a more reactive element.	Reduction of iron oxide in the blast furnace.
METALS AT THE BOTTOM OF THE SERIES eg. silver, platinum and gold	These metals are unreactive and exist naturally. They are obtained by physical processes such as panning.	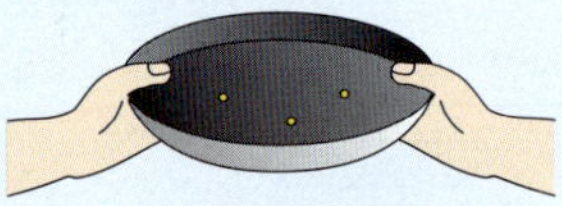 Panning for gold.

Extraction Of Iron – The Blast Furnace

Iron is BELOW CARBON in the Reactivity Series.
It is one of the most widely used metals in the world ... for building, transport and everyday objects.
Haematite is the name of the ore from which iron is extracted.
It contains IRON OXIDE.

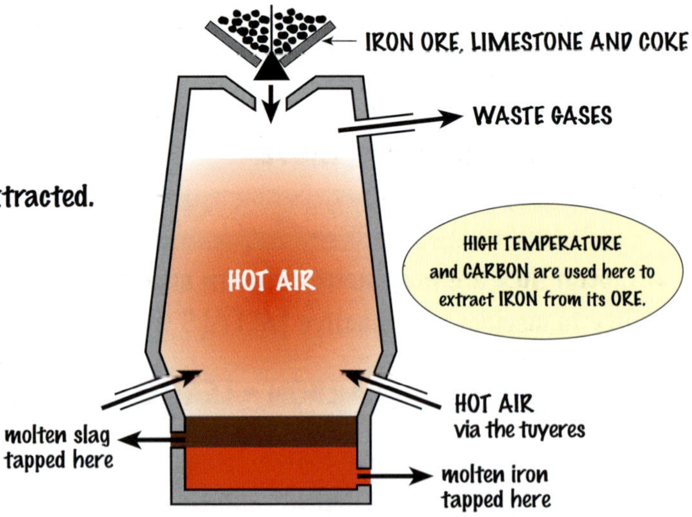

- HAEMATITE (iron ore), limestone and coke (carbon) are fed into the top of the furnace ... ... hot air is blasted in at the bottom.
- The CARBON REACTS WITH OXYGEN to form CARBON DIOXIDE and a great deal of heat energy. At these high temperatures the carbon dioxide will react with more carbon to form carbon monoxide.
- CARBON MONOXIDE IS A REDUCING AGENT and will take the oxygen from the iron oxide leaving just iron. ie. it 'reduces' the iron oxide to molten iron which flows to the bottom of the furnace where it can be tapped off. Carbon itself is often used to reduce oxides as it is quite high in the Reactivity Series. However, here it is CARBON MONOXIDE which acts as the REDUCING AGENT.

IRON OXIDE + CARBON MONOXIDE → IRON + CARBON DIOXIDE

This process by which carbon monoxide combines with oxygen from iron oxide to form carbon dioxide is called OXIDATION. The limestone reacts with impurities, including sand, to form the slag.

Extraction Of Aluminium - By Electrolysis

- Aluminium must be obtained from its ore by electrolysis because it is too reactive to be extracted by heating with carbon. (Look at their positions in the Reactivity Series).
- When substances which are made up of ions are dissolved in WATER or MELTED, ...
  ... they can be broken down (decomposed) into simpler substances, ...
  ... by passing an ELECTRIC CURRENT through them.
- This process is called ELECTROLYSIS and depends on +ve and -ve ions being free to move about, which can only happen when the substance is in solution or melted.
- During electrolysis, positively charged ions (eg. metal ions) move to the NEGATIVE ELECTRODE ...
  ... and negatively charged ions move to the POSITIVE ELECTRODE.
- This can cause gases to be given off, or metals to be deposited at the electrodes.

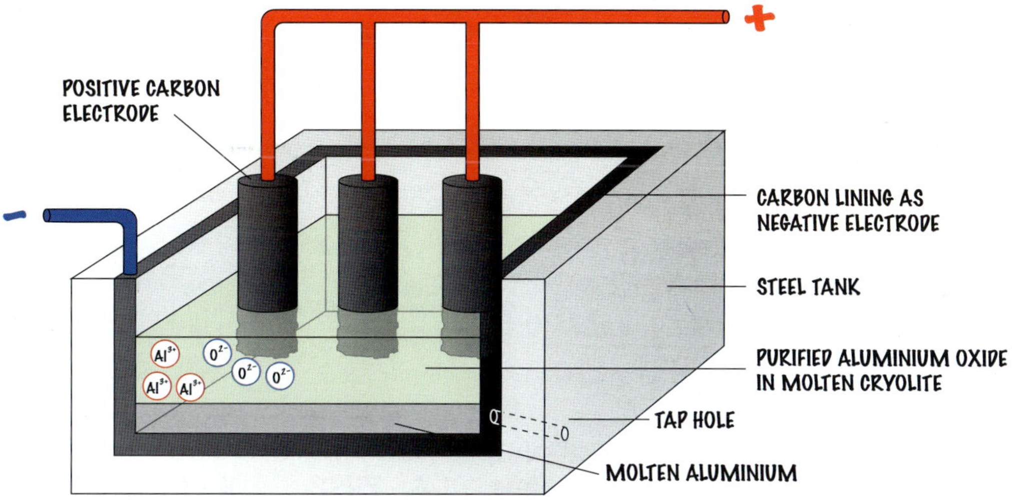

- ALUMINIUM ORE (BAUXITE) is purified to leave aluminium oxide.
- Aluminium oxide is MIXED WITH CRYOLITE (a compound of aluminium) TO LOWER ITS MELTING POINT.
- The Aluminium oxide and cryolite mixture is melted ...
  ... so that the IONS CAN MOVE.
- When a CURRENT passes through the molten mixture ...
- ... AT THE **NEGATIVE ELECTRODE** ...
- ... POSITIVELY CHARGED ALUMINIUM IONS MOVE TOWARDS IT and ALUMINIUM FORMS and ...
- ... AT THE **POSITIVE ELECTRODES** ...
- ... NEGATIVELY CHARGED OXIDE IONS MOVE TOWARDS THEM and OXYGEN FORMS.
- This causes the positive electrodes to burn away quickly and they frequently have to be replaced.

Redox Reactions

During electrolysis ...

- ... at the NEGATIVE ELECTRODE POSITIVELY CHARGED IONS GAIN ELECTRONS.
- This gain of electrons is known as REDUCTION.
- At the POSITIVE ELECTRODE NEGATIVELY CHARGED IONS LOSE ELECTRONS.
- This loss of electrons is known as OXIDATION.
- A chemical reaction where BOTH REDUCTION and OXIDATION occurs is called

a REDOX REACTION. It will help you to remember the above if you apply the word 'OILRIG'.

OXIDATION **I**S **L**OSS **O I L**
OF ELECTRONS.

REDUCTION **I**S **G**AIN **R I G**
OF ELECTRONS.

Purification Of Copper By Electrolysis

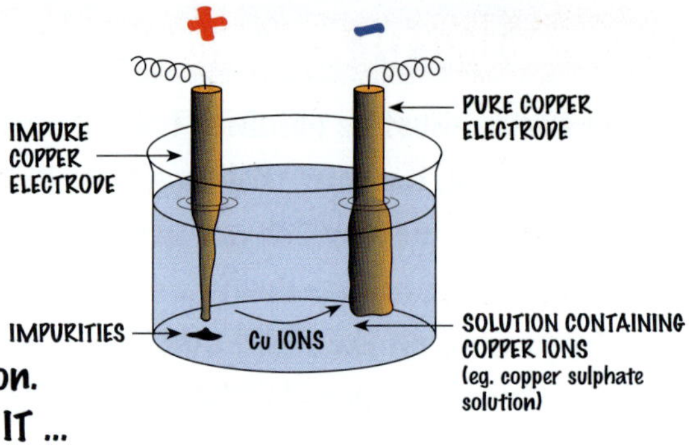

Copper can easily be extracted by REDUCTION but when it is needed in a pure form it is purified by ELECTROLYSIS.

- The POSITIVE ELECTRODE is made of IMPURE COPPER.
- The NEGATIVE ELECTRODE is made of PURE COPPER.
- The solution MUST contain COPPER IONS
- AT THE POSITIVE ELECTRODE COPPER IONS pass into the solution.
- AT THE NEGATIVE ELECTRODE COPPER IONS MOVE TOWARDS IT ...
  ... TO FORM COPPER ATOMS ...
  ... which stick to the pure copper electrode.

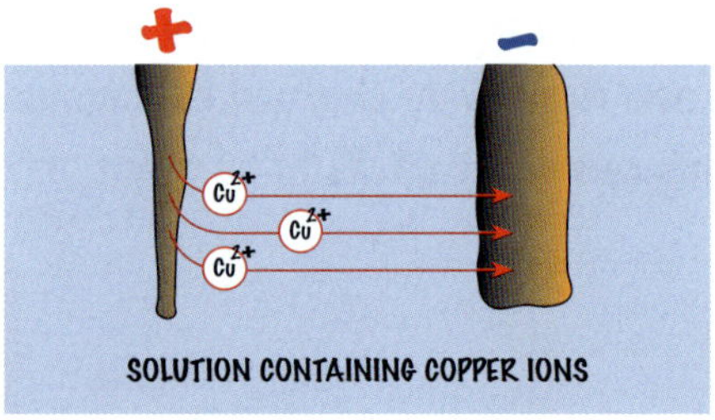

- Consequently the negative electrode gets bigger and bigger as the positive electrode seems to 'dissolve' away to nothing.
- The impurities in the positive electrode simply fall to the bottom as the process takes place.

The Rusting Of Iron

When iron reacts with water and oxygen ...

- ... rust (hydrated iron oxide) is formed ...
- ... and this weakens the iron.
- Rusting is an example of an OXIDATION REACTION ...
  ... but it is not very useful to us!

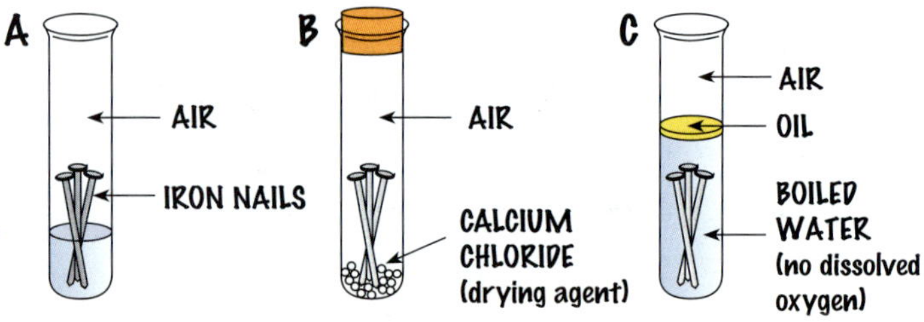

BOTH OXYGEN AND WATER are needed for rusting.
Salt (sodium chloride) can speed up the rate of rusting.

THREE DAYS LATER ...
A - RUST B - NO RUST C - NO RUST

Sacrificial Protection

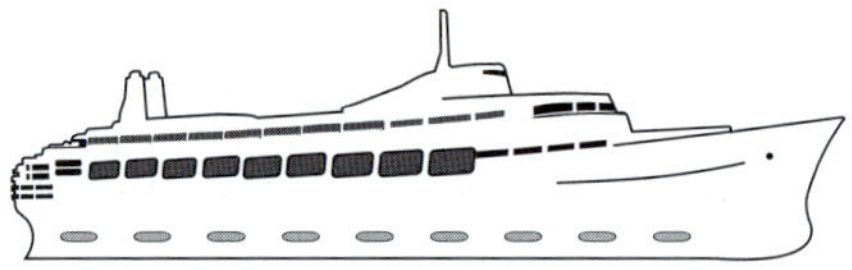

ZINC BARS ATTACHED TO THE HULL

- Iron (or steel) corrodes more quickly than most other transition metals but this can be prevented by connecting the iron to a more reactive metal such as zinc or magnesium.
- The more reactive metal reacts preferentially with the water and oxygen thus preventing it reacting with the iron.
- Zinc bars are attached to the hulls of ships, and magnesium strips to underground steel pipes to prevent corrosion. Only when these have corroded will the iron or steel begin to corrode.
- GALVANISING relies on coating iron objects with zinc. Even if they are scratched they still won't corrode until ALL the zinc has gone.
- Some objects, such as knives and forks, are made from non-rusting alloys such as STAINLESS STEEL which is an alloy containing chromium.

Aluminium - A Special Case

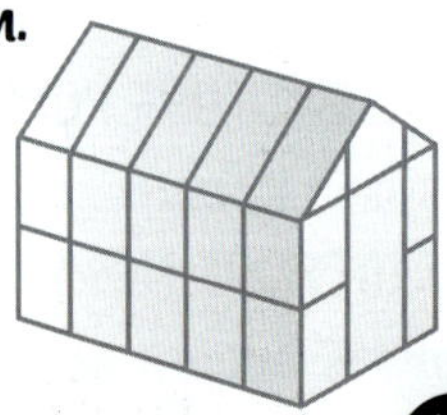

Although aluminium is a quite reactive metal it doesn't oxidise (corrode) as quickly as you would think. This is due to the formation of a thin 'skin' of oxide which forms on the surface and prevents further rusting. It's for this reason that greenhouses don't have to be painted. Aluminium can be made HARDER, STRONGER, and STIFFER, by mixing it with small amounts of other metals (magnesium, titanium) to make alloys.

pH Scale

- When a substance dissolves in water it forms an AQUEOUS solution.
- The solution may be ACIDIC, ALKALINE or NEUTRAL.
- Water itself is neutral.

The pH scale is a measure of the acidity or alkalinity of an aqueous solution, across a 14 point scale.

VERY ACIDIC ⟷					SLIGHTLY ACIDIC	NEUTRAL	SLIGHTLY ALKALINE ⟷						VERY ALKALINE
1	2	3	4	5	6	7	8	9	10	11	12	13	14

- When substances dissolve in water, they dissociate into their individual IONS.
- Alkalis contain HYDROXIDE ions. $OH^{-}_{(aq)}$
- Acids contain HYDROGEN ions. $H^{+}_{(aq)}$

Indicators

These are really useful dyes which CHANGE COLOUR ...

... depending on whether they're in ACIDIC or ALKALINE solutions.

- Some are just simple substances such as LITMUS which changes from RED to BLUE or vice versa ...
- ... whereas others are mixtures of dyes, such as UNIVERSAL INDICATOR, which ...
- ... show a RANGE OF COLOUR to indicate just how ACIDIC or ALKALINE a substance is.

	1	2	3	4	5	6	7	8	9	10	11	12	13	14
eg.	Battery Acid Stomach Acid		Lemon Juice Vinegar		Soda Water		Water	Soap	Baking Powder	Washing Soda		Oven Cleaner		Potassium Hydroxide

Neutralisation

Because acids and alkalis are 'chemical opposites', if they are added together in the correct amounts they can 'cancel' each other out. This is called NEUTRALISATION because the solution which remains has a neutral pH of 7.

ACID + ALKALINE HYDROXIDE SOLUTION ⟶ NEUTRAL SALT SOLUTION + WATER

eg. HCl (containing universal indicator)

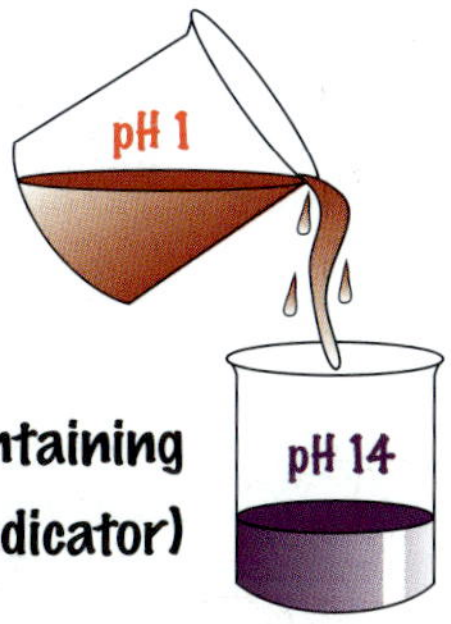

KOH (containing universal indicator)

⟶

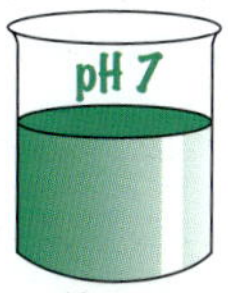

KCl + H_2O (containing universal indicator)

Both beakers must contain the same number of acid and alkali molecules if they are to neutralise each other exactly!

$$HCl + KOH \longrightarrow KCl + H_2O$$

HYDROCHLORIC ACID + POTASSIUM HYDROXIDE ⟶ POTASSIUM CHLORIDE + WATER

This can all be summarised more simply if we look at what's happening to the hydrogen ions $H^{+}_{(aq)}$ and the hydroxide ions $OH^{-}_{(aq)}$ in the acid and alkali:-

$$H^{+}_{(aq)} + OH^{-}_{(aq)} \longrightarrow H_2O_{(l)}$$

Salts of Alkali Metals

Compounds of alkali metals, called SALTS, can be made by reacting solutions of their hydroxides (which are alkaline) with a particular acid. This is called a NEUTRALISATION REACTION and as we saw on the previous page, can be represented as follows:

ACID + ALKALINE HYDROXIDE SOLUTION ⟶ NEUTRAL SALT SOLUTION + WATER

The particular salt produced depends on the METAL IN THE ALKALI, and the ACID USED.

eg. SODIUM HYDROXIDE + HYDROCHLORIC ACID ⟶ SODIUM CHLORIDE + WATER

OTHER EXAMPLES

	HYDROCHLORIC ACID	SULPHURIC ACID	NITRIC ACID
+ SODIUM HYDROXIDE	→ SODIUM CHLORIDE + WATER	→ SODIUM SULPHATE + WATER	→ SODIUM NITRATE + WATER
+ POTASSIUM HYDROXIDE	→ POTASSIUM CHLORIDE + WATER	→ POTASSIUM SULPHATE + WATER	→ POTASSIUM NITRATE + WATER

Ammonia also dissolves in water to produce an alkaline solution. This can be neutralised with acids to produce ammonium salts.

+ AMMONIA	→ AMMONIUM CHLORIDE	→ AMMONIUM SULPHATE	→ AMMONIUM NITRATE

REMEMBER! THIS RULE ALWAYS APPLIES ...

- HYDROCHLORIC ACID produces CHLORIDE salts.
- SULPHURIC ACID produces SULPHATE salts.
- NITRIC ACID produces NITRATE salts.

Salts of Transition Metals

Bases are the OXIDES and HYDROXIDES of metals. Those which are soluble are called ALKALIS. Unfortunately the OXIDES and HYDROXIDES of TRANSITION METALS are INSOLUBLE, which means that preparing their salts is a little less straightforward ...

- The metal OXIDE or HYDROXIDE is added to an acid until no more will react.
- The excess metal OXIDE or HYDROXIDE is then filtered off, ...
- ... to leave a solution of the salt which can then be evaporated to produce crystals of copper sulphate.

SULPHURIC ACID + COPPER OXIDE ⟶ COPPER SULPHATE + WATER

or generally speaking ...

ACID + BASE ⟶ NEUTRAL SALT SOLUTION + WATER

ALKALI AND TRANSITION METALS IN THE PERIODIC TABLE

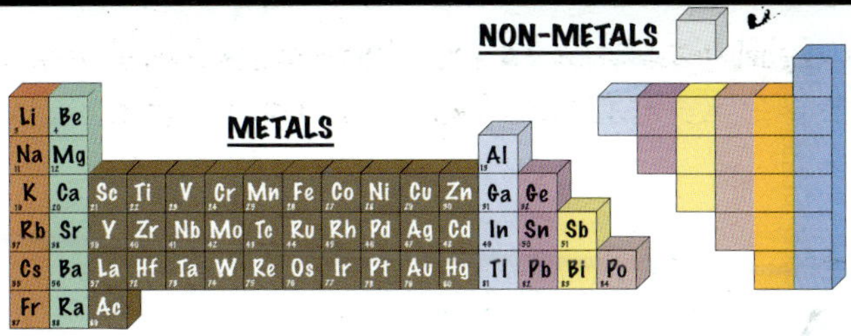

ALKALI METALS

- GROUP 1
- INCLUDES LITHIUM, SODIUM & POTASSIUM.
- Form IONIC COMPOUNDS which form COLOURLESS SOLUTIONS
- React with WATER releasing HYDROGEN and forming HYDROXIDES which dissolve in water to give ALKALINE SOLUTIONS
- LOW DENSITY

TRANSITION METALS

- Occupy central block of table
- Include IRON, COPPER, ZINC and TIN
- EASILY BENT
- GOOD CONDUCTORS OF HEAT & ELEC.
- HIGH MELTING POINTS
- HARD & TOUGH
- Not too reactive
- FORM COLOURED COMPOUNDS
- Some are used as CATALYSTS.

REACTIVITY OF METALS

1. OXYGEN — METAL + OXYGEN → METAL OXIDE
   e.g. Magnesium + Oxygen → Magnesium Oxide
2. WATER — METAL + WATER → *METAL HYDROXIDE + HYDROGEN
   *(some form oxides)
   e.g. Calcium + Water → Calcium Hydroxide + Hydrogen
3. ACIDS — METAL + ACID → SALT + HYDROGEN
   e.g. Zinc + Hydrochloric Acid → Zinc Chloride + Hydrogen

REACTIVITY SERIES

Depending on how vigorously they react with the above substances, metals (and carbon + hydrogen) can be placed in order ...

POTASSIUM SODIUM CALCIUM	VERY REACTIVE
MAGNESIUM ALUMINIUM ZINC	QUITE REACTIVE
IRON TIN LEAD COPPER	NOT VERY REACTIVE
SILVER GOLD PLATINUM	UNREACTIVE

- Some reactions such as adding sodium or potassium to acid are dangerous and should not be attempted.
- Carbon and hydrogen, although non-metals, can be placed according to their reactivity.
- This series can then be used to predict which metals will displace other metals from metal compounds.

DISPLACEMENT REACTIONS

'A metal higher up in the reactivity series will displace a less reactive metal from its compound'.

The more REACTIVE iron ... ... takes the sulphate from the copper ... ... to form iron sulphate ... ... and copper.

EXAMPLES OF DISPLACEMENT REACTIONS ...

1. ZINC + COPPER SULPHATE → ZINC SULPHATE + COPPER ✓
2. COPPER + LEAD NITRATE → LEAD NITRATE + COPPER ✗
3. MAGNESIUM + COPPER SULPHATE → MAGNESIUM SULPHATE + COPPER ✓
4. SILVER + IRON SULPHATE → SILVER + IRON SULPHATE ✗
5. CARBON + LEAD OXIDE → LEAD + CARBON DIOXIDE ✓
6. HYDROGEN + COPPER OXIDE → COPPER + WATER ✓
7. ALUMINIUM + IRON OXIDE → ALUMINIUM OXIDE + IRON. ✓

EXTRACTING METALS

METHODS OF EXTRACTION ...

1. Metals above carbon in the Reactivity Series are extracted by ELECTROLYSIS eg. aluminium.
2. Metals below carbon in the Reactivity Series are extracted by HEATING WITH CARBON eg. iron.
3. Metals at the bottom of the Series are UNREACTIVE and are found naturally eg. gold.

EXTRACTION OF IRON - THE BLAST FURNACE ...

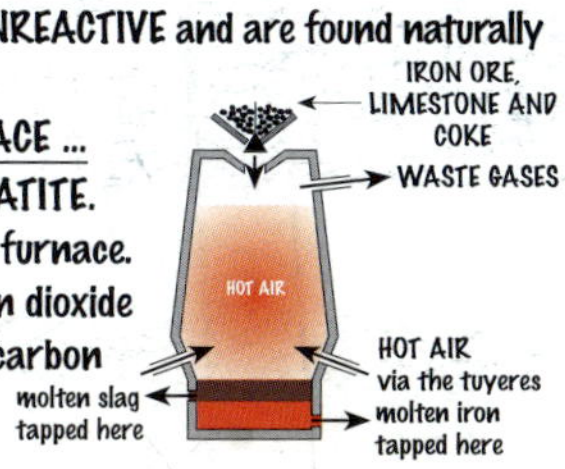

- The ore, rich in iron oxide is called HAEMATITE.
- With limestone and coke it is fed into the furnace.
- Carbon reacts with oxygen to form carbon dioxide which reacts with more carbon to form carbon monoxide (a reducing agent).

IRON OXIDE + CARBON MONOXIDE → IRON + CARBON DIOXIDE.

EXTRACTION OF ALUMINIUM - ELECTROLYSIS ...

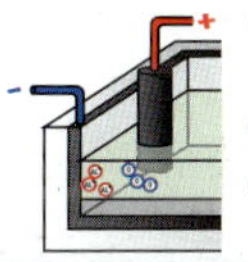

- Aluminium ore, BAUXITE is mixed with CRYOLITE to lower its melting point.
- At the -ve electrode, Al^{3+} → Aluminium
- At the +ve electrode, O^{2-} → Oxygen

The Oxygen causes the electrodes to burn away.

PURIFICATION OF COPPER/CORROSION/REDOX REACTIONS

PURIFICATION OF COPPER BY ELECTROLYSIS ...

copper, extracted by reduction, can be purified by electrolysis ..

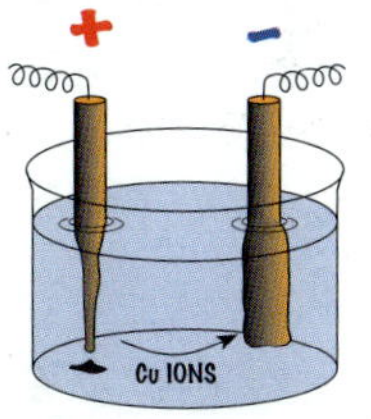

- At the +ve electrode copper ions pass into solution
- At the -ve electrode copper ions become copper atoms and are deposited making the electrode grow bigger.

SACRIFICIAL PROTECTION ...

this is when a more reactive metal is attached to a less reactive metal in order that it corrodes first leaving the less reactive metal intact. eg. zinc bars are attached to ship's hulls, magnesium strips are stuck to underground pipes and outdoor objects may be GALVANISED using molten zinc.

REDOX REACTIONS ...

during electrolysis, positively charged ions gain electrons at the -ve electrode, while negatively charged ions lose electrons at the +ve electrode. This is REDUCTION and OXIDATION respectively i.e. a REDOX REACTION.

'OILRIG' = Oxidation is loss of electrons; Reduction is gain of electrons.

pH, INDICATORS, NEUTRALISATION + SALTS

Acids contain HYDROGEN H^+ ions. Alkalis contain HYDROXIDE OH^- ions.
Universal indicator is a mixture of dyes which changes colour at different pHs.

NEUTRALISATION ...

ACID + ALKALINE HYDROXIDE → NEUTRAL SALT SOLUTION + WATER

eg. Hydrochloric Acid + Potassium Hydroxide → Potassium Chloride + Water

$H^+(aq)$ + $OH^-(aq)$ → $H_2O(l)$

PREPARING SALTS ...

the salt produced in a reaction between an acid and an alkali depends on ...
.. • THE ACID USED .. • THE METAL IN THE ALKALI.

HYDROCHLORIC ACID + SODIUM HYDROXIDE → SODIUM CHLORIDE + WATER

In neutralisation reactions ...

HYDROCHLORIC ACID produces CHLORIDE SALTS
SULPHURIC ACID produces SULPHATE SALTS
NITRIC ACID produces NITRATE SALTS

SALTS OF TRANSITION METALS ...

because their OXIDES and HYDROXIDES are INSOLUBLE they must be added to acid until no more will react, then filtered and evaporated to dryness.

SULPHURIC ACID + COPPER OXIDE → COPPER SULPHATE + WATER

1. Choose words from the list for each of the spaces 1 to 4 to complete the sentences.
   A. TRANSITION
   B. ALKALI
   C. CATALYSTS
   D. IONIC

Elements in group 1 of the periodic table are known as the ____1____ metals. They form ____2____ compounds when they react with non-metals. ____3____ metals are found in the centre of the periodic table between groups 2 and 3. Some of them can be used as ____4____ to speed up certain chemical processes.

2. <u>Sodium</u> reacts faster than calcium with cold water. <u>Copper</u> displaces silver from silver nitrate solution. <u>Zinc</u> reacts more slowly than <u>magnesium</u> with dilute acid.
   Match each of the underlined metals with each of the numbers 1 - 4 in the reactivity series.

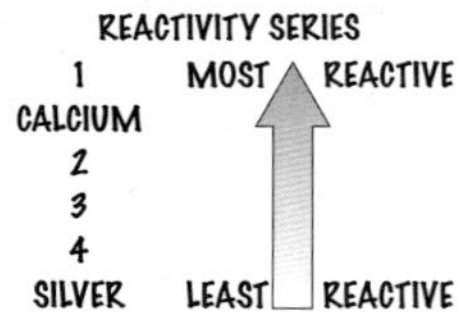

3. Copper is a metal which is used to make electrical wiring. Which <u>TWO</u> properties of copper make it a good choice?
   A. It is a good conductor.
   B. It is a shiny metal.
   C. It is a good conductor of electricity.
   D. It has a high melting point.
   E. It can be bent and pulled into different shapes.

4. The diagram below shows apparatus which can be used to purify copper. Which <u>TWO</u> of the following statements are true regarding this process?

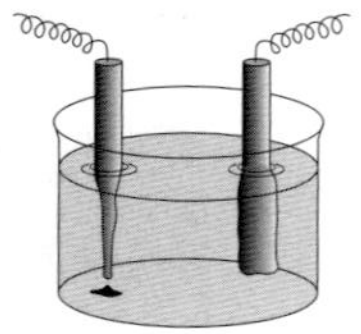

   A. The positive electrode is made of pure copper.
   B. Copper ions travel from the +ve electrode to the -ve electrode.
   C. Copper ions travel from the -ve electrode to the +ve electrode.
   D. The solution contains copper ions.
   E. The negative electrode is made of impure copper.

5. The following chart shows the colour that universal indicator becomes at different pH values:

Colour:	Red	Orange	Yellow	Green	Blue	Navy Blue	Purple
pH:	0 - 2	3 - 4	5 - 6	7	8 - 9	10 - 12	13 - 14
	ACID			NEUTRAL		ALKALINE	

5.1 All acids contain which one of the following ions ...
   A. Sulphate
   B. Hydrogen
   C. Carbonate
   D. Hydroxide

5.2 Sodium hydroxide is a metal hydroxide which makes green universal indicator turn ...
   A. Purple
   B. Green
   C. Red
   D. Orange

5.3 If pure water is added to green universal indicator it ...
   A. Turns yellow
   B. Turns blue
   C. Stays green
   D. Turns orange

5.4 If a strong alkali, potassium hydroxide is added to an equal volume of equal strength hydrochloric acid, a neutralisation reaction occurs. What is formed in this reaction?
   A. A metal hydroxide and hydrogen.
   B. A salt and hydrogen.
   C. A metal oxide and water.
   D. A salt and water.

6. Aluminium is extracted from aluminium oxide by dissolving it in molten cryolite and passing an electric current through it.

6.1 Which of the following describes best what has happened to the aluminium oxide?
   A. It has been neutralised.
   B. It has been reduced.
   C. It has been oxidised.
   D. It has been purified.

6.2 Aluminium is produced at the negative electrode because ...
   A. Positively charged aluminium ions are attracted to it.
   B. Negatively charged aluminium ions are attracted to it.
   C. Aluminium ions have a negative charge.
   D. Aluminium is a metal and conducts electricity.

6.3 Why is cryolite used in this reaction?
   A. To break the aluminium oxide into ions.
   B. To conduct the electric current through the molten mixture.
   C. To reduce the aluminium oxide.
   D. To reduce the temperature needed to melt the aluminium oxide.

6.4 Aluminium powder will react with iron oxide to form aluminium oxide and iron in a displacement reaction. The reason for this is ...
   A. Aluminium is less reactive than iron.
   B. Aluminium is higher on the reactivity series than iron.
   C. Aluminium is more reactive than oxygen.
   D. Aluminium is less reactive than oxygen.

7. Iron can be extracted from iron ore using the blast furnace below.

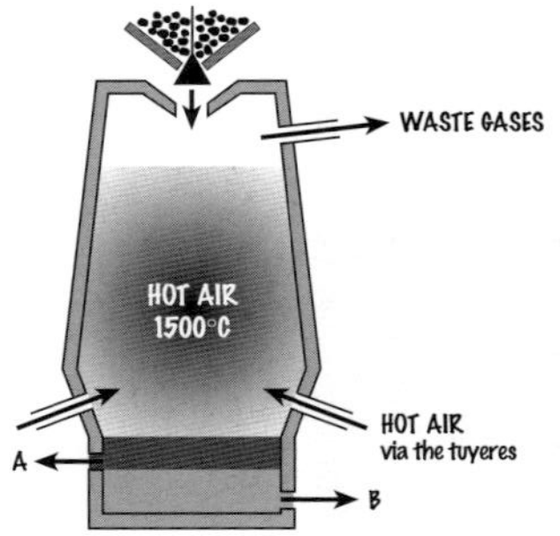

7.1 Which substances are fed into the top of the blast furnace?
   A. Iron ore.
   B. Iron ore and coke.
   C. Iron ore, limestone and coke.
   D. Iron ore and limestone.

7.2 Which two substances marked A + B are tapped off at the bottom of the furnace?
   A. Carbon and iron.
   B. Carbon and slag.
   C. Slag and iron.
   D. Carbon, slag and iron.

7.3 Which substance is responsible for removing the oxygen from iron oxide?
   A. Carbon monoxide.
   B. Carbon dioxide.
   C. Carbon.
   D. Oxygen.

7.4 The process by which iron oxide becomes iron in the blast furnace is called ...
   A. Precipitation.
   B. Oxidation.
   C. Replacement.
   D. Reduction.

LIMESTONE

Limestone is a SEDIMENTARY ROCK ...
... which consists mainly of CALCIUM CARBONATE.
It is cheap ...
... easy to obtain ...
... and has many uses:

1. Neutralising Agent

- Excess ACIDITY of soils can cause crop failure.
  - Alkalis can be 'washed out' by acid rain.
    - Powdered limestone can correct this ...
      - ... but it works quite slowly.
- However, when CALCIUM CARBONATE is heated in a kiln...

... a THERMAL DECOMPOSITION reaction takes place ...
... and the calcium carbonate breaks down into the more ...
... simple substances, CALCIUM OXIDE (QUICKLIME) and carbon dioxide.

> **NB**
> Other carbonates behave very similarly when they are heated.

CALCIUM CARBONATE (limestone) —HEAT→ CALCIUM OXIDE (quicklime) + CARBON DIOXIDE

- This can then be 'SLAKED' with water to produce CALCIUM HYDROXIDE (SLAKED LIME).

CALCIUM OXIDE (quicklime) —WATER→ CALCIUM HYDROXIDE (slaked lime)

- This, being a HYDROXIDE, is quite strongly ALKALINE ...
  - ... and so can neutralise soils and lakes much faster than just using powdered limestone.

2. Building Material

- Can be QUARRIED and cut ...
  - ... into BLOCKS, and used directly ...
    - ... to build WALLS of houses, ...
      - ... in regions where it is plentiful!
        - It is badly affected by ACID RAIN, ...
          - ... but this takes a long time.

3. Glass Making

- Glass is made by mixing ...
  - ... LIMESTONE, SAND and ...
    - ... SODA (sodium carbonate) ...
      - ... and heating the mixture until it melts.
        - When cool, it is TRANSPARENT.

LIMESTONE + SAND + SODA —HEAT→ GLASS

4. Cement Making

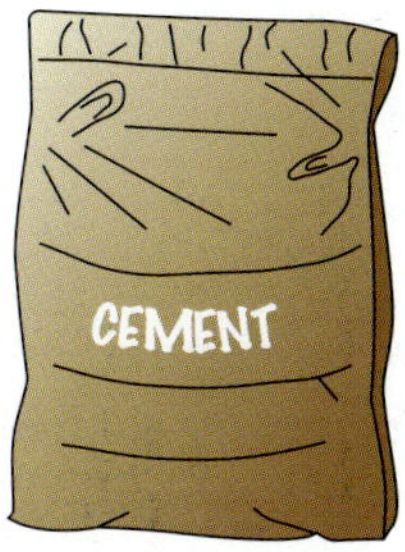

- Powdered limestone and powdered CLAY ...
  - ... are roasted in a ROTARY KILN, ...
    - ... to produce dry cement.
      - When the cement is mixed with ...
        - ...WATER, SAND and GRAVEL (crushed rock) ...
          - ... a slow reaction takes place where ...
            - ... a HARD, STONE-LIKE BUILDING MATERIAL, ...
              - ... called CONCRETE, is produced.

Formation Of Crude Oil

- Crude oil, coal and natural gas are FOSSIL FUELS.
- These are fuels which have formed over MILLIONS of years ...
- ... by the action of HEAT and PRESSURE, in the absence of oxygen,
- ... on ORGANIC material from ANIMALS and PLANTS.
- This material gets trapped by layers of sedimentary rock.

Crude oil and natural gas were formed from animals that lived in the sea.

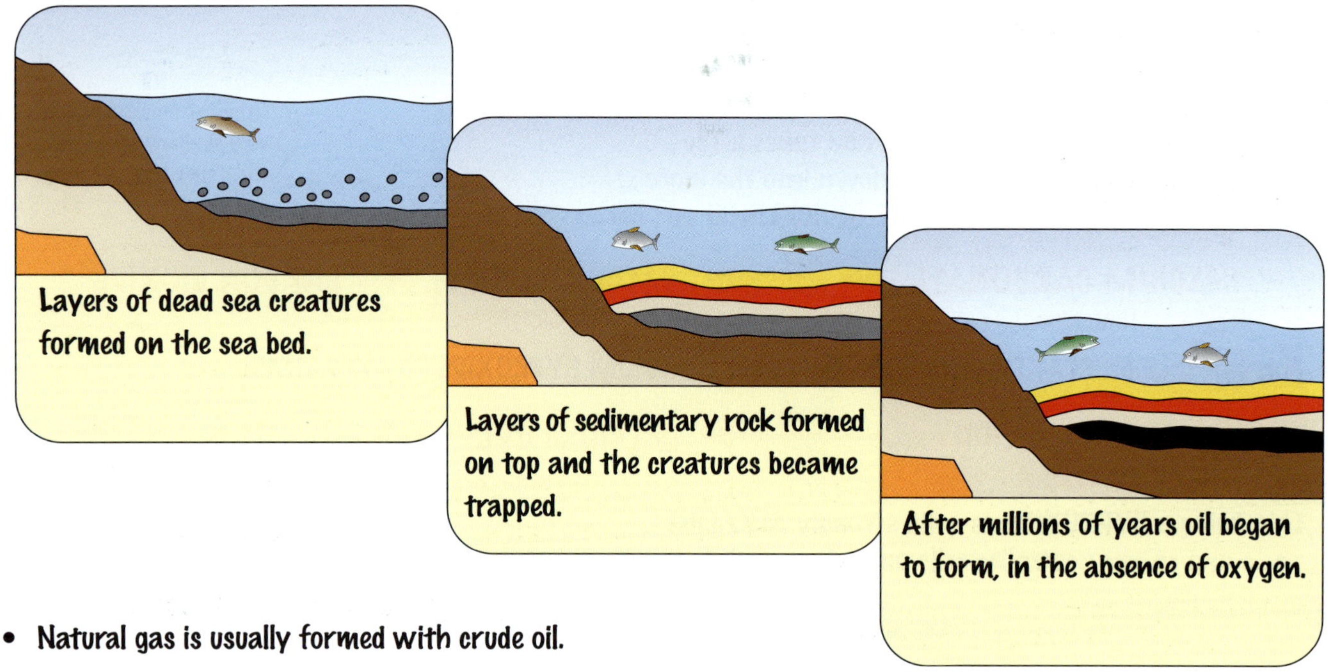

- Natural gas is usually formed with crude oil.

What Crude Oil Is

- Crude oil is a mixture of compounds most of which ...
- ... are MOLECULES made up of CARBON and HYDROGEN atoms only, called HYDROCARBONS.

These hydrocarbon molecules vary in size. This affects their properties.

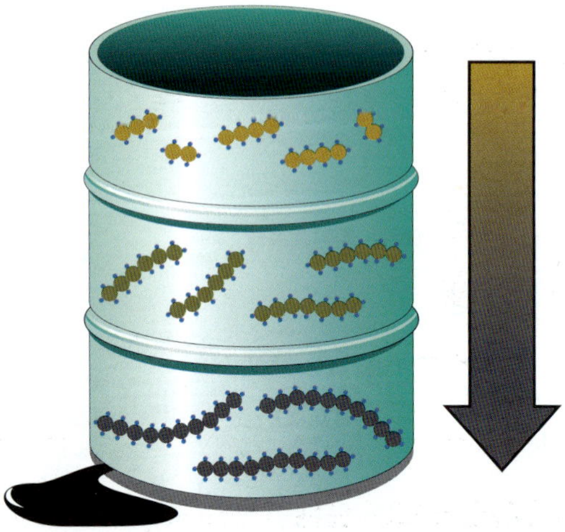

The LARGER the HYDROCARBON
ie. the greater the number of carbon atoms in a molecule:

1. The **LESS EASILY IT FLOWS** ...
   ... ie. the more viscous it is.
2. The **LESS EASILY IT IGNITES** ...
   ... ie. the less flammable it is.
3. The **LESS VOLATILE IT IS** ...
   ... ie. it doesn't vaporise as easily.
4. The **HIGHER ITS BOILING POINT.**

Because a mixture consists of two or more elements or compounds, which aren't chemically combined together, the properties of the substances in the mixture remain unchanged and specific to that substance. This makes it possible to separate the substances in a mixture by physical methods such as DISTILLATION. (See next page)

Fractional Distillation Of Crude Oil

Crude oil on its own isn't a great deal of use. However, different hydrocarbons have different **BOILING POINTS** which means that they can be separated into their individual parts, or **FRACTIONS**, by **FRACTIONAL DISTILLATION**.

EVAPORATE the oil by heating ...
... and then allow it to **CONDENSE** ...
... at a **RANGE OF DIFFERENT TEMPERATURES** ...
... where it forms **FRACTIONS** ...
... each of which contains ...
... hydrocarbon molecules ...
... with a **SIMILAR NUMBER** ...
... of **CARBON ATOMS**.
This is done in a ...
... **FRACTIONATING COLUMN**

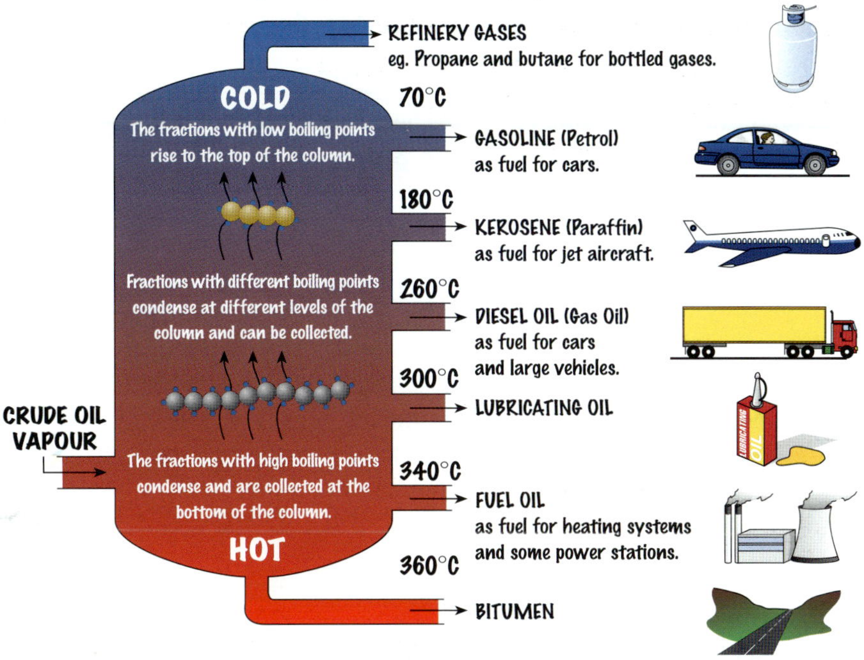

Cracking

Because the **SHORTER CHAIN HYDROCARBONS** release energy more quickly by **BURNING**, there is a greater demand for them as fuels. Therefore **LONGER CHAIN HYDROCARBONS** are **'CRACKED'** or broken down into shorter chains.

This is done by heating them until they vaporise; the vapour is then passed over a heated catalyst, ...
... where a **THERMAL DECOMPOSITION** reaction takes place.

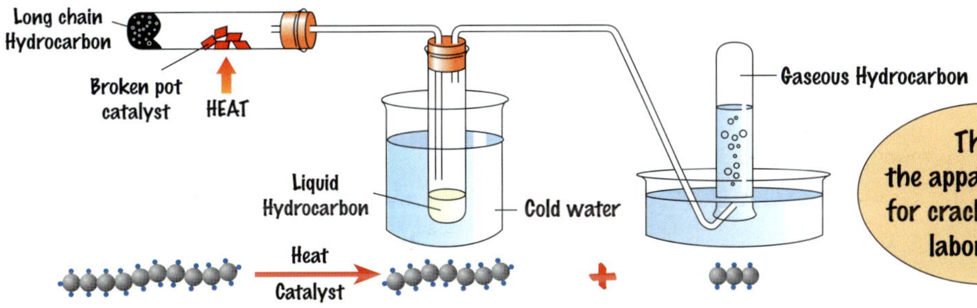

This is the apparatus used for cracking in the laboratory.

The products of cracking are used ...

① ... as **FUELS** which burn to produce **WASTE PRODUCTS**, which are then released into the atmosphere. The waste product produced depends on which element is present in the fuel eg.

- **CARBON** PRODUCES **CARBON DIOXIDE**
- **HYDROGEN** PRODUCES **WATER VAPOUR** (an oxide of hydrogen)
- **SULPHUR** PRODUCES **SULPHUR DIOXIDE**

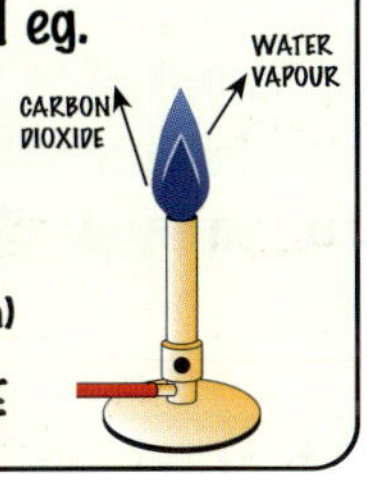

② ... to **MAKE PLASTICS (POLYMERS)** such as ... **POLY(ETHENE)** and **POLY(PROPENE)**.

However ...

- Burning fuels does produce carbon dioxide which contributes to the **GREENHOUSE EFFECT** and sulphur dioxide which helps produce **ACID RAIN**.
- Most plastics including poly(ethene) and poly(propene) are not **BIODEGRADABLE**. Microorganisms have no effect on them; they will not decompose and rot away. This causes problems when we throw plastics away as they can build up in landfill sites.

Alkanes - Saturated Hydrocarbons

The 'SPINE' of a HYDROCARBON is made up of a chain of CARBON ATOMS.

- When these are joined together by single covalent carbon—carbon bonds ...
- ... we say the HYDROCARBON is SATURATED and it is known as an ALKANE.

To put it simply ...

Hydrogen atoms can make ...
... 1 BOND EACH

Carbon atoms can make ...
... 4 BONDS EACH

The simplest alkane, METHANE, is made up of ...
... 4 HYDROGEN ATOMS and 1 CARBON ATOM.

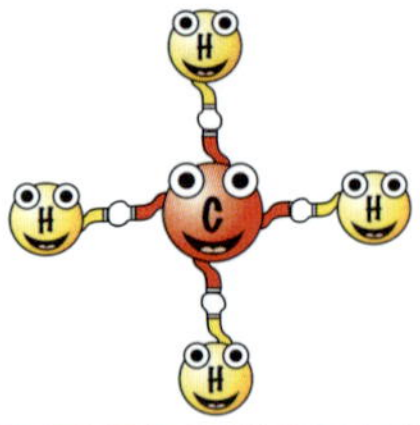

CH_4

A more convenient way of representing alkanes is as follows ...

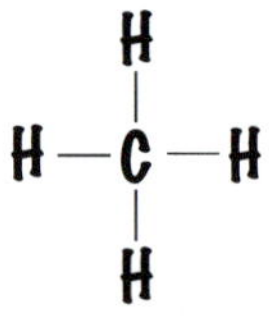

METHANE, CH_4

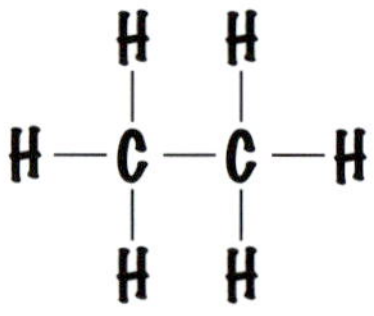

ETHANE, C_2H_6

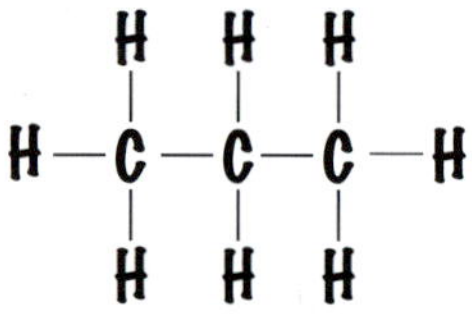

PROPANE, C_3H_8

- ALL THE CARBON ATOMS ARE LINKED TO 4 OTHER ATOMS.
- THEY ARE ALL 'FULLY OCCUPIED' OR SATURATED.
- ALL THE BONDS ARE SINGLE COVALENT BONDS.

Because all their bonds are 'occupied' they are fairly UNREACTIVE, although they do burn well.

Alkenes - Unsaturated Hydrocarbons

- Carbon atoms can also form DOUBLE COVALENT BONDS with other atoms, and ...

... amongst the products of cracking are HYDROCARBON MOLECULES which have ...
... at least ONE DOUBLE COVALENT BOND.
We say that the HYDROCARBON is UNSATURATED and it is known as an ALKENE.
The simplest alkene is ETHENE, C_2H_4 which ...

... is made up of 4 HYDROGEN ATOMS ...
... and 2 CARBON ATOMS.
As you can see ethene contains ...
... ONE DOUBLE CARBON=CARBON COVALENT BOND.

Yet again, there is a convenient way of representing alkenes ...

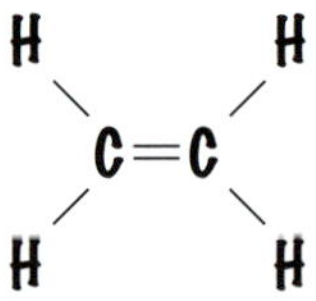

ETHENE, C_2H_4

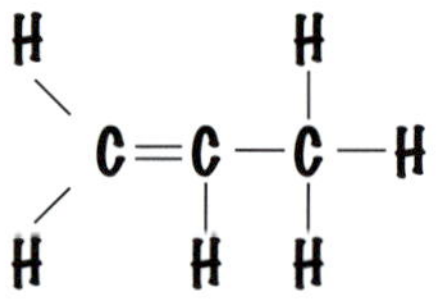

PROPENE, C_3H_6

- NOT ALL THE CARBON ATOMS ARE LINKED TO 4 OTHER ATOMS.
- THEY ARE NOT ALL 'FULLY OCCUPIED' ie. THEY ARE UNSATURATED.
- A DOUBLE BOND IS PRESENT.

Because of this DOUBLE BOND (=) the ALKENES have the potential to join with other atoms and so they are REACTIVE. This makes them useful for making other molecules, especially POLYMERS.
Polymers are very large molecules which are formed when the small alkene molecules above, called MONOMERS, join together. This process is known as POLYMERISATION.

Test For An Alkene

Alkenes will DECOLOURISE BROMINE WATER as the ALKENE REACTS WITH IT.

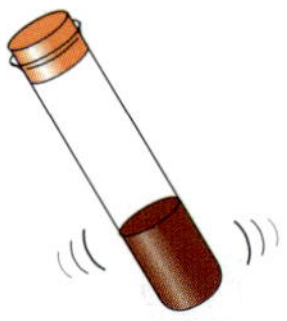

Monomers To Polymers

One of the important uses of the alkenes which are produced during cracking, is the production of **POLYMERS**;... ... these are **LONG CHAIN MOLECULES**, some of which make up **PLASTICS**.

Because **ALKENES** are **UNSATURATED**, they are very good at joining together and when they do so without producing another substance, we call this **ADDITION POLYMERISATION**.

eg. the formation of poly(ethene) from ethene.

1

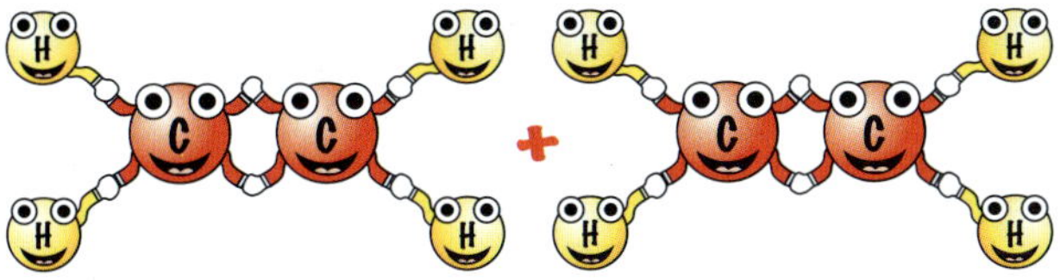

The small alkene molecules are called **MONOMERS**.

2

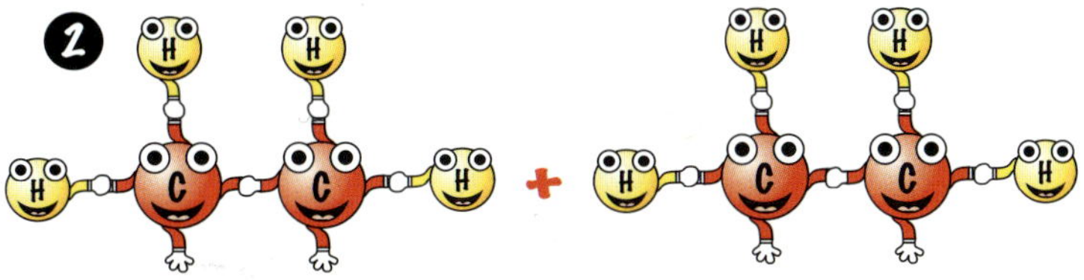

Their double bonds are easily broken.

... large numbers of molecules can therefore be joined in this way.

3

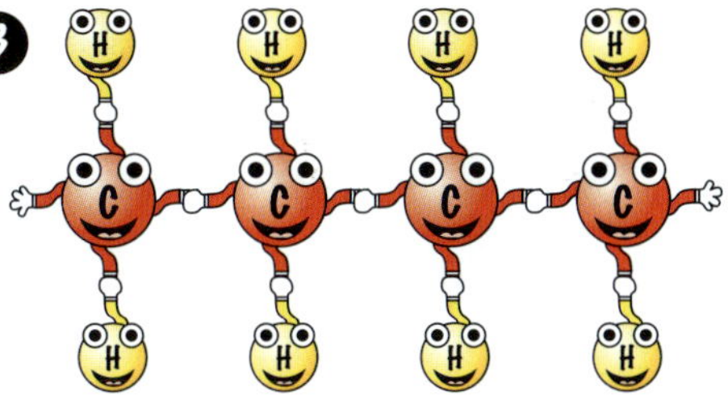

The resulting long chain molecule is a **POLYMER** - in this case **POLY(ETHENE)** ... often called **POLYTHENE**

A more convenient form of representing addition polymerisation is ...

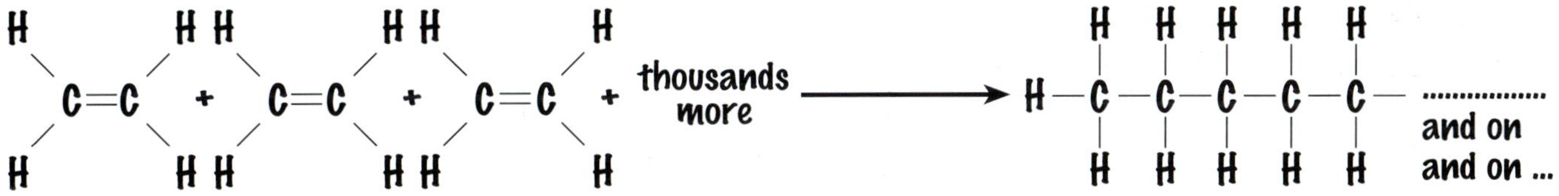

ethene monomers (unsaturated)

poly(ethene) polymer (saturated)

General Formula For Addition Polymerisation

This can be applied to any **ADDITION POLYMERISATION** ...
... to represent the formation of a simple addition polymer.

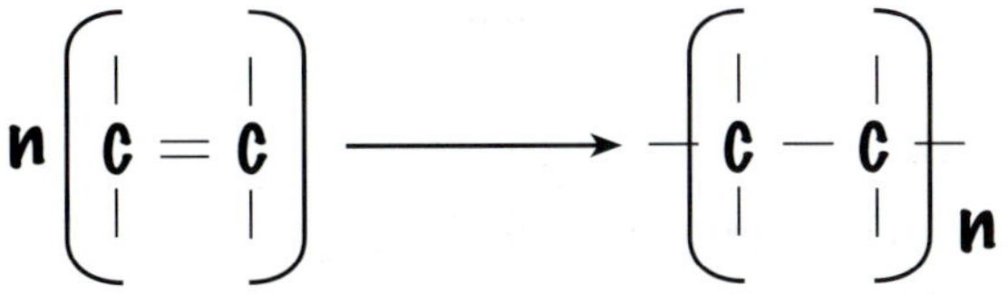

... where 'n' is a very large number.

For example, if we take ...

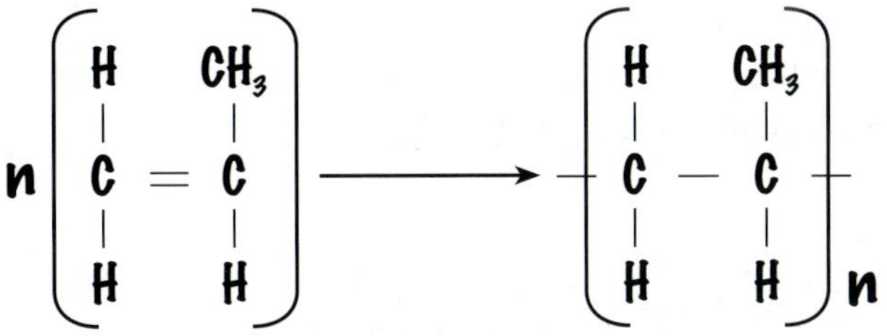

... 'n' molecules of propene to produce poly(propene), which is used to make crates and ropes (see P.53).

Since the formation of the earth 4.6 billion years ago the atmosphere has changed very dramatically. The timescale, however, is enormous because one billion years is one thousand million years! (1,000,000,000)

COMPOSITION OF THE ATMOSPHERE

TIME SCALE

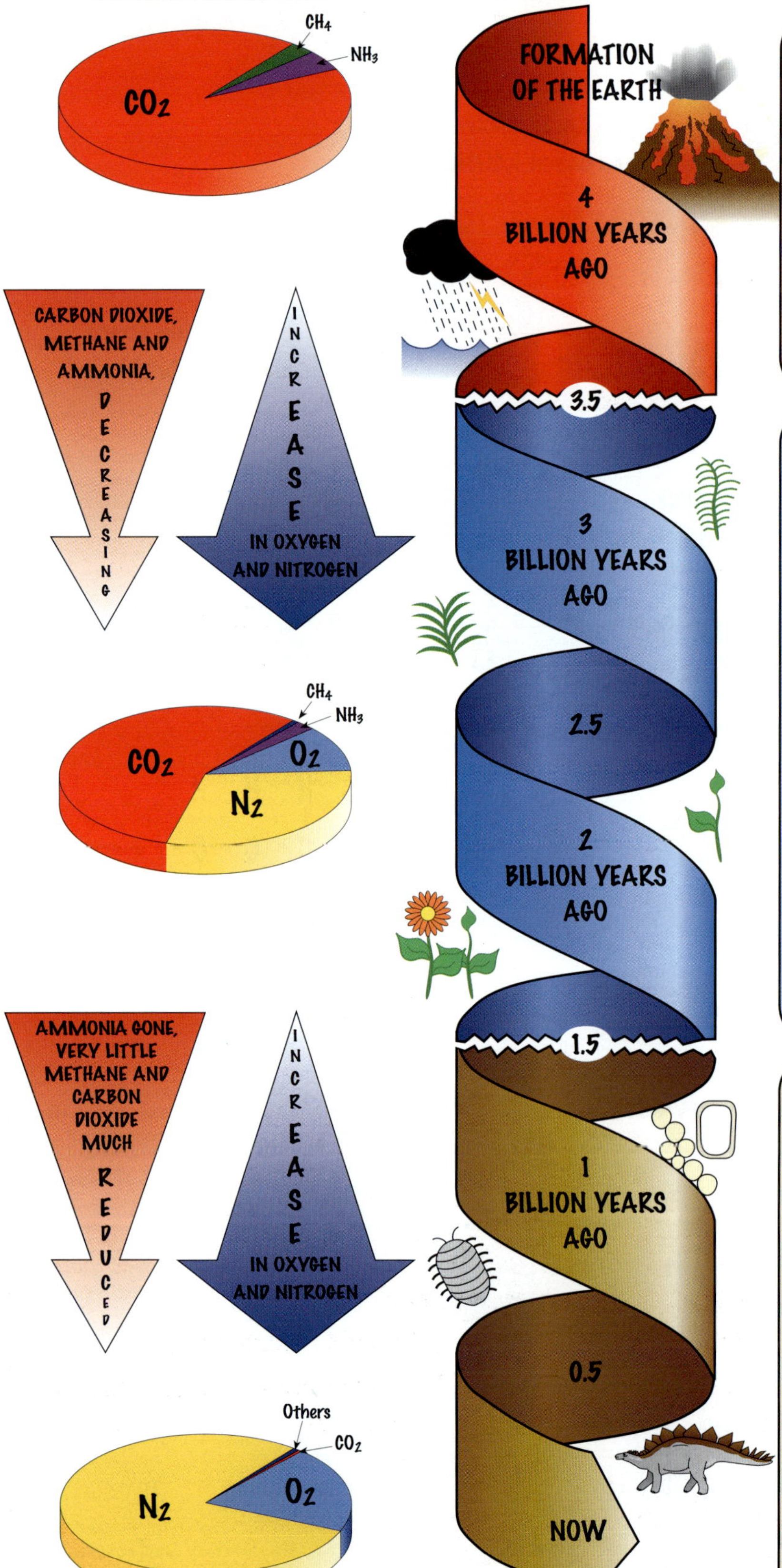

KEY FACTORS AND EVENTS WHICH SHAPED THE ATMOSPHERE

Volcanic activity releases ...

- ... mainly CARBON DIOXIDE, and ...
- ... small amounts of METHANE ...
  ... and AMMONIA.
- WATER VAPOUR is also released which condenses to form the oceans.

Green plants evolve and ...

- CARBON DIOXIDE is reduced as the plants take it in and give out OXYGEN.
- Microorganisms which can't tolerate OXYGEN are killed off.
- Carbon from CARBON DIOXIDE in the air becomes locked up in sedimentary rocks as carbonates and fossil fuels.
- METHANE and AMMONIA react with the OXYGEN now available.
- This releases NITROGEN (from the AMMONIA), which is also produced as a result of the action of DENITRIFYING BACTERIA on nitrates from decaying plant material.

- The OXYGEN in the atmosphere is now much increased and some of it is converted into OZONE.
- This OZONE forms a thin layer in the atmosphere which filters out harmful U.V. light from the sun.
- The reduction in harmful ultra-violet light falling onto the surface of the planet allows the evolution of new living organisms.

Composition Of The Atmosphere

Our atmosphere has been more or less the same for 200 million years!!!

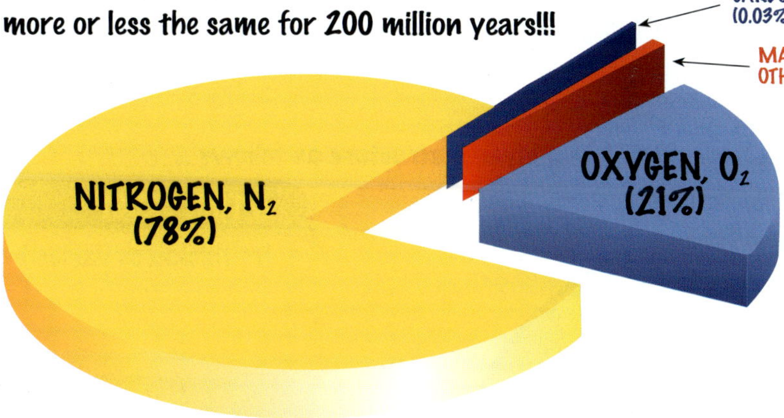

- WATER VAPOUR may also be present in varying quantities (0-3%).

Modern Day Changes To The Level Of Carbon Dioxide In The Atmosphere

The level of CARBON DIOXIDE in the atmosphere is INCREASED due to ...

VOLCANIC ACTIVITY

Geological activity moves ...
... CARBONATE ROCKS deep ...
... into the EARTH.

During volcanic activity, ...
... they may release CARBON DIOXIDE ...
... back into the atmosphere.

+

BURNING OF FOSSIL FUELS

The burning of the carbon, ...
... which has been locked up ...
... in FOSSIL FUELS for ....

... millions of years, releases ...
... CARBON DIOXIDE into ...
... the atmosphere.

The level of CARBON DIOXIDE in the atmosphere is REDUCED by...

THE REACTION BETWEEN CARBON DIOXIDE AND SEA WATER

- Increased CARBON DIOXIDE in the atmosphere increases the reaction between ...
... CARBON DIOXIDE and SEA WATER, which produces INSOLUBLE CARBONATES (mainly calcium) ...
... which are deposited as SEDIMENT and SOLUBLE HYDROGENCARBONATES (mainly calcium and magnesium).

CO_2 CO_2 CO_2 CO_2 CO_2 CO_2 CO_2 CO_2 CO_2 CO_2 CO_2 CO_2 CO_2

Unfortunately this reaction does NOT remove ALL of the CO_2 which is ...
... released into the atmosphere, through volcanic activity and fossil fuel burning, ...
... which means that the LEVEL OF CARBON DIOXIDE CONTINUES TO RISE!!

EARTH STRUCTURE AND MOVEMENT

Although there doesn't seem to be much going on, the Earth and its crust are very dynamic. Rocks at the Earth's surface are continually being broken up, reformed and changed in an ongoing, cycle of events, known as the rock cycle. It's just that things take such a long time.

Structure Of The Earth

The Earth is nearly spherical and has a layered structure as follows ...

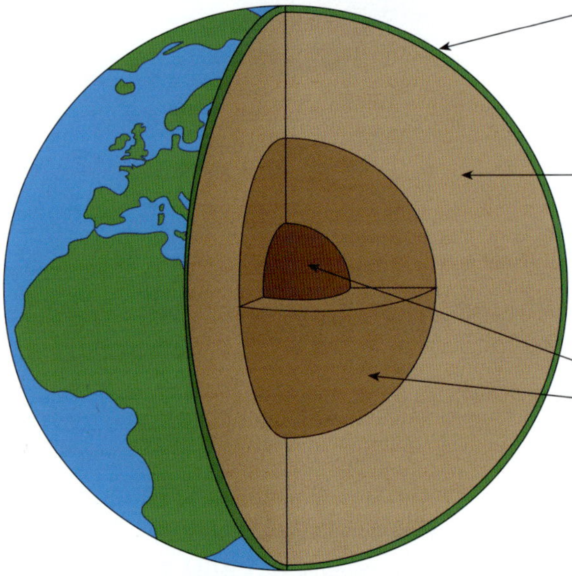

A THIN CRUST
- Its thickness varies between 10 Km and 100 Km.

A MANTLE
- Extends almost HALFWAY TO THE CENTRE.
- Has all the properties of a SOLID ...
  ... even though it does flow very slowly.

A CORE
- Made of NICKEL and IRON.
- Over HALF of the Earth's RADIUS with a ...
  ... LIQUID OUTER PART and a SOLID INNER PART.

- The average density of the Earth is MUCH GREATER than ...
- ... the average density of the rocks which form the CRUST.
- This proves that the INTERIOR OF THE EARTH ...
- ... is made of a DIFFERENT and DENSER MATERIAL than that of the crust.

The Crust

At the surface of the Earth sedimentary rocks exist mainly in LAYERS ...
... where the younger sedimentary rocks USUALLY lie on top of older rocks.
A typical cross-section could look like this ...

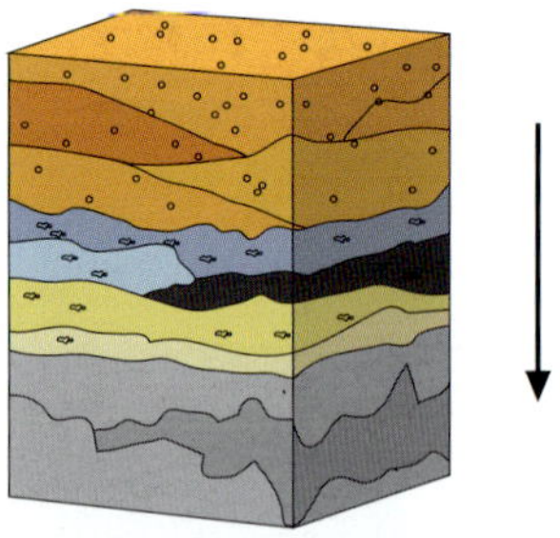

Examination of the sediments can provide evidence of how they were formed.
- Layers are formed due to the deposition of the sediments at interrupted intervals.
- Ripple marks may be found due to the movement of currents or waves.

However, sedimentary rock layers are often found ...

... TILTED ... FOLDED ... FRACTURED ... TURNED UPSIDE DOWN.

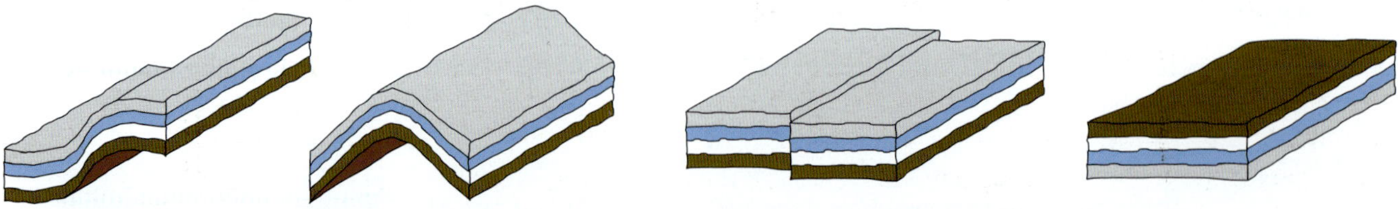

- All this shows ...
- ... that the EARTH'S CRUST HAS BEEN SUBJECTED TO VERY LARGE FORCES, ...
- ... to cause this movement of the sedimentary rock layers, and that it is very UNSTABLE!

Movement Of The Lithosphere

The Earth's LITHOSPHERE ie. the CRUST and the UPPER PART OF THE MANTLE ...
... is 'cracked' into several large pieces called TECTONIC PLATES.

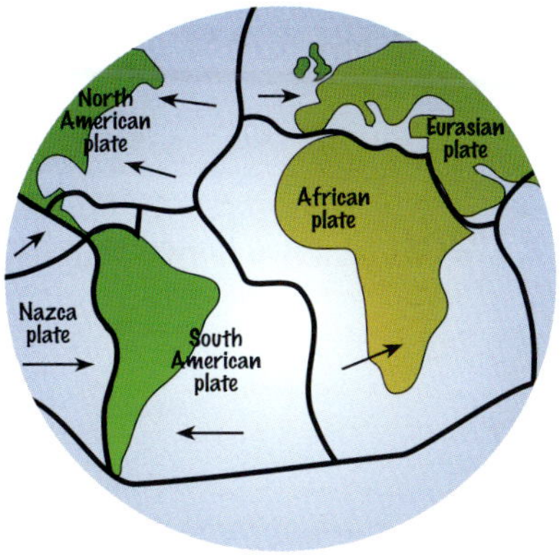

These plates move slowly, at speeds of a few cm per year, ...
... driven by CONVECTION CURRENTS in the MANTLE, ...
... which are caused by HEAT released by RADIOACTIVE DECAY.

Hot molten rock comes ...
.. up to the surface ...
... at the boundary ...
... between the plates.

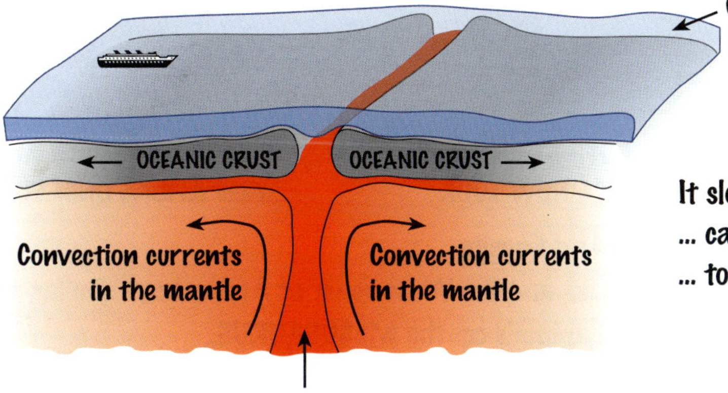

It slowly spreads sideways ...
... causing the plates ...
... to gradually move apart.

<u>In other words:</u>
New crust is formed where the rising convection current reaches the surface ...
...and old crust disappears where the convection current starts to fall (see P.61).
This causes the land masses on these plates to move slowly across the globe.

EARTHQUAKES and VOLCANIC ERUPTIONS are common occurrences ...
... at the boundary between two plates.
As yet, scientists cannot predict when these events will occur, ...
... due to the difficulty in taking appropriate measurements, ...
... but at least they do know where these events are likely to occur.

This may form the basis of a data handling question in your TERMINAL EXAMINATION.

Forming Mountain Ranges

- Mountain ranges can form where plates collide. This causes the continental crust to crumple and fold at the point of impact.
- This can cause sedimentary rocks in the continental crust to be subjected to intense PRESSURE and HIGH TEMPERATURE, causing them to change structure and become METAMORPHIC rocks. eg. Limestone may change into marble.
- This movement of the crust causes mountain ranges to form very slowly over millions of years. An example of this is where the continental crust which is India, has collided with the Asian crust, to form the Himalayas. These mountains are still being forced upwards as the two plates pile into each other but of course, they are simultaneously being worn away due to weathering and erosion.

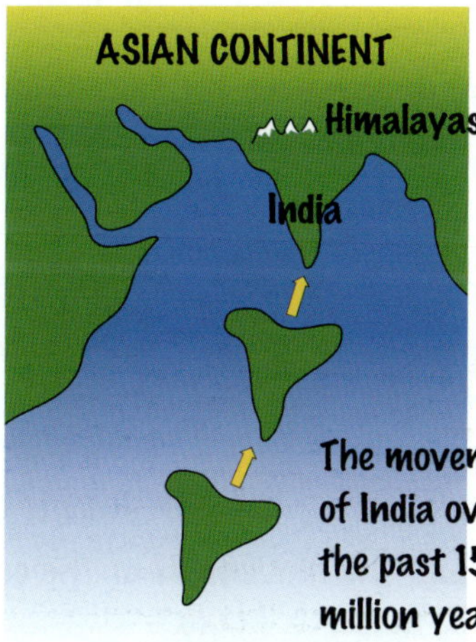

The movement of India over the past 150 million years.

The Evidence

At one time people used to believe that the features of the Earth's surface were caused by **SHRINKAGE** when the Earth cooled, following its formation.
Today, this is rejected in favour of the **TECTONIC THEORY** ...
Evidence has been gained by comparing the **EAST COAST** of **SOUTH AMERICA** and the **WEST COAST** of **AFRICA**.
Although separated by thousands of kilometres of ocean, they have ...

1 Closely Matching Shapes

Geologists have long noticed that their coastlines are closely matched and were, therefore, once joined together.

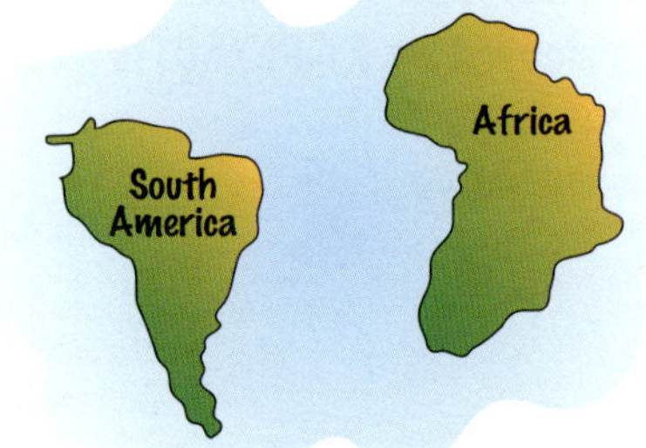

HOW SOUTH AMERICA AND AFRICA NOW LOOK

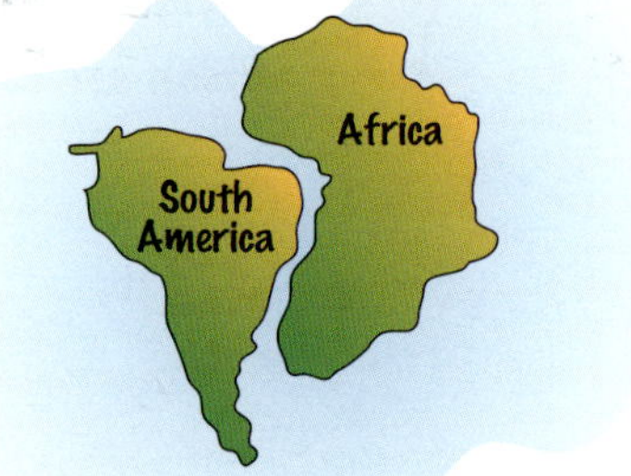

IS THIS HOW SOUTH AMERICA AND AFRICA ONCE LOOKED?

2 Similar Patterns Of Rocks And Fossils

The East coast of South America and the West coast of Africa have similar patterns of rocks and contain fossils of the same plants and animals eg. the **MESOSAURUS**.

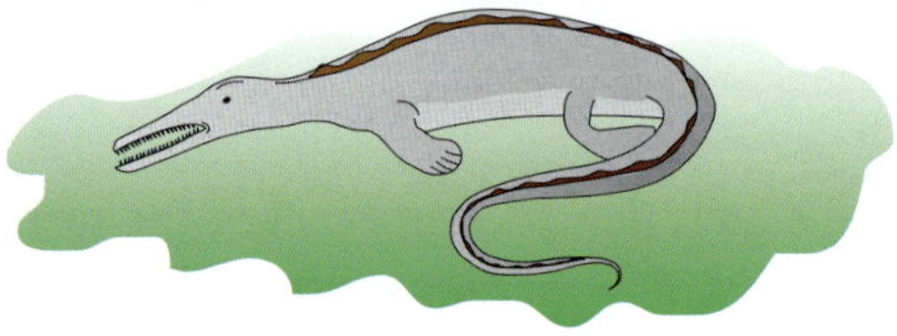

The Theory

The evidence above led Alfred Wegener to propose that ...
... **MOVEMENT OF THE CRUST** or **CONTINENTAL DRIFT** was responsible for their separation ...
... and indeed that they had at one time both been part of a single land mass.
Unfortunately Wegener was unable to explain how the crust moved ...
... and it took more than 50 years for scientists to realise ...
... that the enormous heat released during radioactive decay inside the Earth ...
... generates convection currents in the mantle, causing movement of the crust.
The hard evidence for this comes from magnetic reversal patterns alongside oceanic ridges ...
... which confirm sea floor spreading.

This may form the basis of a data handling question in your **TERMINAL EXAMINATION**.

We now favour his **TECTONIC THEORY** which explains **MOUNTAIN BUILDING** ...

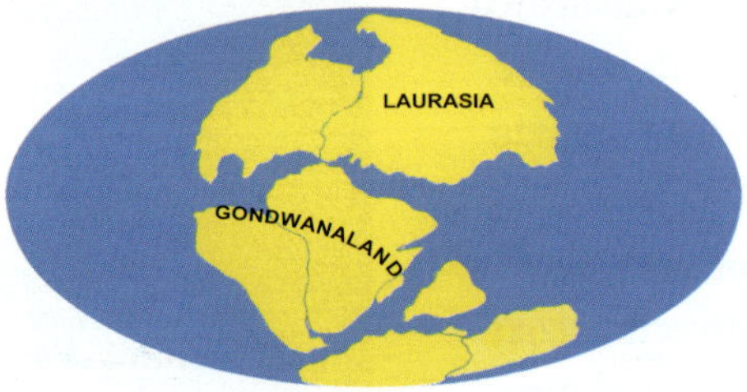

HOW IT ONCE WAS

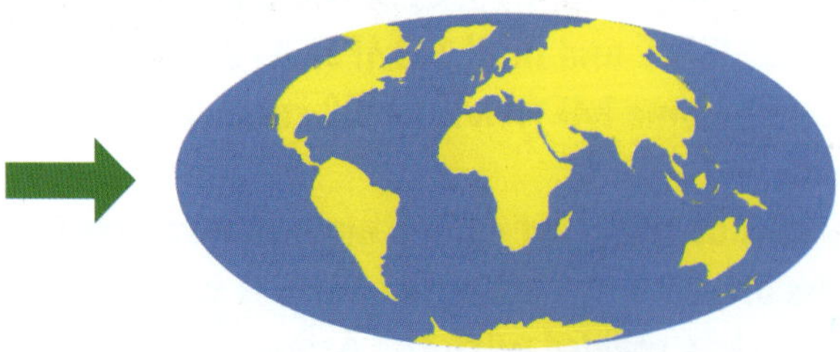

HOW IT IS TODAY

... and the movement of the continents from how they were (as **GONDWANALAND** and **LAURASIA**) to what they look like today.

Three Things That Can Happen

The 'plates' on the previous page can basically only do THREE things:

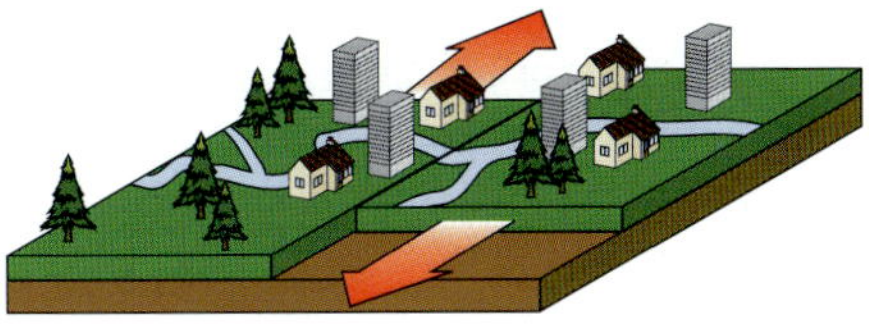

1 Slide Past Each Other

When plates SLIDE, HUGE STRESSES AND STRAINS build up in the crust ...
... which eventually have to be RELEASED in order for MOVEMENT to occur.
This 'release' of energy results in an EARTHQUAKE.
A classic example of this is the West Coast of North America (esp. California).

2 Move Away From Each Other – Constructive Plate Margins

When plates MOVE AWAY FROM EACH OTHER, at an oceanic ridge, FRACTURES OCCUR, ...
... these are filled by MAGMA to produce NEW BASALTIC OCEAN CRUST, ...
... at a rate of 2cm per year.
This is known as SEA FLOOR SPREADING.

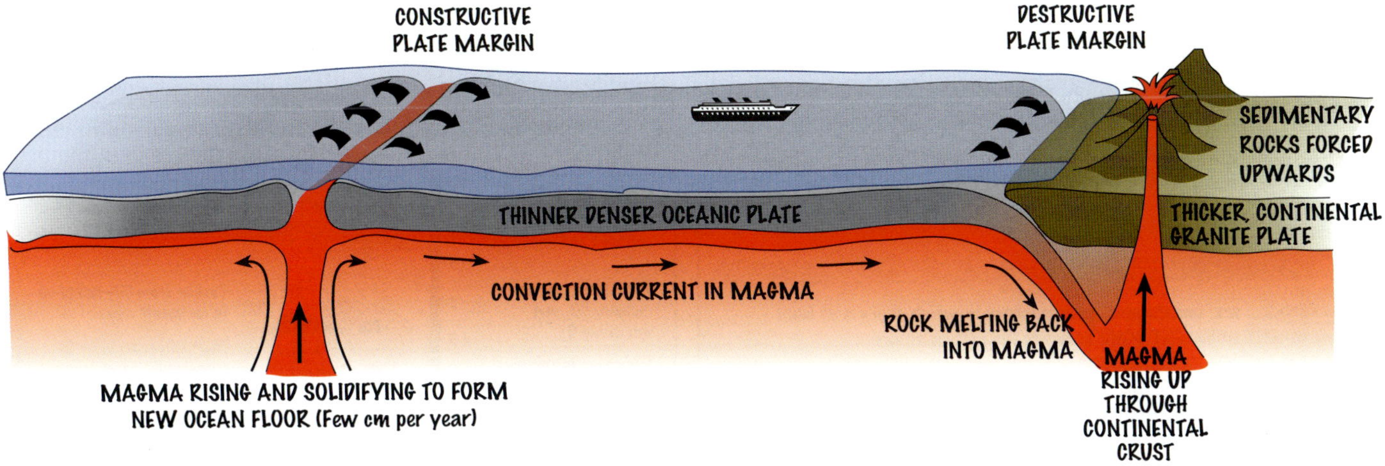

3 Move Towards Each Other – Destructive Plate Margins

As plates are moving away from each other in some places ...
... it follows that they must be MOVING TOWARDS EACH OTHER in other places.
This always results in the THINNER, DENSER, OCEANIC PLATE being FORCED DOWN (SUBDUCTED) beneath ...
... the THICKER CONTINENTAL GRANITE PLATE, where it partially MELTS.
This subduction forces continental crust to be compressed resulting in folding and metamorphism.
EARTHQUAKES are common and even VOLCANOES are formed ...
... due to magma rising up through the continental crust eg. West Coast of South America (Andes).

Evidence for Sea Floor Spreading

As Magma rises and solidifies, to form new Basaltic Ocean Crust, ...
... IRON-RICH minerals ORIENTATE themselves in the DIRECTION OF THE EARTH'S MAGNETIC FIELD, ...
... forming MAGNETIC REVERSAL PATTERNS parallel to the OCEANIC RIDGE ...
The magnetic field of the Earth has changed NINE times in the last 3.6 million years, and ...
... this is 'mirrored' in these REVERSAL PATTERNS.

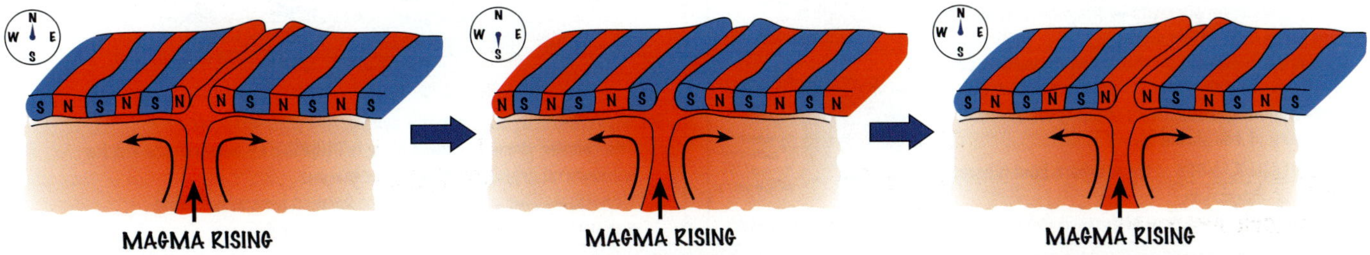

LIMESTONE AND INTRODUCTION TO CRUDE OIL

LIMESTONE ... is made mainly of CALCIUM CARBONATE.

- It can be used as a NEUTRALISING AGENT either directly or as CALCIUM HYDROXIDE

CALCIUM CARBONATE (limestone) $\xrightarrow{\text{HEAT}}$ CALCIUM OXIDE (quicklime) + CARBON DIOXIDE

CALCIUM OXIDE (quicklime) $\xrightarrow{\text{WATER}}$ CALCIUM HYDROXIDE (slaked lime)

- It can be used as a building material but is prone to erosion from acid rain.
- It is used in glass making LIMESTONE + SAND + SODA $\xrightarrow{\text{HEAT}}$ GLASS
- It is used in cement making where it is heated in a kiln with powdered clay.

INTRODUCTION TO CRUDE OIL ... formed by HEAT and PRESSURE in the ABSENCE of OXYGEN on ORGANIC MATERIAL trapped beneath layers of sedimentary rocks for millions of years.

- Crude oil is a mixture of compounds most of which are made up of CARBON and HYDROGEN atoms only, called HYDROCARBONS.

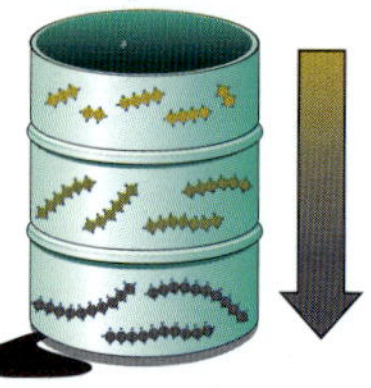

The larger the hydrocarbon molecule ...
- ... the LESS EASILY IT FLOWS.
- ... the LESS EASILY IT IGNITES.

This mixture can be separated by DISTILLATION.

FRACTIONAL DISTILLATION AND CRACKING

FRACTIONAL DISTILLATION ...
- The crude oil is heated and allowed to CONDENSE at a RANGE OF DIFFERENT TEMPERATURES.
- The 'fractions' formed contain HYDROCARBON molecules with a similar number of carbon atoms.
- This is done in a fractionating column shown opposite.

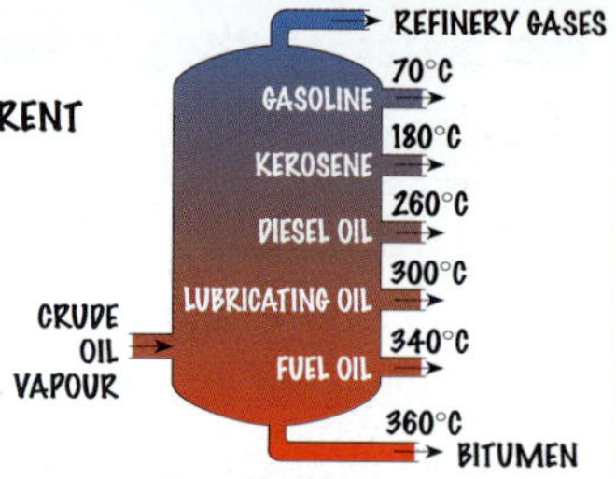

CRACKING ...
- Shorter chain hydrocarbons are in greater demand because they release ENERGY QUICKLY.
- Long chain hydrocarbons are therefore 'CRACKED' into shorter chains by passing their vapour over a heated catalyst causing THERMAL DECOMPOSITION.

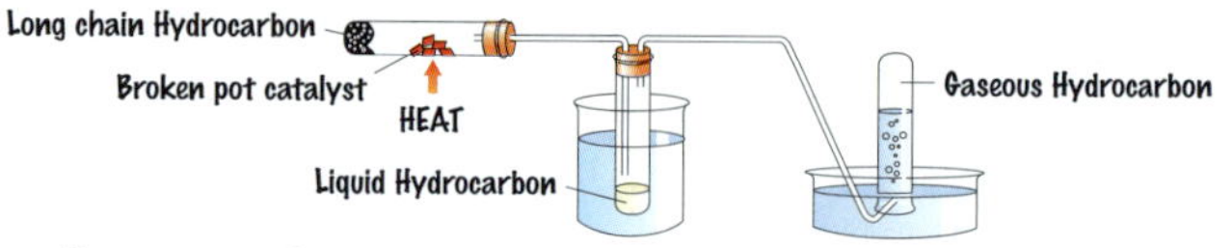

- The products of cracking are used as FUELS and also to make PLASTICS eg. polythene, polypropene.

ALKANES, ALKENES AND ADDITION POLYMERISATION

ALKANES ... are 'saturated' hydrocarbons in which the carbon atoms are joined together by SINGLE COVALENT BONDS.

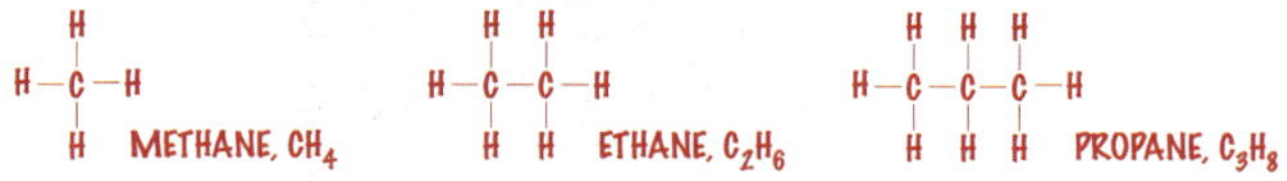

ALKENES ... are 'unsaturated' hydrocarbons in which there is at least one DOUBLE COVALENT BOND between the carbon atoms.

They are reactive because the double bond allows them to join with other molecules to form POLYMERS. Alkenes are identified by decolourising BROMINE WATER.

ADDITION POLYMERISATION ... is when alkene monomers join together to form a polymer and no other substance eg. lots of ETHENE molecules join up to form POLYETHENE.

The general formula is ...

Plastics are polymers and made in this way.

THE EARTH'S ATMOSPHERE

HOW IT EVOLVED ...

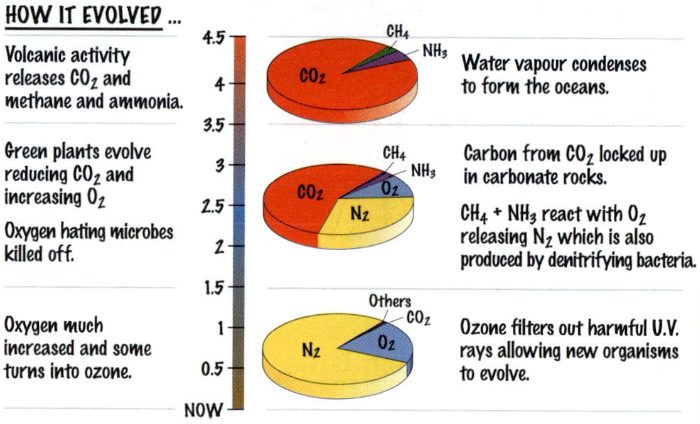

CHANGES IN CO_2 LEVELS ...

decreased by ... dissolving in sea water to form INSOLUBLE (calcium) CARBONATES and SOLUBLE HYDROGENCARBONATES

increased by ... geological and volcanic activity and by ... burning fossil fuels for our energy needs.

MOVEMENTS OF THE EARTH'S CRUST

- The average density of the Earth is much denser than the average density of the crust.
- Therefore the interior of the earth must be made of a different and denser material.

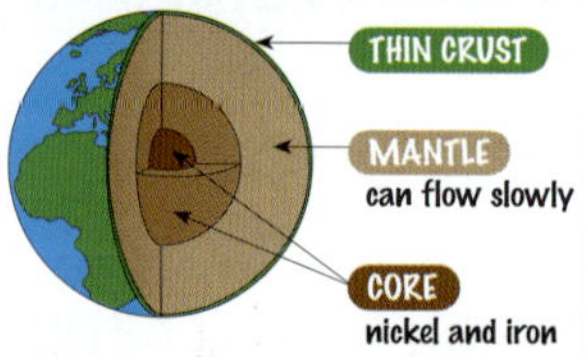

Younger rocks are normally on top of older rocks. Rocks may be ...

... TILTED ... FOLDED ... FRACTURED ... TURNED UPSIDE DOWN.

TECTONIC PLATES ... formed in the lithosphere (crust and upper part of the mantle), move slowly due to convection currents in the mantle caused by heat from radioactive decay.

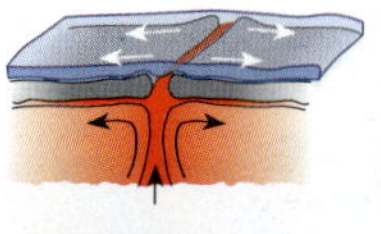

New crust is formed by the rising convection current and old crust disappears where the current falls. Earthquakes and volcanoes often occur at the boundary of the plates.

MOUNTAIN RANGES ... form where land masses collide eg. Himalayas.

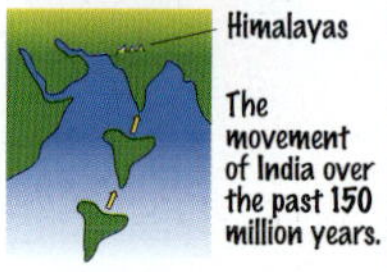

Metamorphic rocks may be formed due to the high pressure and temperature.

TECTONIC ACTIVITY

THE EVIDENCE ... for tectonic theory is based on

(a) Closely matching shapes of South America and Africa.
(b) Similar patterns of rocks and fossils near the coasts of the two continents.
(c) Sea floor spreading confirmed by magnetic reversal patterns.

Wegener's theory was only accepted 50 years after it was proposed.

THE EFFECTS ... tectonic plates can ...

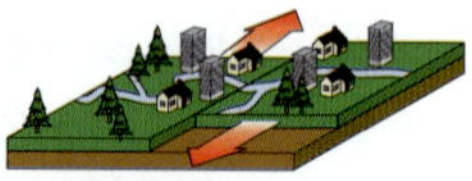

(a) Slide past each other causing EARTHQUAKES eg. Coast of California.
(b) Move away from each other - constructive plate margins. The fractures are filled by magma producing new basaltic ocean crust along the oceanic ridges.

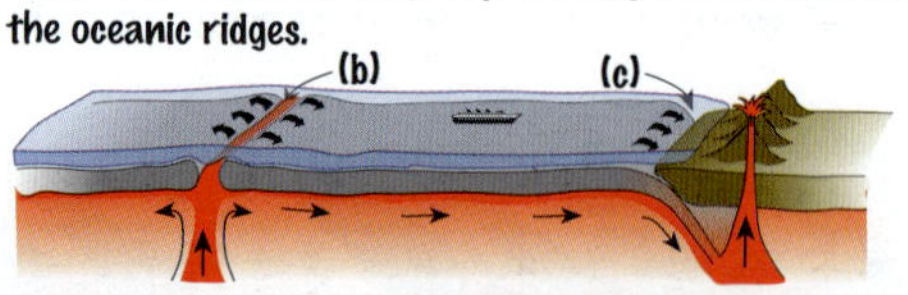

(c) Move towards each other - destructive plate margins. The thinner, denser oceanic plate is SUBDUCTED beneath the thicker continental granite plate into the magma. Mountains and volcanoes may be formed here and folding and metamorphism are common eg. the Andes

1. Limestone can be used as a neutralising agent, and also to make glass. Choose words from the list for each of the spaces 1 - 4 in the word equations.
   A. CARBON DIOXIDE
   B. SAND
   C. SODIUM CARBONATE
   D. CALCIUM HYDROXIDE

CALCIUM CARBONATE $\xrightarrow{\text{HEAT}}$ CALCIUM OXIDE + ___1___

CALCIUM OXIDE $\xrightarrow{\text{WATER}}$ ___2___

LIMESTONE + ___3___ + ___4___ $\xrightarrow{\text{HEAT}}$ GLASS

2. The diagram shows a fractionating column which can be used to separate crude oil into its different fractions. Choose words from the list for each of the fractions labelled 1 to 4 on the diagram.
   A. LUBRICATING OIL
   B. BITUMEN
   C. REFINERY GASES
   D. KEROSENE

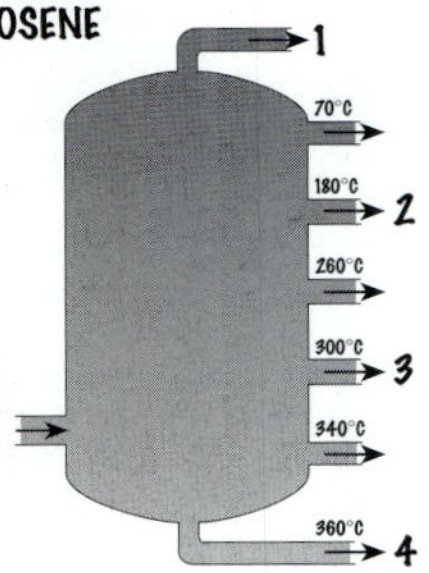

3. Which TWO of the following statements are correct about hydrocarbons. The fewer the number of carbon atoms in a molecule ...
   A. The less flammable it is.
   B. The higher its boiling point.
   C. The less viscous it is.
   D. The more volatile it is.
   E. The denser it is.

4. The general formula for a type of hydrocarbon is C_nH_{2n+2}. Which TWO of the following substances do NOT belong to this particular type?

A.
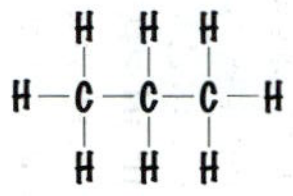

B.
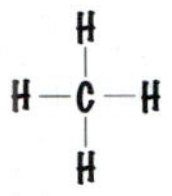

C.
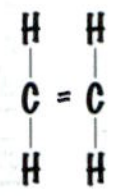

D.
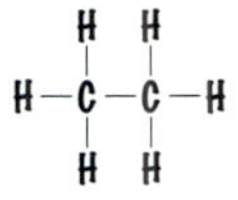

E.
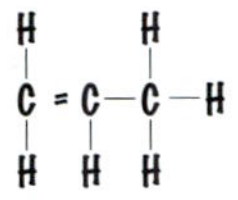

5. The composition of the atmosphere has changed dramatically since the formation of the earth.

5.1 Which one of the following gases has ALWAYS been present in the atmosphere?
   A. Oxygen
   B. Ammonia
   C. Carbon dioxide
   D. Nitrogen

5.2 Which of the following statements best describes the composition of the atmosphere at the formation of the earth.
   A. Mainly carbon dioxide, with small amounts of ammonia and nitrogen.
   B. Mainly carbon dioxide, with small amounts of oxygen and ammonia.
   C. Mainly carbon dioxide, with small amounts of ammonia and methane.
   D. Mainly carbon dioxide, with small amounts of methane and oxygen.

5.3 Our atmosphere has been much the same for the past 200 million years. Which of the following represents the correct proportions of gases in our atmosphere?
   A. Three fifths nitrogen, two fifths oxygen plus small amounts of other gases.
   B. Three fifths oxygen, one fifth nitrogen plus one fifth other gases.
   C. Four fifths oxygen, one fifth nitrogen plus small amounts of other gases.
   D. Four fifths nitrogen, one fifth oxygen plus small amounts of other gases.

5.4 Which of the following is NOT responsible for increasing the level of carbon dioxide in the atmosphere.
   A. Burning coal.
   B. Eruptions from volcanoes.
   C. Production of insoluble carbonates in the sea.
   D. Generating electricity at a fossil fuel power station.

6. The hydrocarbon ethene can be represented by the following ...

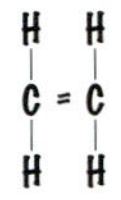

6.1 Ethene can be best described as ...
   A. An alkene
   B. A polymer
   C. A heavy hydrocarbon
   D. A saturated hydrocarbon.

6.2 Ethene molecules can be joined together by addition polymerisation. These long chain molecules can be represented by ...

A.
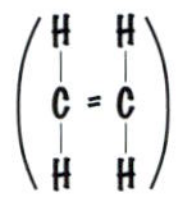

B.
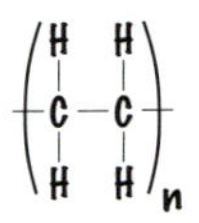

C.
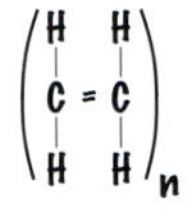

D.
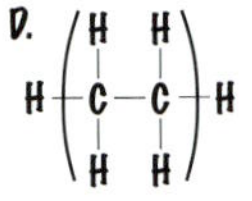

6.3 Ethene can be formed when long chain hydrocarbons are broken down into much smaller ones. The name of this process is ...
   A. Polymerisation.
   B. Fractionation.
   C. Neutralisation.
   D. Cracking.

6.4 When ethene molecules are joined together in addition polymerisation they produce ...
   A. Poly(styrene) and water.
   B. Poly(ethene) and water.
   C. Poly(ethene).
   D. Polymerised ethene and water.

7. The Earth's crust is 'cracked' into several large pieces called tectonic plates which are constantly moving at speeds of a few cm per year.

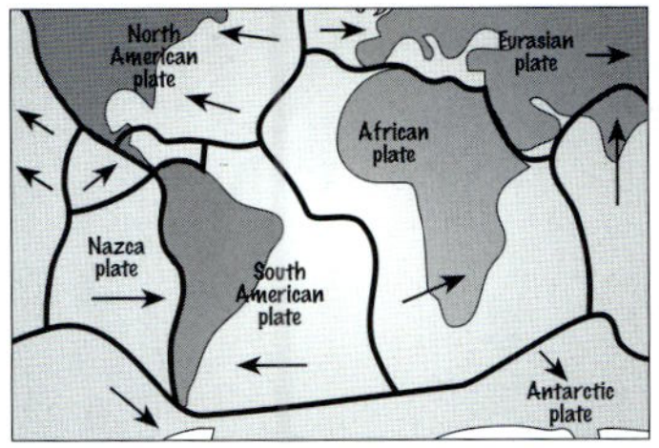

7.1 The energy which drives these plates around the globe comes from ...
   A. Ocean currents deep within the Atlantic and Pacific.
   B. The cooling of the Earth's core.
   C. Convection currents caused by heat from radioactive decay.
   D. The moon's gravitational pull on the earth.

7.2 What happens when these plates collide?
   A. The thinner, denser oceanic plate is forced down beneath the continental plate.
   B. The thinner, denser oceanic plate is forced upwards above the continental plate.
   C. Both oceanic and continental plates are forced downwards.
   D. Both oceanic and continental plates are forced upwards.

7.3 What happens when plates slide past each other?
   A. Mountain ranges are formed.
   B. Valleys are formed.
   C. Volcanoes occur.
   D. Earthquakes occur.

7.4 Magnetic reversal patterns parallel to the oceanic ridge provide evidence of ...
   A. Interlocking continents
   B. Sea floor spreading
   C. Subduction
   D. Similar fossils on different continents.

Heat (thermal) energy is transferred from HOTTER PLACES to COOLER PLACES by three different methods ...

1. CONDUCTION - Transfer of heat energy WITHOUT THE SUBSTANCE ITSELF MOVING.
2. CONVECTION - Transfer of heat energy by THE MOVEMENT OF THE SUBSTANCE ITSELF.
3. RADIATION - Transfer of heat energy by WAVES with no particles of matter being involved.

Conduction

Conduction occurs in metals because as the metal becomes hotter its vibrating ions gain more kinetic energy. This energy is transferred to cooler parts of the metal by FREE ELECTRONS as they DIFFUSE through the metal, colliding with ions and other electrons.

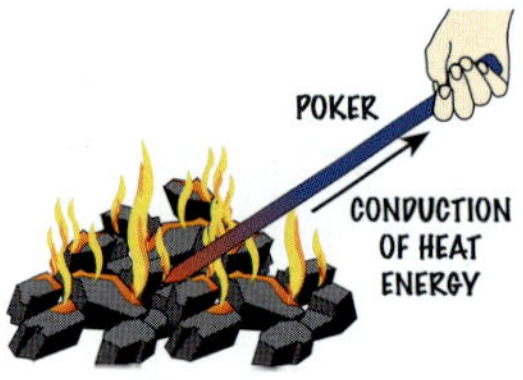

GOOD CONDUCTORS ... • ALL METALS especially COPPER and ALUMINIUM. ... or POOR INSULATORS.

METALS are particularly GOOD CONDUCTORS as they allow energy to spread through them quickly. NON-METALS on the other hand are poor conductors (but good INSULATORS) as energy spreads through them much more slowly.

GOOD INSULATORS ... • Most NON-METALS especially WOOD, PLASTIC and GLASS • AIR ... or POOR CONDUCTORS.

Here is an everyday example of a conductor and insulator in action ...

The pan is made of a good conductor eg. copper or aluminium.

The handle is made of a good insulator eg. wood or plastic

Convection

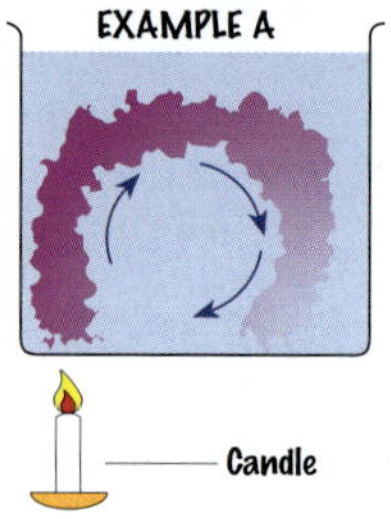

Red dye crystals placed in water over a heat source

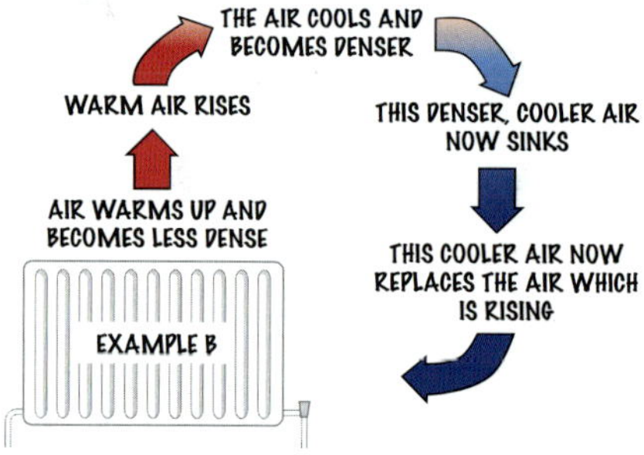

Circulation of air caused by a radiator.

- Convection currents can occur in LIQUIDS and GASES.
- As the liquid or gas gets hotter, its particles move faster causing it to EXPAND and become LESS DENSE than colder regions.
- The warm liquid or gas will now RISE UP and be replaced by COLDER, DENSER regions.

Radiation

Hot objects emit mainly INFRA-RED radiation, and the hotter the object, the more energy it radiates. How much radiation is GIVEN OUT or TAKEN IN by an object depends on its SURFACE.

DARK MATT SURFACES EMIT MORE RADIATION ...

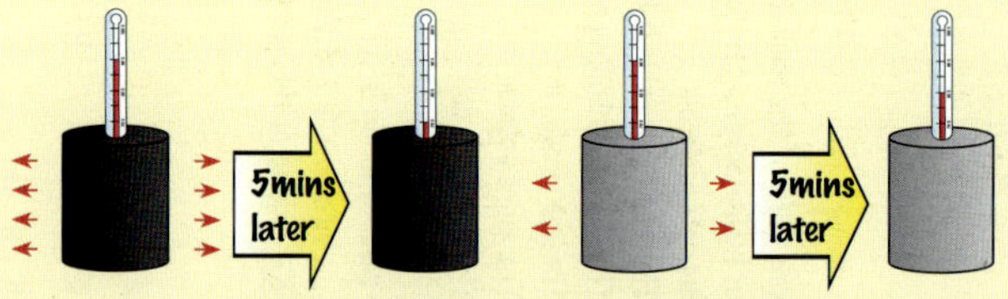

... THAN LIGHT SHINY SURFACES AT THE SAME TEMPERATURE

DARK MATT SURFACES ARE BETTER ABSORBERS (POORER REFLECTORS) ...

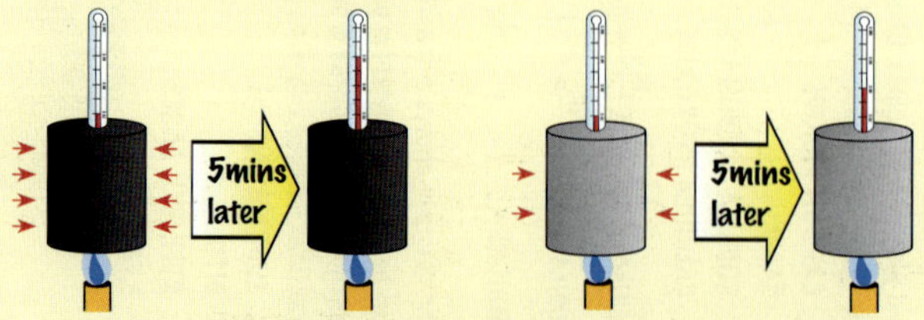

... OF RADIATION THAN LIGHT SHINY SURFACES AT THE SAME TEMPERATURE.

Reducing Energy Consumption In Buildings

There are many different ways in which heat losses from a building can be reduced.

FIBREGLASS ROOF INSULATION

Reduces heat loss by conduction and convection, because of the layer of air (a good insulator) trapped between the fibres (up to 25% heat lost).

DOUBLE GLAZING

Reduces heat loss by conduction and convection, because of the air between the panes of glass (up to 10% heat lost).

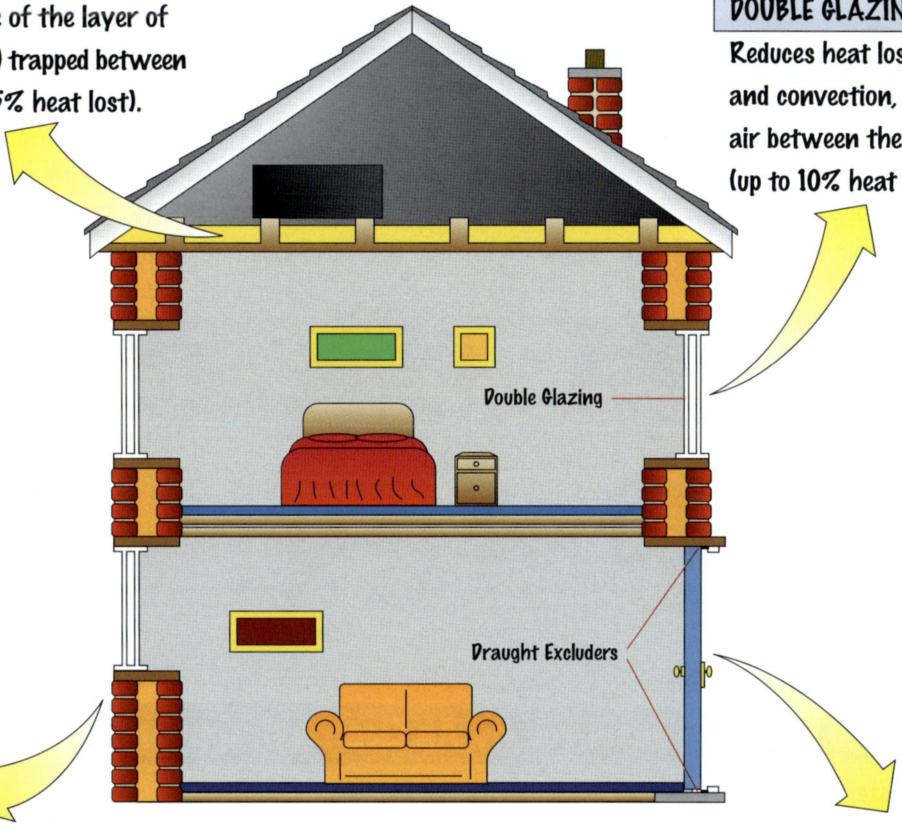

CAVITY WALL INSULATION

Reduces heat loss by conduction and especially convection by trapping the air in foam (up to 35% heat lost).

DRAUGHT EXCLUDERS

Reduces heat loss by convection by keeping as much warm air as possible inside (up to 15% heat lost).

Effectiveness And Cost-Effectiveness Of Different Forms Of Insulation

Here is some typical data about the various methods of insulation above:

FORM OF INSULATION	ORIGINAL COST	ANNUAL AMOUNT SAVED	HOW LONG TO PAY FOR ITSELF
Roof Insulation	£400	£80	5 years
Cavity Wall Insulation	£600	£30	20 years
Double Glazing	£1,800	£60	30 years
Draught Excluders	£40	£20	2 years

The most EFFECTIVE of these methods is the one which saves the most money each year.
In this case the ROOF INSULATION with draught excluders being the least effective.
However...
... to work out the most COST-EFFECTIVE we must consider the issue over a longer period of time, say 4 or 5 years. In this case, we can see that draught excluders have paid for themselves and are now well in profit. Nothing else has, so DRAUGHT EXCLUDERS are the most cost-effective.

Most of the Energy transferred in homes and industry is ELECTRICAL ENERGY because it is easily transferred as ...

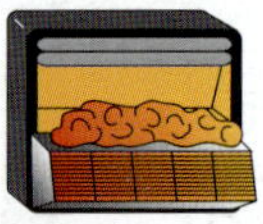

... HEAT (thermal),

LIGHT,

SOUND

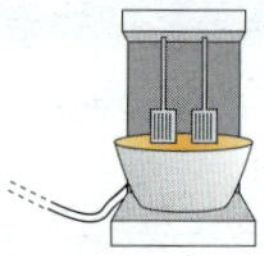

and MOVEMENT (kinetic) energy.

Power Ratings Of Some Domestic Appliances

Most appliances in the home depend on the transfer of ELECTRICAL ENERGY into other FORMS OF ENERGY. All appliances have a POWER RATING which tells us how much ENERGY IS TRANSFERRED by that appliance EVERY SECOND. The rate of energy transfer is measured in WATTS where 1 watt is the transfer of 1 joule of energy in 1 second. The greater the power rating, the more energy is transferred by that appliance EVERY SECOND. Here are some examples ...

APPLIANCE			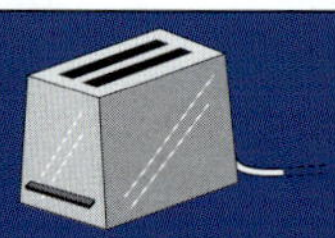	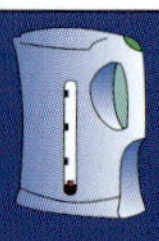
POWER RATING (W)	120 W	600 W	900 W	2000 W
POWER RATING (kW) 1000 watts (W) = 1 Kilowatt (kW)	0.12 kW	0.6 kW	0.9 kW	2 kW
ENERGY TRANSFERRED PER SECOND (J/s)	120 J/s	600 J/s	900 J/s	2000 J/s

Calculating The Energy Transferred By An Electrical Appliance

The energy transferred by an electrical appliance depends on ...

1. How long the appliance is switched on (in seconds).
2. How fast the appliance transfers energy (its POWER in watts)

It is calculated as follows.

ENERGY TRANSFERRED (J) = POWER (W) x TIME (s)

REMEMBER! POWER in WATTS, TIME in SECONDS ⟶ ENERGY in JOULES

EXAMPLE

An 1800W electric kettle is switched on for 2 min 30 secs. How much electrical energy will the kettle transfer to heat energy while it is switched on?

Using our formula: ENERGY TRANSFERRED = POWER x TIME
= 1800W x 150s
= 270,000 joules

TIME must be in SECONDS remember.

Calculating The Power Rating Of An Appliance

If we know the energy transferred and time then we can calculate the power rating of an appliance by rearranging the formula above using the formula triangle.

$$\text{POWER (W)} = \frac{\text{ENERGY TRANSFERRED (J)}}{\text{TIME TAKEN (s)}}$$

EXAMPLE

A toaster transfers 108,000 J of electrical energy into heat in the 120 secs it takes to toast two pieces of bread. Calculate its power rating.

Using our formula: $\text{POWER} = \frac{\text{ENERGY TRANSFERRED}}{\text{TIME TAKEN}} = \frac{108{,}000 \text{ J}}{120 \text{ s}}$ = 900 J/s
= 900W or 0.9 kW

The Electricity Meter In Your Home

Your meter at home may show a reading like this ...

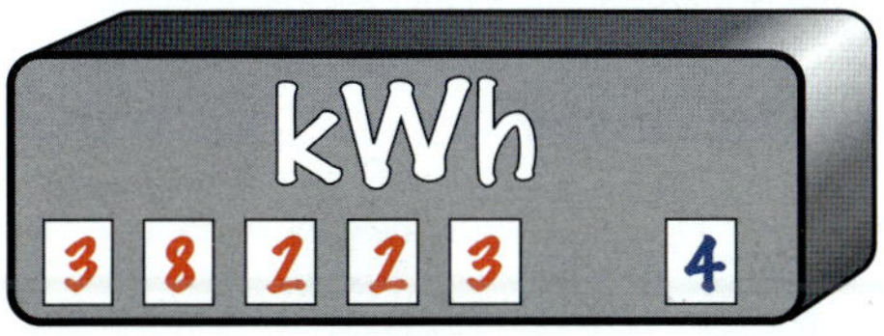

Your latest bill may look like this ...

The letters kWh represent ...
... **kilowatt-hours**, a unit of ENERGY.
These are sometimes called 'Units,' and are a measure of the electrical energy you have used.
1kWh = 3,600,000 joules

REB Regional **Electricity** Board

Meter readings (E=Estimate C=Your Own)

This time	Last time	Units used	Tariff	Pence per unit (kWh)	Amount £
1957	897E	1060	D9	6.5	68.90
Standing charge this quarter					10.00
Total charges this quarter excluding VAT.					78.90
VAT @ 5.0%					3.95
Total Charges this quarter including VAT.					82.85
				BALANCE	**£82.85**

The Kilowatt-hour

The Kilowatt-hour is a unit of ENERGY ...
... please remember it is NOT a unit of power- that's the kilowatt!!
An electrical appliance transfers 1 kWh of energy if it transfers energy at the rate of 1 kilowatt for one hour.

A 200 watt T.V. set  ... transfers 1 kWh of energy if it is switched on for 5 hours.
A 500 watt vacuum cleaner  ... transfers 1 kWh of energy if it is switched on for 2 hours.
A 1,000 watt electric fire  ... transfers 1 kWh of energy if it is switched on for 1 hour.

Kilowatt-hour Calculations

In order to work out the number of kilowatt-hours or 'Units' transferred by an appliance we need the following formula ...

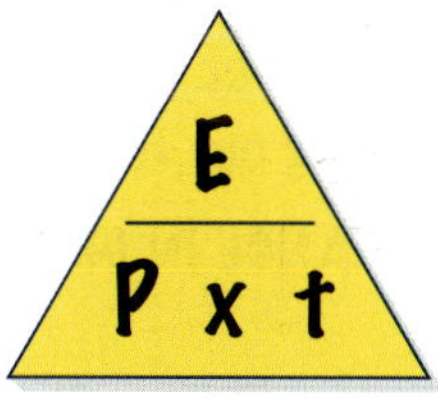

ENERGY TRANSFERRED (kWh) = POWER (kW) x TIME (h)

EXAMPLE

A 2000 watt electric hot plate is switched on for 90 minutes. How much does it cost if electricity is 6p per unit?

Using our formula: ENERGY TRANSFERRED = POWER x TIME
= 2 kW x 1.5h
= 3 kilowatt-hours (or UNITS)

(POWER IN kW; TIME IN HOURS)

But, **TOTAL COST = NUMBER OF UNITS x COST PER UNIT**

Therefore Total Cost = 3 x 6
= 18 pence

And finally, to do these calculations, you must remember ...
... to make sure the POWER is in KILOWATTS, and ...
... to make sure that the TIME is in HOURS.

Weight

WEIGHT is due to the force of GRAVITY on an object.
Near the surface of the Earth EVERY 1KG OF MATTER ...
... experiences a DOWNWARDS FORCE or has a WEIGHT of 10N due to gravity.
In other words, the weight of an object near the surface of the Earth is numerically 10 times bigger than its mass in kilograms ...

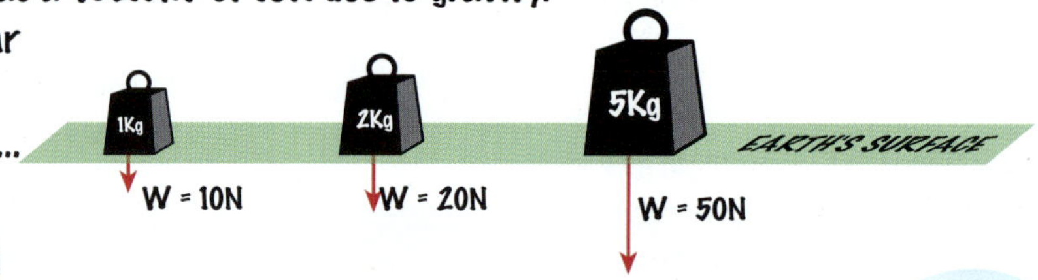

Gravitational Potential Energy

This is the ENERGY STORED in an object because of the HEIGHT ...
... through which the WEIGHT of the object has been LIFTED ...
... AGAINST the force of GRAVITY.
If an OBJECT CAN FALL ...
... IT'S GOT GRAVITATIONAL POTENTIAL ENERGY.

Calculating Change In Gravitational Potential Energy

The formula ...

CHANGE IN GRAVITATIONAL POTENTIAL ENERGY (J) = WEIGHT (N) x CHANGE IN VERTICAL HEIGHT (m)

$$gpe = mg \times \Delta h$$

As you can see the formula triangle looks rather nasty, so we'll explain what it means ...

- CHANGE IN GRAVITATIONAL POTENTIAL ENERGY is represented as 'gpe.'
- WEIGHT is represented as 'mg' which is simply the mass, m, of an object multiplied by 'g' which is a constant called the gravitational field strength and has a numerical value of 10 here on earth.
- CHANGE IN VERTICAL HEIGHT is represented as Δh where Δ means 'change in'.

Anyway if you remember them as change in gravitational potential energy, weight and change in vertical height you can't go wrong.

EXAMPLE 1

A skier who weighs 800N takes the ski lift which takes him from a height of 1,000m to a height of 3,000m above ground. By how much does his gravitational potential energy change?
Using our formula:

CHANGE IN GRAV. POT. ENERGY = WEIGHT x CHANGE IN VERTICAL HEIGHT
= 800N x (3,000m - 1,000m)
= 800N x 2,000m
= 1,600,000J

... and, as the skier has gone UP, it is an INCREASE IN GRAVITATIONAL POTENTIAL ENERGY.

This is an example of electrical energy being transferred as gravitational potential energy.

EXAMPLE 2

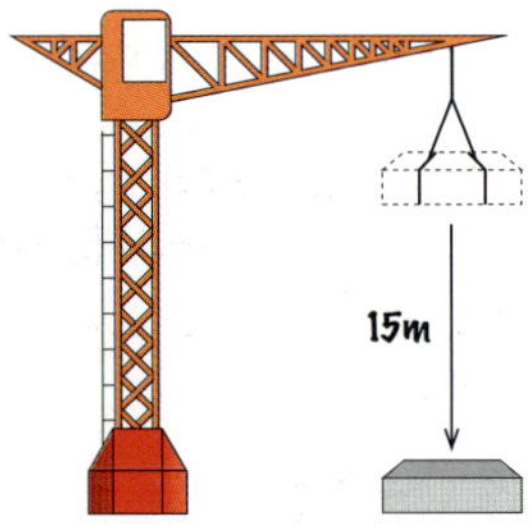

A crane lowers a load of 25,000N from a height of 15m down to the ground.
By how much does the gravitational potential energy of the load change?

Using our formula:

CHANGE IN GRAV. POT. ENERGY = WEIGHT x CHANGE IN VERTICAL HEIGHT
= 25,000N x (15m - 0m)
= 25,000N x 15m
= 375,000J

... and, as the load has gone DOWN, it is a DECREASE IN GRAVITATIONAL POTENTIAL ENERGY.

Transfer Of Energy

When devices transfer energy, only part of it is USEFULLY TRANSFERRED to where it is wanted and in the form that it is wanted. The remainder is transferred in some non-useful way and is therefore 'wasted'. Here are four examples of the intended energy transfer and wastage in everyday devices.

1. Tungsten filament light bulb.

2. Low energy light bulb.

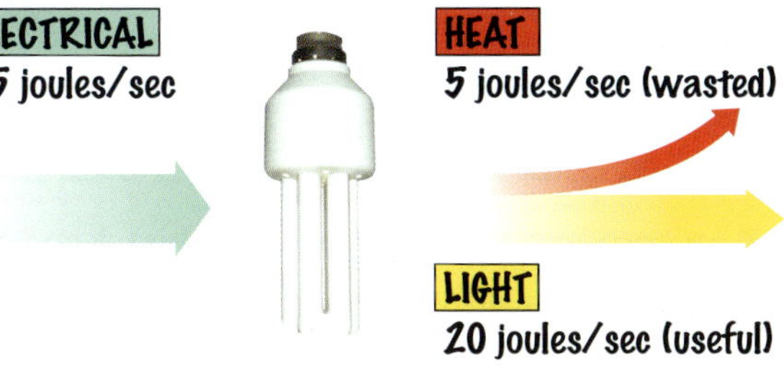

3. Electric kettle.

4. Electric Motor (a drill includes one).

The 'wasted' energy and the 'useful' energy are both eventually transferred to the surroundings which become WARMER.

Unfortunately ...

... this energy becomes so spread out that it becomes difficult for any further useful energy transfers to occur.

Efficiency Of Devices

The greater the proportion of energy supplied to a device, THAT IS USEFULLY TRANSFERRED, the more efficient we say the device is.

For Example ...

... a car engine is 20% efficient - a lot more energy is wasted than is usefully transferred.

... a microwave is 60% efficient - more energy is usefully transferred than is wasted.

Calculating Efficiency

To calculate the efficiency of any device you need to use the following formula.

$$\text{EFFICIENCY} = \frac{\text{USEFUL ENERGY TRANSFERRED BY DEVICE}}{\text{TOTAL ENERGY SUPPLIED TO DEVICE}}$$

Remember! A T.V. has both LIGHT and SOUND as useful energy transferred.

In the case of the T.V. set shown, ... EFFICIENCY $= \frac{50}{200} \times 100 = 25\%$

(100: to convert it to a percentage)

Fuels

Fuels are substances which release useful amounts of energy when they burn.
Typical fuels used by humans for generating energy are ...

NON-RENEWABLE FOSSIL FUELS

... COAL 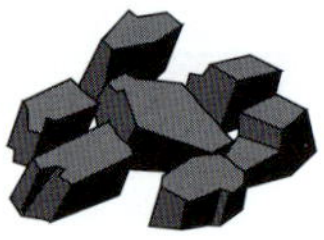 ... OIL  ... GAS 

 ... WOOD

Coal, oil and gas are energy resources which have formed over millions of years from the remains of living things. For this reason they are called FOSSIL FUELS, and most of the energy used by humans comes from these sources.

- However, because these energy resources take so long to form, we are using them up at a far faster rate than they can be replaced. Hence they are called NON-RENEWABLE ENERGY RESOURCES, and will eventually run out.
- **NUCLEAR FUEL** is also a non-renewable, although unlike coal, oil and gas it is not a fossil fuel, and is not burnt to release energy.

AN IMPORTANT POINT!

- Wood is NOT a fossil fuel, nor is it non-renewable. It is classed as a renewable energy resource since, trees can be grown relatively quickly to replace those which are burnt to provide energy for heating.

Generating Electricity From Non-Renewable Energy Resources

The trick in using non-renewables to generate electricity is to ...
... produce heat from the fuel, and use it to make steam which ...
... will eventually turn turbines attached to a generator.

Eg. ❶ Fossil fuels are burnt to release heat energy, ...
... which boils water to produce steam, ...
... which drives the turbines and ultimately the generators.

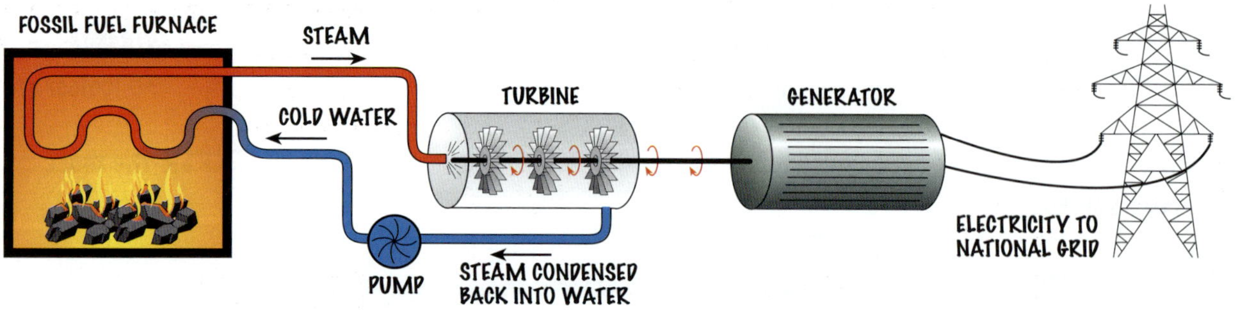

Eg. ❷ Electricity is also generated in a similar way ...
... using NUCLEAR FUEL
eg. URANIUM and PLUTONIUM.
Here a REACTOR is used to generate ...
... HEAT and a HEAT EXCHANGER is used ...
... to transfer this energy from the reactor ...
... to water which turns to steam ...
to turn the turbines.

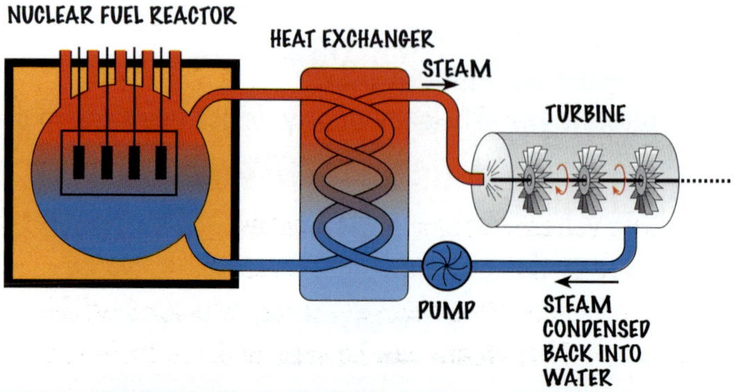

- **RENEWABLE ENERGY RESOURCES** are those that will not run out, because ...
  ... they are continually being replaced.
- This is because many of them are 'powered' by the Sun. For instance, the Sun causes evaporation which results in rain and flowing water, it causes convection currents which result in winds and these winds cause waves.
- Other types of energy resource rely on the gravitational pull of the moon! eg. tides.

Generating Electricity From Renewable Energy Resources

- In renewables, the energy resource is used to drive turbines directly.
  In other words, nothing needs to be burnt to produce heat!

WIND

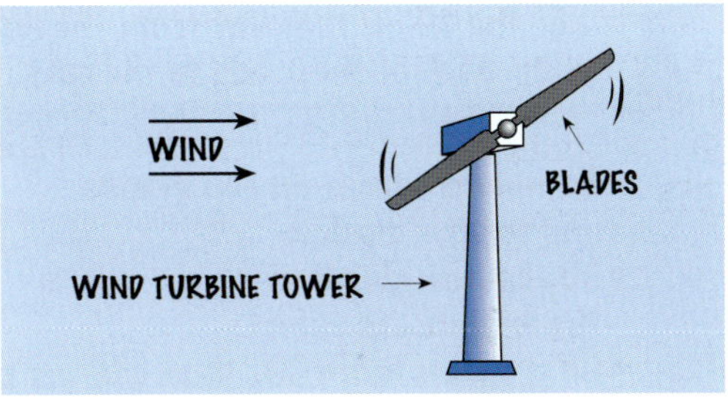

The force of the wind turns the blades of a wind turbine which in turn causes a generator to spin and produce electricity.

TIDAL

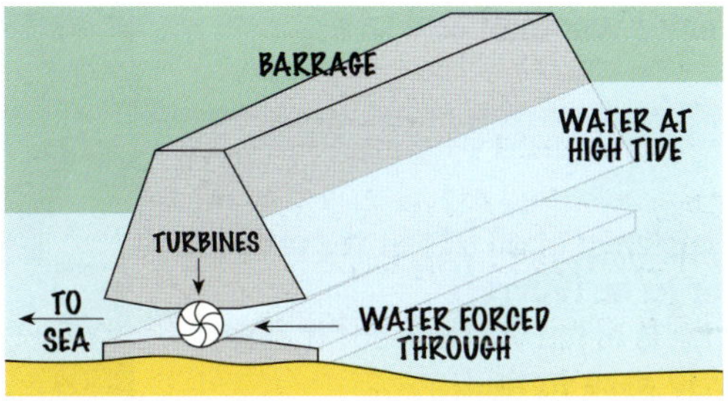

At high tide, water is trapped by a barrage. At low tide the water is released and flows back to the same level as the sea. The movement of this water drives a turbine to generate electricity.

WAVES

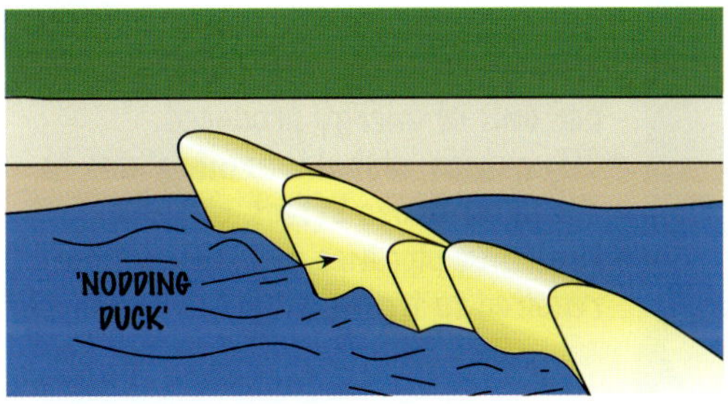

The rocking motion of the waves makes the 'nodding duck' move up and down. This movement is translated into a rotary movement which eventually turns a generator.

HYDRO-ELECTRIC

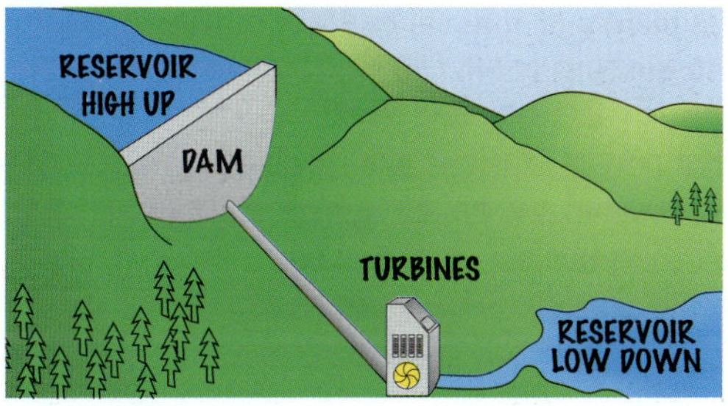

Water stored in reservoirs above the power station is allowed to flow down through pipes to drive the turbines. The water can be pumped back up again when the demand for electricity is low.

GEOTHERMAL

In some volcanic areas, hot water and steam rise naturally to the surface, having been heated up by the decay of radioactive substances (eg. uranium) within the earth. This steam can be used to drive turbines.

SOLAR

Solar cells rely on modern technology to transfer sunlight directly into useful electricity. This has applications in calculators, watches and garden lighting, as well as a more sophisticated use in space probes and satellites.

Comparing Non-Renewable Sources Of Energy

The four energy sources listed below are used to provide most of the electricity we need in this country directly through power stations. Some of the advantages and disadvantages of each one are listed below ...

COAL

- Coal is relatively cheap and sometimes easy to obtain.
- Coal fired power stations are flexible in meeting demand and have a quicker start-up time than their nuclear equivalents.
- Estimates suggest that there may be over a century's worth of coal left.

- Burning produces carbon dioxide (CO_2) and sulphur dioxide (SO_2).
- CO_2 causes 'global warming' due to the Greenhouse Effect.
- Coal produces more CO_2 per unit of energy produced than oil or gas.
- SO_2 causes acid rain unless ...
  ... the sulphur is removed before burning ...
  ... or the SO_2 is removed from the waste gases. Both of these add to the cost.

OIL

- There is plenty of oil left in the short to medium term. (30yrs?)
- The price is often variable but it can be relatively easy to find.
- Oil fired Power Stations are flexible in meeting demand and have a quicker start-up time than both nuclear-powered and coal-fired reactors.

- Burning produces carbon dioxide and sulphur dioxide.
- CO_2 causes 'global warming' due to the Greenhouse Effect.
- Oil produces more CO_2 than gas, per unit of energy produced.
- SO_2 causes acid rain (see coal above).
- Oil is often carried between continents on tankers leading to the risk of spillage and pollution.

NATURAL GAS

- There is plenty of natural gas left in the short to medium term. (30 yrs?)
- As relatively easy to find as oil.
- Gas fired power stations are flexible in meeting demand and have a quicker start-up time than nuclear, coal and oil.
- No sulphur dioxide (SO_2) is produced.

- Burning produces carbon dioxide (CO_2) although it is less than both coal and oil, per unit of energy produced.
- CO_2 causes 'global warming' due to the Greenhouse Effect.
- Expensive pipelines and networks are often required to transport it to the point of use.

NUCLEAR

- The cost and rate of use of fuel is relatively low.
- They can often be situated in sparsely populated areas (and should be!)
- Nuclear power stations are flexible in meeting demand.
- They <u>don't</u> produce carbon dioxide and sulphur dioxide.

- Although there is very little escape of radioactive material in normal use, radioactive waste can stay dangerously radioactive for thousands of years and safe storage is expensive.
- The cost of building and de-commissioning adds heavily to the unit cost of energy produced.
- They have the longest start-up time compared to coal, oil and gas.

Summary

ADVANTAGES
- Produce huge amounts of energy.
- They are reliable.
- They are flexible in meeting demand.
- They don't take up much space (relatively).

DISADVANTAGES
- They pollute the environment.
- They cause 'global warming' and acid rain.
- They will 'soon' run out.
- Fuels may have to be transported long distances.

Comparing Renewable Sources Of Energy

The five energy sources listed below represent the attempts of modern technology to provide us with a clean, safe alternative source of energy. Some of the advantages and disadvantages of each one are listed below ...

WIND

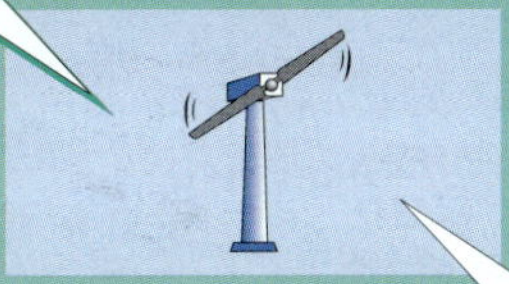

- Wind turbines don't require any fuel and need very little maintenance.
- They don't produce any pollutant gases such as carbon dioxide and sulphur dioxide.
- Once they're built they give 'free' energy when the wind is blowing.

- You need loads of them usually on hills and coastal areas and this can look a bit ugly (visual pollution). Also, noise can be a problem.
- Electricity output depends entirely on the strength of the wind.
- Not very flexible in meeting demand unless the energy is stored.
- Capital outlay can be high in building them.

TIDAL and WAVES

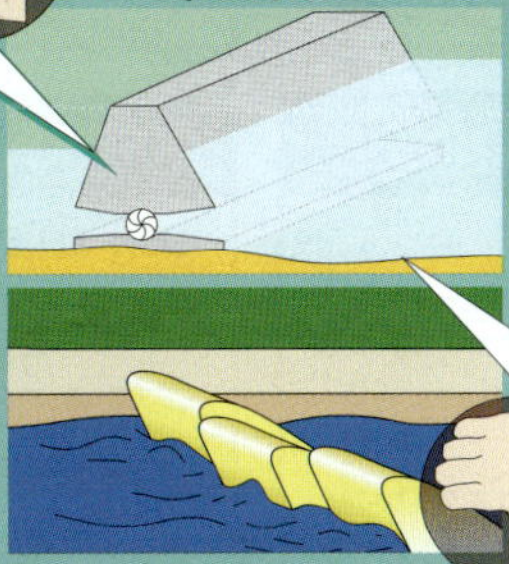

- These devices don't require any fuel.
- They don't produce any pollutant gases such as carbon dioxide and sulphur dioxide.
- Once they're built they provide 'free' energy - at certain times!
- Barrage water can be released when demand for electricity is high.

- Tidal barrages, across estuaries, are unsightly, a hazard to shipping, and destroy the habitats of wading birds etc.
- Output depends on daily variations in the state of the tide and monthly and annual variations in its height, in the case of tidal barrages, and the energy contained in the waves for the 'nodding duck'.
- High initial capital outlay in building them.

HYDRO-ELECTRIC

- No fuel is required unless they are operated in reverse to store energy.
- Very fast start-up time to meet sudden increases in demand.
- Large amounts of clean, reliable electricity can be produced.
- When operated in reverse, by pumping water into the higher reservoir, surplus electricity can be stored to help meet future peak demand.

- Location is critical and often involves damming upland valleys which means flooding farms, forests and natural habitats.
- To actually achieve a net output (aside from pumping) there must be adequate rainfall in the region where the reservoir is.
- Very high initial capital outlay - but worth the investment in the end.

SOLAR

- Ideal for use in situations where a source of electricity is needed in a remote location.
- Excellent energy source when only a small amount of electricity is needed, eg. calculator, watch.
- When in direct sunlight they produce a 'free', clean, although small supply of electricity.

- The amount of electricity produced by solar cells depends on the intensity of light that falls on them. This means they're more useful in sunny places.
- Solar cells have a high cost per unit of electricity produced compared to all other sources except non-rechargeable batteries.

Summary

ADVANTAGES

- No fuel costs during operation.
- No chemical pollution.
- Often low maintenance.
- Don't contribute to 'global warming' and acid rain.

DISADVANTAGES

- With the exception of hydro-electric they produce small amounts of electricity.
- Take up lots of space and are unsightly.
- Unreliable (apart form H-E), weather dependent, and can't match demand.
- High initial capital outlay.

THERMAL ENERGY TRANSFER

CONDUCTION ...
the substance itself does not move. In metals heat is transferred by FREE ELECTRONS, as they diffuse through the metal, colliding with ions and other electrons.

CONVECTION ...
the substance (liquid or gas) actually moves causing the transfer of heat energy from a warmer to a cooler place via CONVECTION CURRENTS, eg. warm air becomes less dense, rises, cools and becomes more dense causing it to fall.

RADIATION ...
no particles are involved. Hot objects emit mainly INFRA RED RADIATION; the amount being dependent upon the surface of the object. DARK, MATT SURFACES EMIT MORE RADIATION THAN LIGHT, SHINY SURFACES AT THE SAME TEMPERATURE. DARK, MATT = GOOD ABSORBERS; LIGHT, SHINY = GOOD REFLECTORS.

REDUCING ENERGY CONSUMPTION ...
the most EFFECTIVE is the one that saves most money each year, BUT ...
the most COST-EFFECTIVE is the one that pays for itself the fastest.

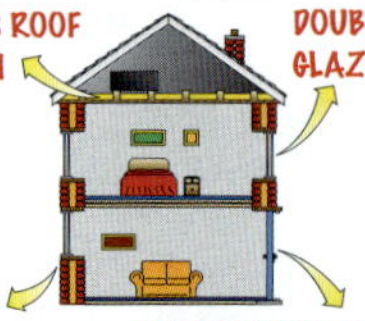

ELECTRICAL ENERGY TRANSFER, POWER AND COST

POWER RATINGS ...
indicate the rate of energy transfer of an appliance eg. a rating of 500 watts (0.5kW) means the appliance transfers energy at the rate of 500 joules per second.

ENERGY TRANSFERRED (J) = POWER (W) X TIME (s)

$$\text{POWER (W)} = \frac{\text{ENERGY TRANSFERRED (J)}}{\text{TIME (s)}}$$

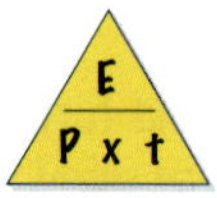

POWER IN WATTS: TIME IN SECONDS: ENERGY IN JOULES

COST OF ELECTRICITY ...
electricity is measured in kilowatt-hours or 'Units.' These are units of ENERGY (not units of power!!). 'An appliance transfers 1kWh of energy if it transfers energy at the rate of 1 kilowatt for 1 hour.'

ENERGY TRANSFERRED (kWh) = POWER (kW) x TIME (h)

TOTAL COST (p) = NUMBER OF 'UNITS' (kWh) x COST PER UNIT (p/kWh)

GRAVITATIONAL POTENTIAL ENERGY AND EFFICIENCY

WEIGHT ...
is due to the force of gravity on an object. 1 kg of matter experiences a downwards force of 10N due to gravity ie. it weighs 10 Newtons.

GRAVITATIONAL POTENTIAL ENERGY ...
is the energy, stored in an object due to its height above the Earth's surface.

CHANGE IN GRAVITATIONAL POTENTIAL ENERGY (J) = WEIGHT (N) x CHANGE IN VERTICAL HEIGHT (m)

Remember, weight must be in Newtons, so its mg, and it's the change in vertical height (Δh).

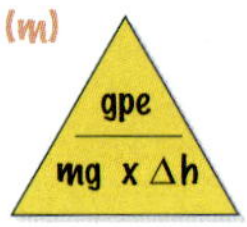

EFFICIENCY OF ENERGY TRANSFER ...
when devices transfer energy some of it is transferred in a non-useful way and is therefore wasted.
This energy is eventually transferred to the surroundings. Efficient devices waste a smaller proportion of energy.

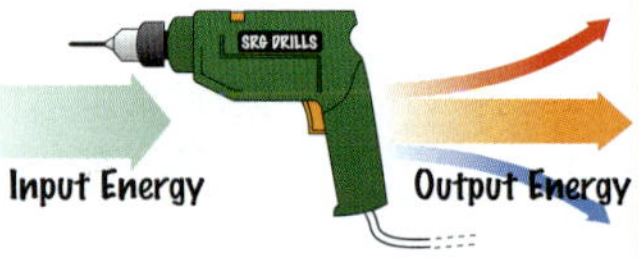

$$\text{EFFICIENCY} = \frac{\text{USEFUL ENERGY TRANSFERRED BY DEVICE}}{\text{TOTAL ENERGY SUPPLIED TO DEVICE}}$$

NON-RENEWABLE AND RENEWABLE ENERGY RESOURCES

NON-RENEWABLES ...

COAL  OIL  GAS  NUCLEAR 

FOSSIL FUELS

- Fossil fuels are formed over millions of years from the remains of living things.
- Both fossil fuels and nuclear fuels are used to produce HEAT, which is used to make steam, which eventually turns turbines.

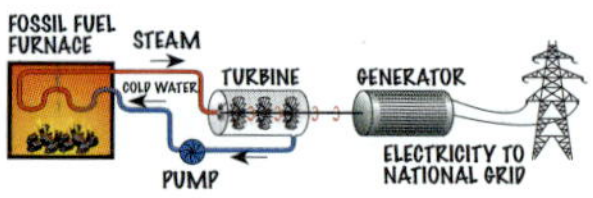

RENEWABLES ...

These will not run out because they are continuously being replaced. Many of them are 'powered' by the sun eg. evaporation and convection currents.

ANALYSIS OF NON-RENEWABLE ENERGY RESOURCES

COMPARING NON-RENEWABLE SOURCES OF ENERGY

Source	+	−
COAL	• Cheap, easy to obtain. • Flexible, quicker start-up time than nuclear. • A century's worth of coal left.	• Produces SO_2 and more CO_2 than oil or gas. • CO_2 causes 'global warming' • SO_2 causes acid rain; costs to remove it.
OIL	• Plenty left. • Relatively easy to find. • Flexible. • Quicker start-up than coal or nuclear.	• Produces SO_2 and more CO_2 than gas. • CO_2 causes 'global warming'. • SO_2 causes acid rain; costs to remove it. • Transportation risks spillage and pollution.
GAS	• Plenty left. • Relatively easy to find. • Flexible - quicker start-up time than nuclear, coal and oil. • No SO_2 produced.	• Produces CO_2 (less than coal and oil) • CO_2 causes 'global warming'. • Expensive pipelines and networks to point of use.
NUCLEAR	• Cost and rate of use is low. • Situated in sparsely populated areas. • Flexible in meeting demand. • DOESN'T produce CO_2 or SO_2.	• Waste is dangerous for thousands of years; safe storage is expensive. • Building and decommissioning is costly. • Longest start-up time of these four.

- Huge amounts of Energy
- Reliable
- Flexible
- Compact

- Pollute Environment
- Global warming and acid rain
- Will soon run out
- Transportation cost and dangers

ANALYSIS OF RENEWABLE ENERGY RESOURCES

COMPARING RENEWABLE SOURCES OF ENERGY

Source	+	−
WIND	• Require no fuel and little maintenance. • Doesn't produce any CO_2 or SO_2 • Once built, energy is free.	• Need lots; visual and noise pollution. • Output depends on strength of wind. • Not very flexible. • High capital outlay.
TIDAL & WAVES	• No fuel required. • Don't produce CO_2 or SO_2. • Once built energy is free. • High demand - release barrage water.	• Unsightly tidal barrages, destroy habitats. • Daily variations affect output. • High capital outlay.
HYDRO-ELECTRIC	• No fuel required unless storing energy, to meet future peak demand. • Fast start-up time. • Produces large amounts; clean; reliable.	• Farms, forests and natural habitats may be flooded when damming. • Rainfall must be adequate. • Very high capital outlay.
SOLAR	• Electricity source in remote locations. • Excellent source for small amounts. eg. calculator, watch. • Free and clean supply.	• Depends on light intensity. • High cost per unit of electricity.

- No fuel costs
- No chemical pollution
- Low maintenance
- No global warming or acid rain

- Only H.E produces much energy
- Unsightly - take up space
- Unreliable - weather dependant
- High capital outlay

1. Choose words from the list for each of the spaces 1 - 4 in the sentences which describe the fire (electric) used to heat a room in a house.
   A. CONDUCTION
   B. CONVECTION
   C. RADIATION
   D. INSULATION

The on/off switch is made of plastic which provides ___1___ to prevent your hand being burnt. Heat travels through the metal casing of the fire by ___2___, but hot air rises from the fire and warms the room by ___3___. If you stand with your back against the same wall that the fire is on, thermal energy will not reach you by ___4___.

2. The amount of energy transferred by a kettle can be worked out by multiplying together which two of the following?
   A. EFFICIENCY.
   B. TIME.
   C. COST PER UNIT.
   D. POWER.
   E. NEWTONS.

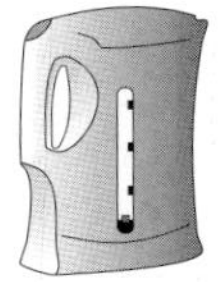

3. Which TWO of these statements are referring to convection?
   A. The liquid or gas expands when hot as its particles move faster.
   B. Thermal energy is transferred by waves.
   C. The liquid or gas becomes less dense and starts to rise.
   D. Thermal energy is passed from electron to electron.
   E. Free electrons diffuse through the substance carrying thermal energy.

4. The diagram below shows a power drill which can be either used from the mains supply or has a battery attachment.

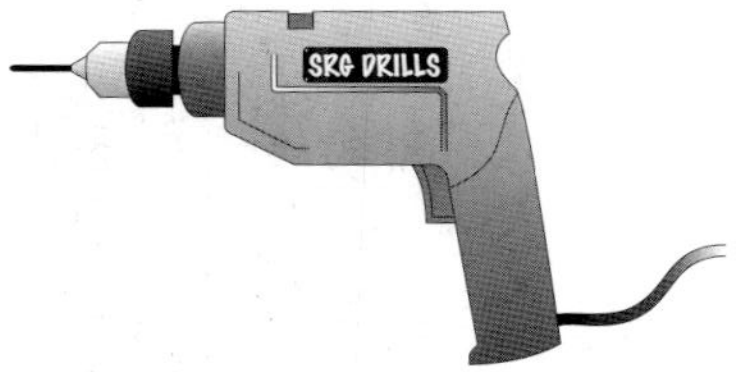

4.1 Which of the following statements accurately describes the energy transfer when the drill is plugged into the mains supply?
   A. ELECTRICAL ⟶ LIGHT + SOUND
   B. CHEMICAL ⟶ MOVEMENT + HEAT + SOUND
   C. ELECTRICAL ⟶ MOVEMENT + HEAT + SOUND
   D. CHEMICAL ⟶ MOVEMENT + HEAT + LIGHT

4.2 If the drill is attached to a battery which statement describes the energy transfer?
   A. ELECTRICAL ⟶ MOVEMENT + HEAT + SOUND
   B. CHEMICAL ⟶ MOVEMENT + HEAT + SOUND
   C. ELECTRICAL ⟶ CHEMICAL ⟶ HEAT + MOVEMENT + SOUND
   D. CHEMICAL ⟶ ELECTRICAL ⟶ MOVEMENT + HEAT + SOUND

4.3 If the drill converts 600 joules/sec of electrical energy into 350 joules/sec of useful energy and 250 joules/sec of 'waste' energy, what is it's efficiency?
   A. 58.3%
   B. 71.4%
   C. 41.7%
   D. 26.3%

4.4 How could the drill be made more efficient?
   A. Supply it with more power.
   B. Increase the amount of useful energy it transfers.
   C. Increase the amount of energy supplied to it.
   D. Provide a higher voltage.

5. The vacuum cleaner has a power rating of 600 watts.

5.1 If it is switched on for 5 minutes, how much energy does it transfer?
   A. 180,000 joules.
   B. 600 joules.
   C. 3000 joules.
   D. 120 joules.

5.2 How much energy will be transferred in kilowatt-hours if the vacuum cleaner is left on for 15 minutes?

ENERGY TRANSFERRED (kWh) = POWER (kW) x TIME (h)

   A. 9000 kWh.
   B. 150 kWh.
   C. 9 kWh.
   D. 0.15 kWh.

5.3 If electricity costs 12p per unit. How much will it cost to run for 1 hour?
   A. £7.20p.
   B. 0.72p.
   C. 7.2p.
   D. 12p.

5.4 What types of energy are transferred as 'waste energy' by the vacuum cleaner?
   A. Light and sound.
   B. Heat and sound.
   C. Movement and sound.
   D. Movement and heat.

6. The diagram shows a 'pumped storage' hydroelectric power station, through which water with a weight of 3000N flows every second. The water falls through a vertical height of 200 metres and drives the turbines to produce electricity when needed. At times of low demand, electricity is used to pump water to the higher resevoir.

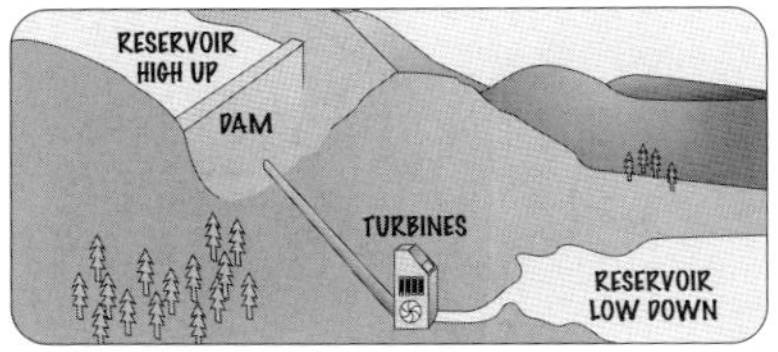

CHANGE IN GRAVITATIONAL POTENTIAL ENERGY (J) = WEIGHT (N) X CHANGE IN VERTICAL HEIGHT (m)

6.1 What is the gravitational potential energy lost by the water in one second?
   A. 600,000 J.
   B. 15 J.
   C. 60,000 J.
   D. 6,000 J.

6.2 During times of low electricity demand what energy transfers take place at the power station.
   A. Electrical ⟶ Heat + Kinetic
   B. Gravitational ⟶ Electrical
   C. Gravitational ⟶ Electrical + Kinetic
   D. Electrical ⟶ Gravitational

6.3 These types of power station are ideal to support peak electricity demand because ...
   A. They have a very fast start up time.
   B. They can recycle water.
   C. They rely on natural rainfall.
   D. They are inexpensive to construct.

6.4 Which of the following statements is NOT true?
   A. Hydro-electric power stations have fast start up times.
   B. Hydro-electric power stations affect wildlife and ecosystems.
   C. Hydro-electric power stations produce heavy pollution.
   D. Hydro-electric power stations are usually in hilly or mountainous regions.

7. The diagram shows an electric kettle.

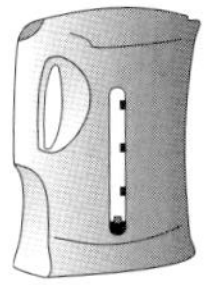

7.1 The hotter water is at the top of the kettle because...
   A. Free electrons diffuse upwards carrying heat.
   B. Water conducts heat upwards.
   C. Heat is radiated upwards from heating element.
   D. Hot water is less dense than cold water.

7.2 Some kettles have shiny silver exteriors so that ...
   A. They conduct less heat to the surroundings.
   B. They convect less heat to the surroundings.
   C. They radiate less heat to the surroundings.
   D. They reflect heat back into the water.

7.3 Only filling the kettle with as much water as you need is good for the environment because ...
   A. Less steam is released into the atmosphere.
   B. Less heat is radiated into the atmosphere.
   C. Less heat is convected into the atmosphere.
   D. Less carbon dioxide is released into the atmosphere by the power station.

7.4 We need to be careful to avoid over using electrical appliances because ...
   A. They may quickly burn out.
   B. Energy is precious and some power stations contribute to the greenhouse effect.
   C. The demand may not be able to match the supply.
   D. They radiate heat out and cause global warming.

An ELECTRIC CURRENT will flow through an ELECTRICAL COMPONENT (or device) ...
... if there is a VOLTAGE or POTENTIAL DIFFERENCE (p.d.) across the ends of the component.
In the following circuits each cell and lamp are identical ...

CIRCUIT 1

Cell provides p.d. ...
... across the lamp.

A current flows and ...
... the lamp lights up.

The amount of current that flows through the component above depends on two things ...

1. The Potential Difference (P.D.) Across The Component

The GREATER the POTENTIAL DIFFERENCE or VOLTAGE across a component ...
... the GREATER the CURRENT that flows through the component.

CIRCUIT 2

Two cells together provide ...
... a bigger p.d. across the lamp.

A bigger current now flows and ...
... the lamp lights up more brightly...
... compared to circuit 1.

2. The Resistance Of The Component

COMPONENTS RESIST the FLOW of CURRENT THROUGH THEM. They have RESISTANCE (measured in ohms).
The GREATER the RESISTANCE of a COMPONENT or COMPONENTS ...

... the SMALLER the CURRENT that ...
... flows for a PARTICULAR VOLTAGE.

OR

... the GREATER the VOLTAGE needed ...
... to maintain a PARTICULAR CURRENT.

CIRCUIT 3

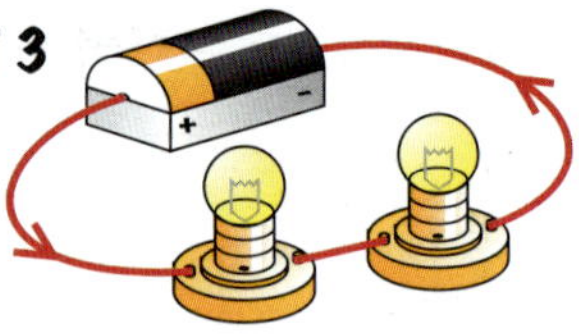

Two lamps together have a GREATER RESISTANCE.
A smaller current now flows and ...
... the lamps light up less brightly (compared to circuit 1).

CIRCUIT 4

Two cells together provide a GREATER VOLTAGE ...
... and the same current as in circuit 1 will now flow and ...
... the lamps light up more brightly (compared to circuit 3).

Measurement Of Potential Difference And Current

The potential difference (p.d.) across a component in a circuit is measured in volts (V) using a VOLTMETER connected in PARALLEL across the component.

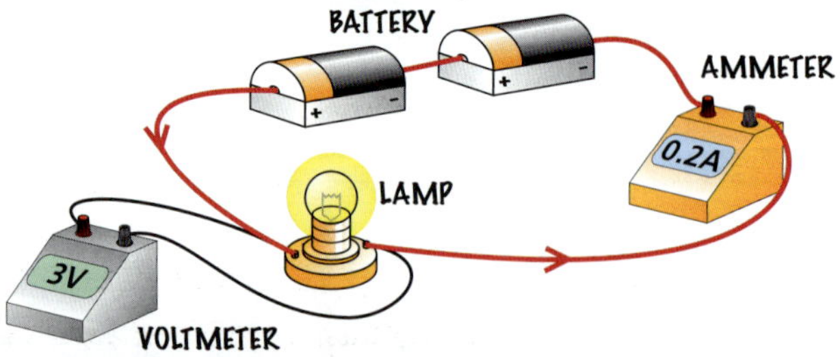

The current flowing through a component in a circuit is measured in amperes (A), using an AMMETER connected in SERIES.

Standard Symbols For Drawing Circuit Diagrams

The following standard symbols should be known. You may be asked to interpret and/or draw circuits using the following standard symbols.

Switch (open)	Variable Resistor	Lamp	Voltmeter
Switch (closed)	Fuse	Diode	Ammeter
Cell			
Battery	LDR	Resistor	Thermistor

Components Connected In Series

In a series circuit, ALL COMPONENTS are connected ONE AFTER THE OTHER in ONE LOOP, going from ONE TERMINAL of the BATTERY to the OTHER. When components are connected in series ...

1. The same CURRENT flows through each COMPONENT.
   ie. $A_1 = A_2 = A_3$
   eg. each ammeter reading is 0.1A.

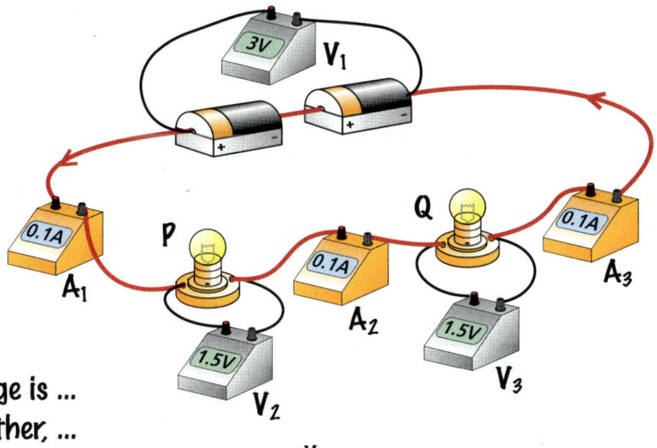

2. The POTENTIAL DIFFERENCE (p.d.) or VOLTAGE ...
   ... supplied by the battery is DIVIDED UP ...
   ... between the TWO COMPONENTS in the circuit.
   ie. $V_1 = V_2 + V_3$
   However ...
   ... in our circuit both bulbs have the same resistance and the voltage is ...
   ... divided equally, but if one bulb had twice the resistance of the other, ...
   ... then the voltage would be divided differently ie. 2V and 1V.
3. Each component has a RESISTANCE and ...
   ... the TOTAL RESISTANCE is the sum of ...
   ... each individual resistance added together.
   eg. if both P and Q each have a resistance of 15 ohms ...
   ... the total resistance = 15 ohms + 15 ohms = 30 ohms.

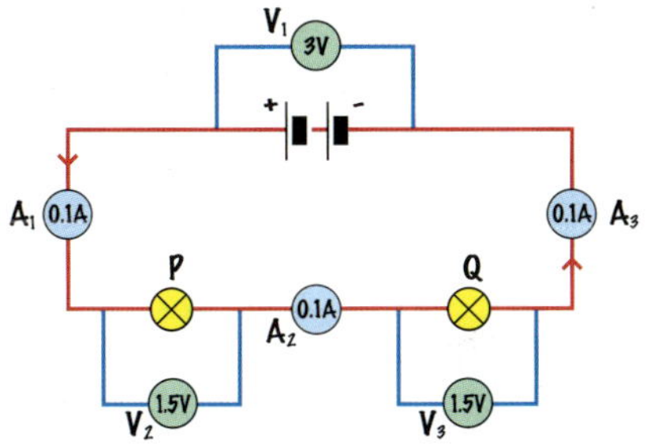

Components Connected In Parallel

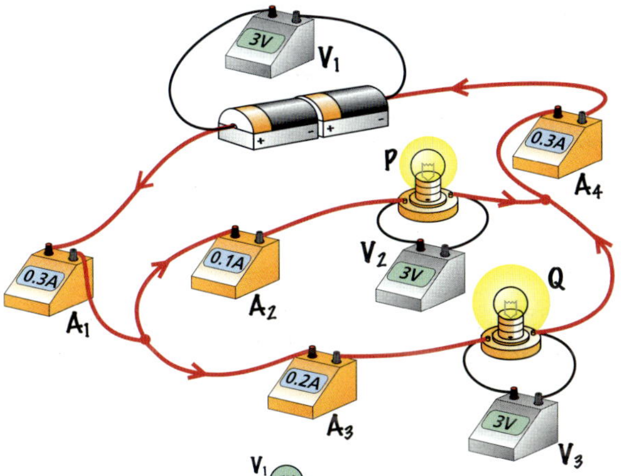

Components connected in parallel are connected SEPARATELY in their OWN LOOP going from ONE TERMINAL of the BATTERY to the OTHER. When components are connected in parallel ...

1. The TOTAL CURRENT in the main circuit ...
   ... is equal to the SUM of the CURRENTS ...
   ... through the separate components.
   ie. $A_1 = A_2 + A_3 = A_4$
   eg. 0.3A = 0.1A + 0.2A = 0.3A
2. The POTENTIAL DIFFERENCE ACROSS ...
   ... EACH COMPONENT is the SAME.
   (... and is equal to the p.d. of the battery)
   ie. $V_1 = V_2 = V_3$
   eg. each bulb has a p.d. of 3V across it.

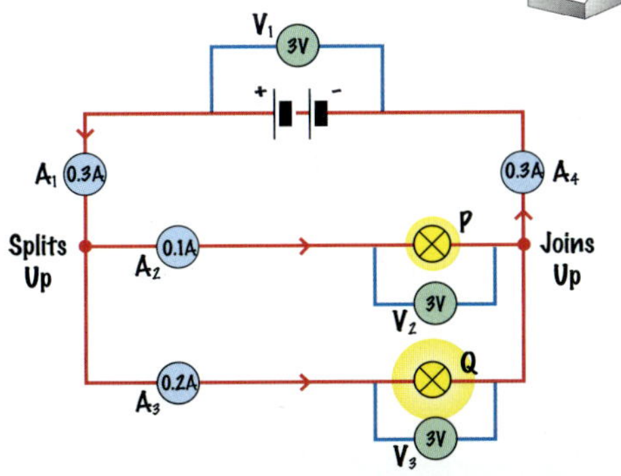

3. The AMOUNT OF CURRENT which passes ...
   ... through EACH COMPONENT depends on the ...
   ... RESISTANCE OF EACH COMPONENT.
   The greater the resistance, the smaller the current.
   Bulb P has TWICE the RESISTANCE of bulb Q ...
   ... and so only 0.1A passes through bulb P ...
   ... while 0.2A passes through bulb Q.

Connecting Cells In Series

The TOTAL POTENTIAL DIFFERENCE provided by cells CONNECTED in SERIES is the SUM of the P.D. ...
... of EACH CELL SEPARATELY, providing that they have been connected in the same direction.
Each of the following cells has a p.d. of 1.5V ...

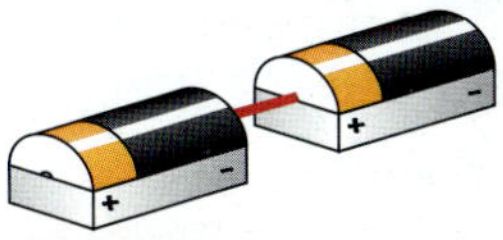

Total p.d. = 2 x 1.5V = 3V

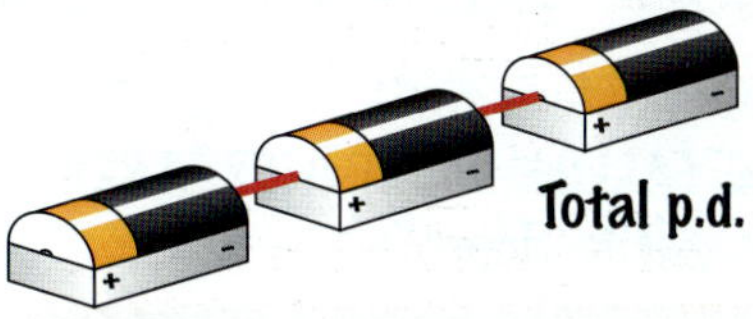

Total p.d. = 3 x 1.5V = 4.5V

V = IR

RESISTANCE is a measure of how hard it is to get a CURRENT through a component at a PARTICULAR POTENTIAL DIFFERENCE or VOLTAGE.
Potential difference, current and resistance are related by the formula:

POTENTIAL DIFFERENCE (volt, V) = CURRENT (ampere, A) x RESISTANCE (ohm, Ω)

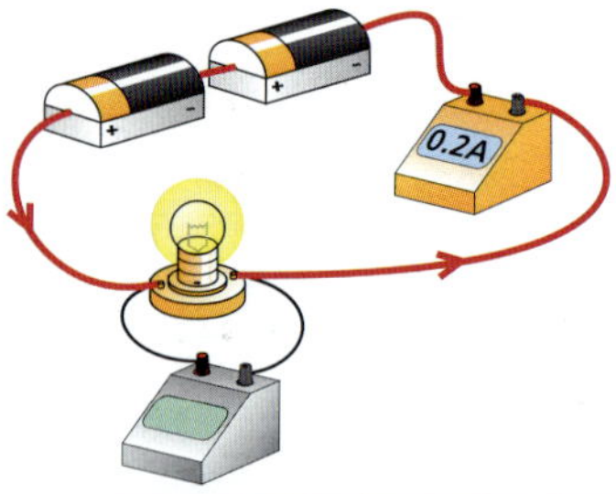

Example
Calculate the reading on the voltmeter in the circuit opposite if the bulb has a resistance of 15 ohms.

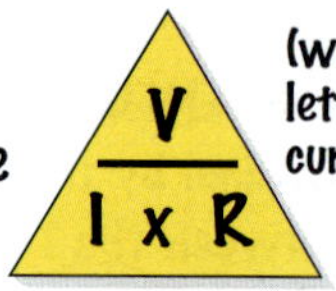

(we use the letter I for current)

Using our formula: POTENTIAL DIFFERENCE = CURRENT x RESISTANCE
= 0.2A x 15Ω
= 3V

The reading on the ammeter is the current.

Resistance Of Components

These can be investigated using the circuit above with a power pack instead of batteries.
You could then draw CURRENT-VOLTAGE graphs which show how the CURRENT THROUGH the component varies with the VOLTAGE ACROSS IT.

① RESISTOR

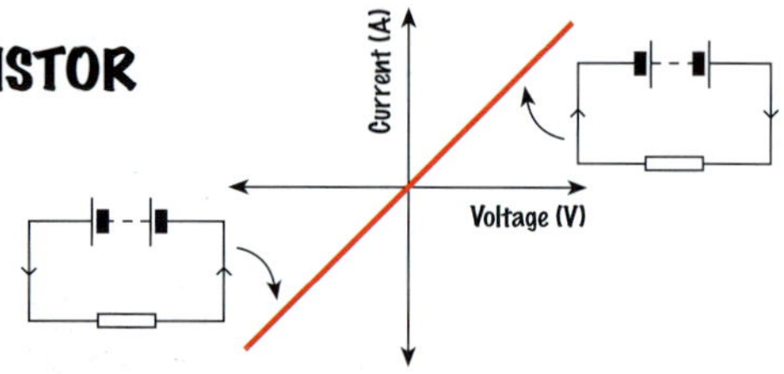

Providing the TEMPERATURE of the RESISTOR ...
... STAYS CONSTANT then ...
... THE CURRENT THROUGH THE RESISTOR IS DIRECTLY PROPORTIONAL TO THE VOLTAGE ACROSS THE RESISTOR ...
... ie. if one doubles, the other doubles etc ...
... regardless of which direction the current is flowing.

② FILAMENT LAMP

As the TEMPERATURE of the ...
... FILAMENT INCREASES and the ...
... bulb gets brighter then the ...
... RESISTANCE OF THE FILAMENT LAMP INCREASES, ...
... regardless of which direction the current is flowing.

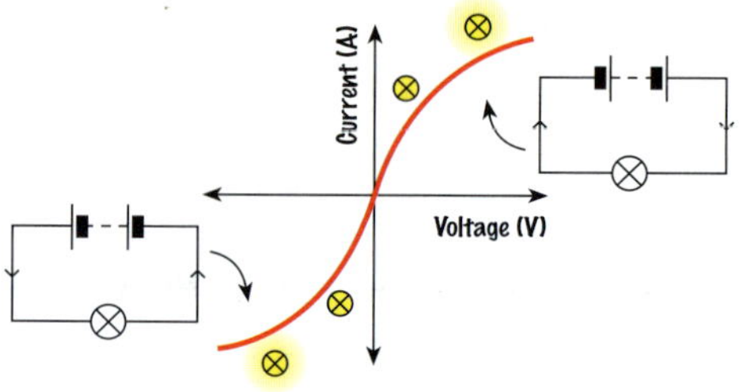

③ DIODE

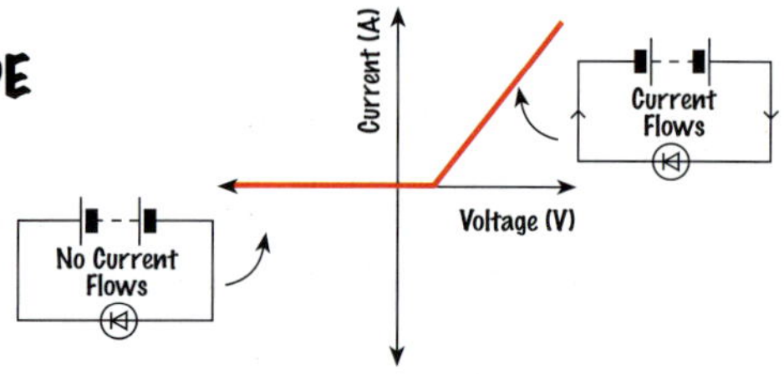

A diode allows a CURRENT to flow through it ...
... in ONE DIRECTION ONLY.
It has a VERY HIGH RESISTANCE ...
... in the REVERSE DIRECTION ...
... and no current flows.

Two Other Components

LIGHT DEPENDENT RESISTOR (LDR)

The resistance of an LDR ...
... depends on the amount of light falling on it.

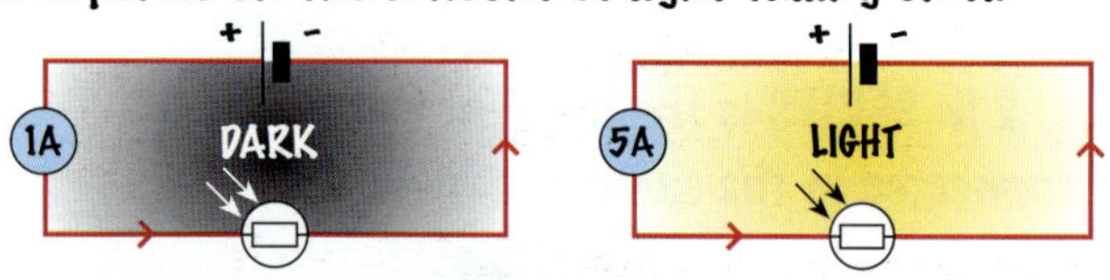

Its RESISTANCE DECREASES as the ...
... AMOUNT OF LIGHT FALLING ON IT INCREASES.
This allows more current to flow.

THERMISTOR

The resistance of a Thermistor ...
... depends on its temperature.

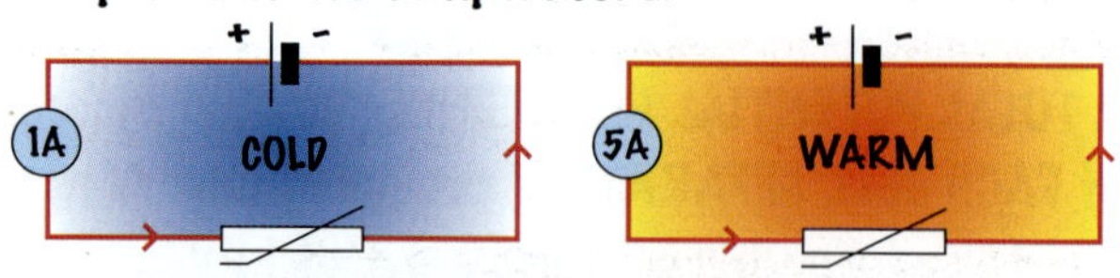

Its RESISTANCE DECREASES as the ...
... TEMPERATURE OF THE THERMISTOR INCREASES.
This allows more current to flow.

STATIC ELECTRICITY

- TWO MATERIALS can become ELECTRICALLY CHARGED when they are RUBBED AGAINST EACH OTHER.
- The materials have become charged with STATIC ELECTRICITY which means ...
- ... that the electricity stays on the material and doesn't move.

You can 'generate' static electricity by rubbing a balloon against a jumper.

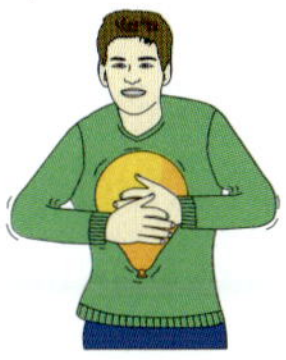

The electrically charged balloon will then attract very small objects.

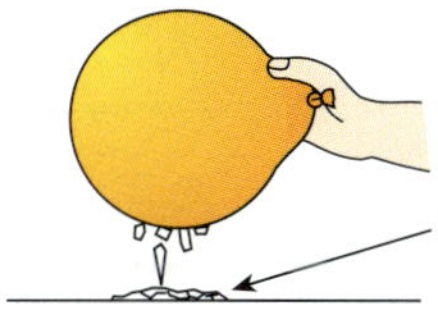

- Electric charge (static) builds up when ELECTRONS (which have a NEGATIVE charge) are 'rubbed off' one material onto another. The material receiving electrons becomes NEGATIVELY CHARGED and the one giving up electrons becomes EQUALLY POSITIVELY CHARGED.

eg. PERSPEX ROD RUBBED WITH A CLOTH

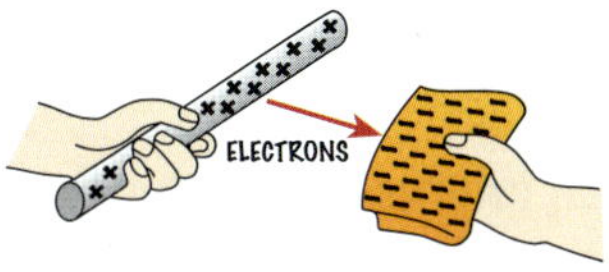

Perspex LOSES electrons ... ... to become ... ... POSITIVELY CHARGED.

Cloth GAINS electrons ... ... to become ... ... NEGATIVELY CHARGED.

eg. EBONITE ROD RUBBED WITH FUR

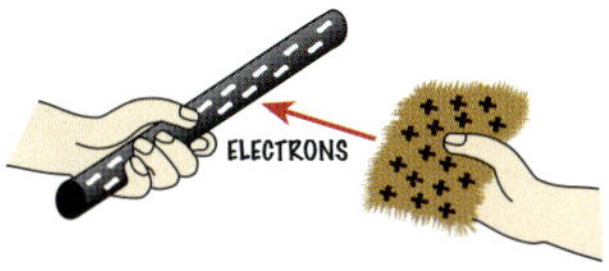

Ebonite GAINS electrons ... ... to become ... ... NEGATIVELY CHARGED.

Fur LOSES electrons ... ... to become ... ... POSITIVELY CHARGED.

Repulsion And Attraction Between Charged Materials

Very simply, two materials with ...

... THE SAME CHARGES REPEL EACH OTHER.

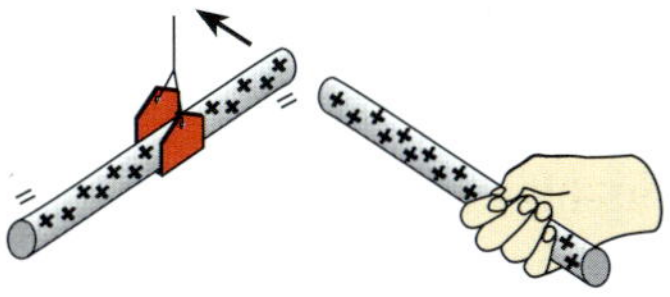

NB
We would get the same with two ebonite rods.

- The SUSPENDED PERSPEX ROD ...
- ... is REPELLED by the OTHER PERSPEX ROD.

... DIFFERENT CHARGES ATTRACT EACH OTHER.

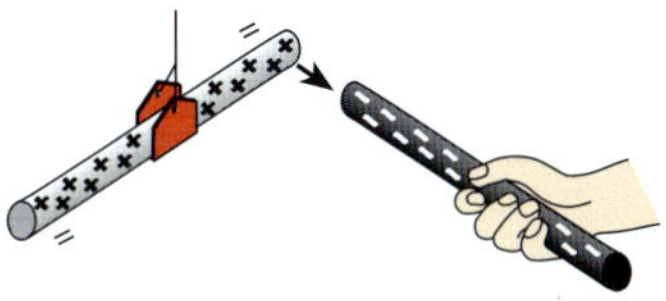

NB
We would get the same if the rods were the other way around.

- The SUSPENDED PERSPEX ROD ...
- ... is ATTRACTED by the EBONITE ROD.

Discharge Of Static Electricity

- A charged conductor can be DISCHARGED ie. have any charge on it removed by connecting it to EARTH with a CONDUCTOR.

Negatively charged dome of Van De Graff generator

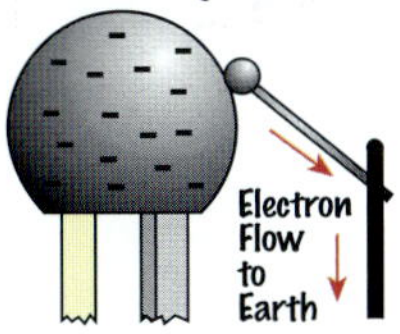

In this case electrons flow from the dome to Earth via the conductor ... until the dome is completely discharged.

Positively charged dome

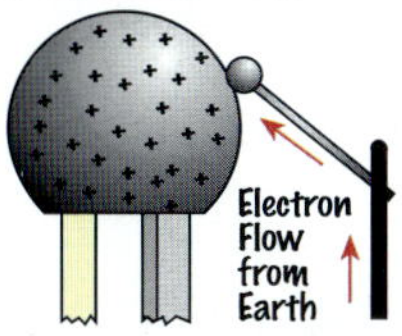

This time the electrons flow from Earth to cancel out the positive charge on the dome ... until the dome is completely discharged.

This flow of electrons through a solid conductor is an ELECTRIC CURRENT and ...

... metals conduct electricity well because electrons from their atoms can move freely throughout the metal structure.

However ...

- ... the GREATER the CHARGE on an ISOLATED OBJECT ...
- ... the GREATER the VOLTAGE (POTENTIAL DIFFERENCE) between the object and Earth.
- If the voltage between the object and a nearby earthed conductor becomes high enough, then ...
- ... this can cause the air molecules to ionise and 'ZAP!', there is a spark as DISCHARGE occurs.

In this case electrons flow from the dome <u>through the air</u> to get to earth via the conductor.

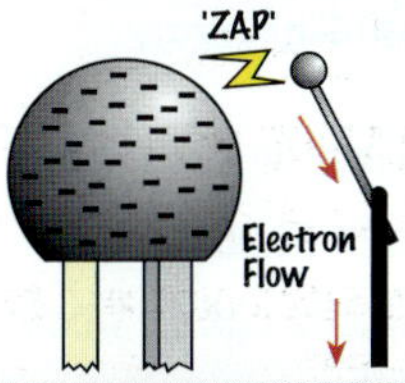

In this case electrons flow from the earthed conductor <u>through the air</u> to cancel out the positive charge on the dome.

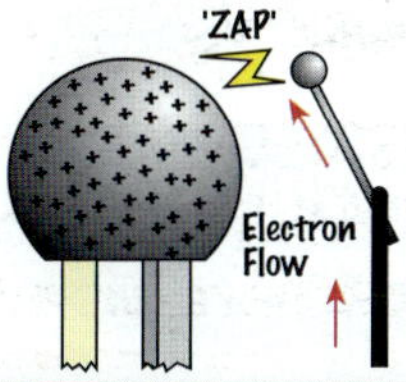

Using Static In Everyday Life

1. THE PHOTOCOPIER

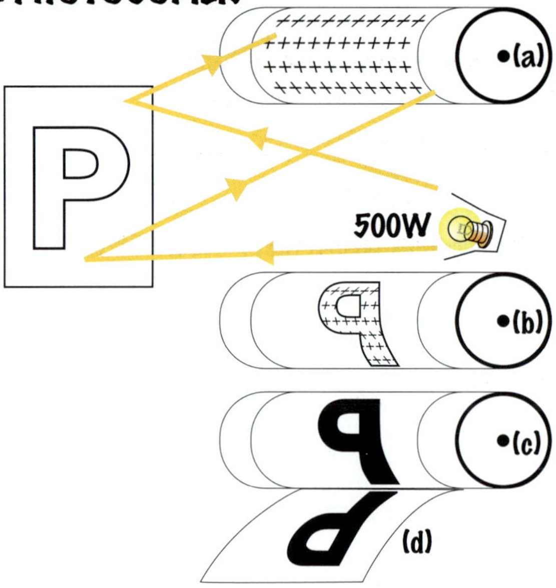

(a) A copying plate is electrically charged (usually positive). An image of the page to be copied is projected onto the plate.

(b) Light causes charge to leak away leaving an 'electrostatic impression' of the page.

(c) This charged impression of the plate attracts tiny specks of black powder.

(d) This powder is then transferred from the plate to paper which is heated to fix the final image.

2. ELECTROSTATIC SMOKE PRECIPITATOR

These are designed to remove solid smoke particles from waste gases before the gases are released into the environment.

- Solid smoke particles become charged as they pass by a charged metal grid. These 'like' charges repel each other causing the particles to move away from the grid.

- The particles are then attracted to the collecting plates which are oppositely charged, where they stick to form a layer of 'soot' which is regularly knocked loose.

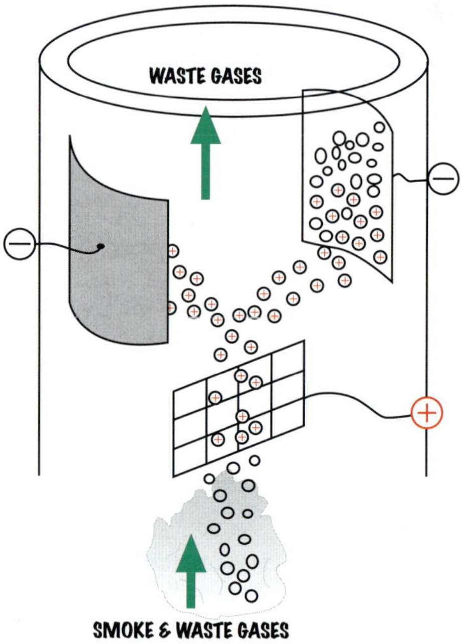

Discharging Unsafe Static

FILLING AIRCRAFT FUEL TANKS

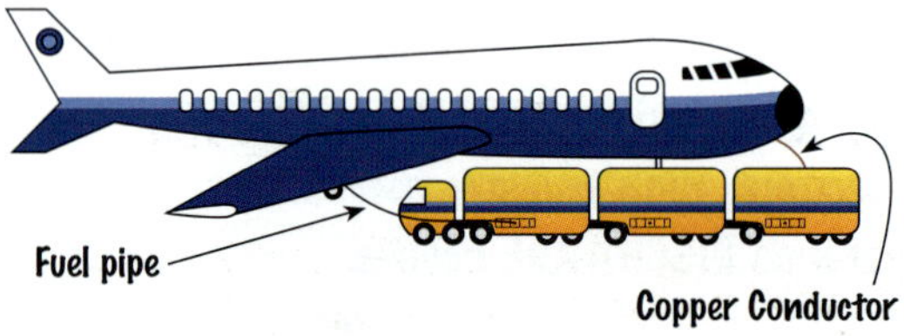

During refuelling the fuel gains electrons from the fuel pipe, making the pipe positively charged and the fuel negatively charged. The resulting voltage between the two can cause a spark (DISCHARGE). You can imagine the rest!!!

SOLVING THE PROBLEM

Earth the fuel tank with a copper conductor, or ...
... link the tanker and the plane by a copper conductor.
Either of these will allow constant safe discharge to occur.

Principles Of Electrolysis

- Some chemical compounds will allow an electric current to flow through them ...
- ... when they are MOLTEN or DISSOLVED IN WATER.
- These compounds contain NEGATIVE and POSITIVE IONS and the electric current is due to BOTH ...
- ... NEGATIVELY CHARGED IONS MOVING TO THE POSITIVE TERMINAL (ELECTRODE) ...
- ... and POSITIVELY CHARGED IONS MOVING TO THE NEGATIVE TERMINAL (ELECTRODE).

When this happens SIMPLER SUBSTANCES are released at the TWO ELECTRODES. This process is called ELECTROLYSIS. If we were to carry out the electrolysis of copper chloride solution ...

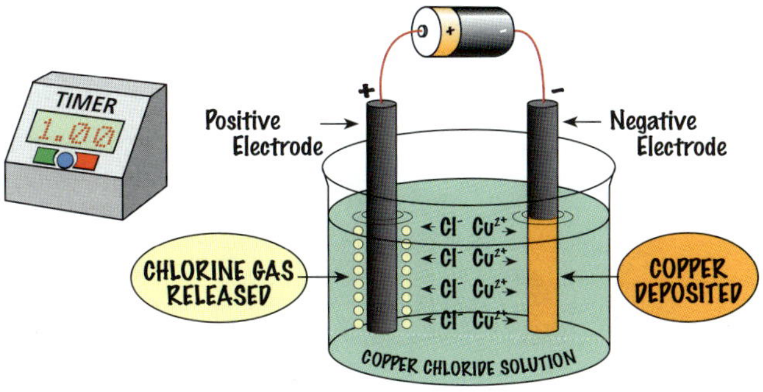

... the simple substances released are Copper at the negative terminal and Chlorine Gas at the positive terminal ...
However, the QUANTITY of these substances released in grams INCREASES IN PROPORTION TO ...

1. THE CURRENT FLOWING.

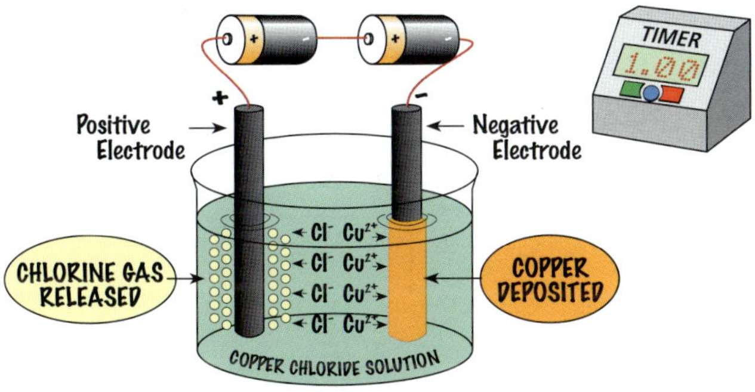

If we DOUBLE THE CURRENT FLOWING ...
... by having two cells, then ...
... the quantity of CHLORINE GAS RELEASED ...
... and COPPER DEPOSITED <u>WILL ALSO DOUBLE</u> ...
... (assuming the same period of time).

2. THE TIME FOR WHICH THE CURRENT FLOWS.

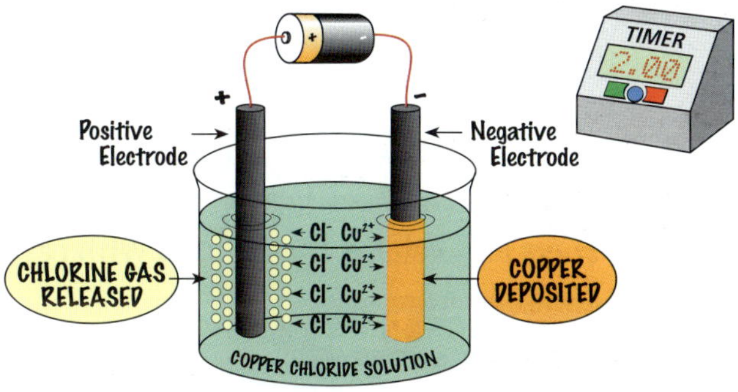

If we DOUBLE THE TIME ...
... FOR WHICH THE CURRENT FLOWS, then ...
... the quantity of CHLORINE GAS RELEASED ...
... and COPPER DEPOSITED <u>WILL ALSO DOUBLE</u> ...
... (assuming the same current).

<u>EXAMPLE</u>

During the electrolysis of copper chloride solution a current of 2 Amps flows for 3 minutes releasing 0.06g of copper. How much copper would be deposited if ...

a) ... a current of 2 Amps flows for 6 minutes?

> THE SAME CURRENT FLOW <u>BUT</u> THE TIME IT FLOWS IS DOUBLED ... ... WHICH MEANS THE COPPER DEPOSITED IS ALSO DOUBLED

Therefore, copper deposited = 2 x 0.06g = 0.12g

b) ... a current of 1 Amp flows for 3 minutes?

> THE TIME CURRENT FLOWS IS THE SAME <u>BUT</u> THE CURRENT FLOW IS HALVED ... ... WHICH MEANS THE COPPER DEPOSITED IS ALSO HALVED

Therefore, copper deposited = $\frac{1}{2}$ x 0.06g = 0.03g

MAINS ELECTRICITY I - THE 3-PIN PLUG

Most electrical appliances are connected to the MAINS ELECTRICITY SUPPLY ...
... using a CABLE and a 3-PIN PLUG which is inserted into a SOCKET on the ring main circuit.
In the UK, the mains supply has a VOLTAGE OF ABOUT 230 VOLTS ...
... which if it's not used safely can kill!!

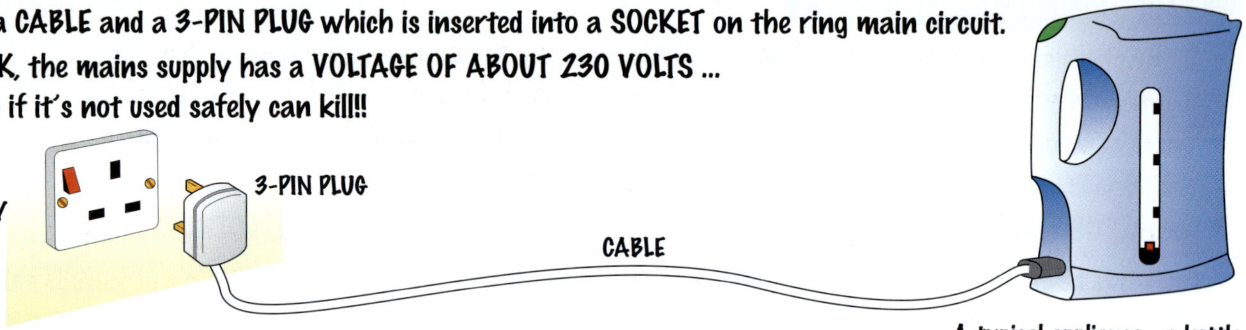

A typical appliance - a kettle

3-Pin Plug

EARTH WIRE (Green & Yellow)
- All appliances with outer metal cases are earthed.

NEUTRAL WIRE (Blue)
- Carries current away from appliance.

CABLE GRIP
- Secures the cable in the plug.

FUSE
- Always part of the live circuit.
- Should be of the proper current rating.

CASING
- Plastic or Rubber because both are good insulators.

LIVE WIRE (Brown)
- Carries current to appliance.

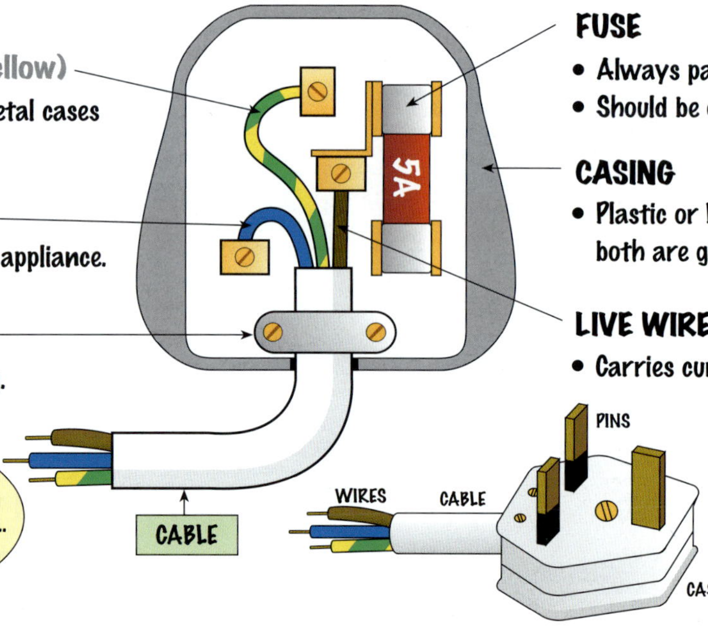

- Inner cores of COPPER ...
- ... because it's a good conductor.
- Outer layers of FLEXIBLE PLASTIC ...
- ... because it's a good insulator.

- The plug has ...
- ... PINS made from BRASS ...
- ... because it's a good conductor.

NB
The LIVE terminal of the mains supply alternates between ...
... a positive and negative voltage with respect to the NEUTRAL terminal, ...
... which stays at a voltage close to zero with respect to EARTH.

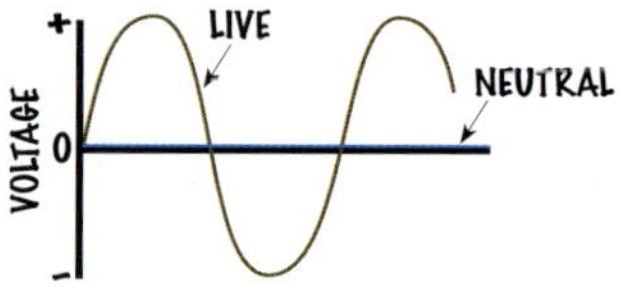

Errors In Wiring Plugs

It is very important that all plugs are wired correctly with NO errors, for our own safety.
Below are five examples of dangerously wired plugs!

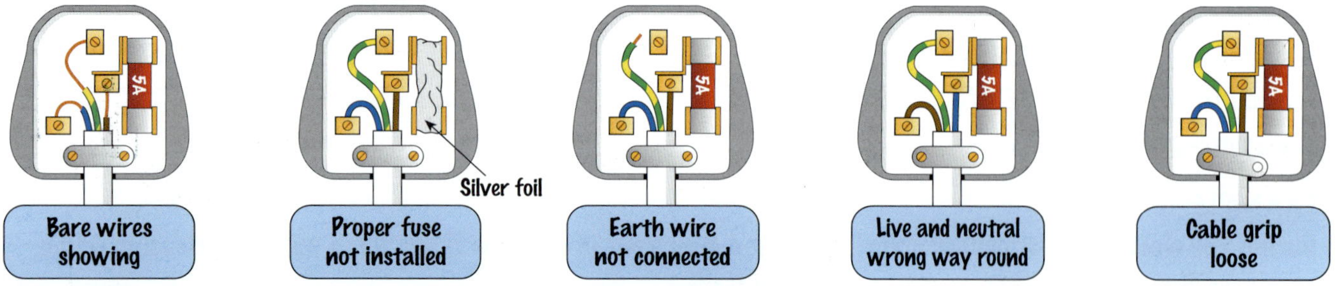

Dangerous Practices In The Use Of Mains Electricity

Apart from making sure that all plugs are wired correctly, here are some 'common sense' practices which should be followed at all times:
- All broken plugs and frayed cables should be replaced.
- Keep plugs and cables away from water or heat.
- Never overload a socket with too many plugs.
- Make sure your hands aren't wet when switching appliances on or off.

Alternating Current

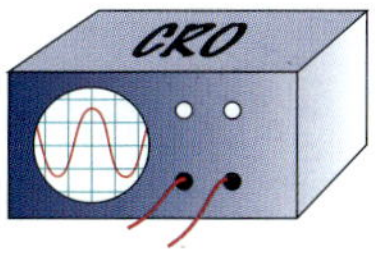

This type of current changes direction of flow back and forth continuously. The number of complete cycles of reversal per second is called the FREQUENCY, and for mains electricity this is 50 cycles per second (Hertz). FREQUENCY and VOLTAGE can be compared using an oscilloscope.

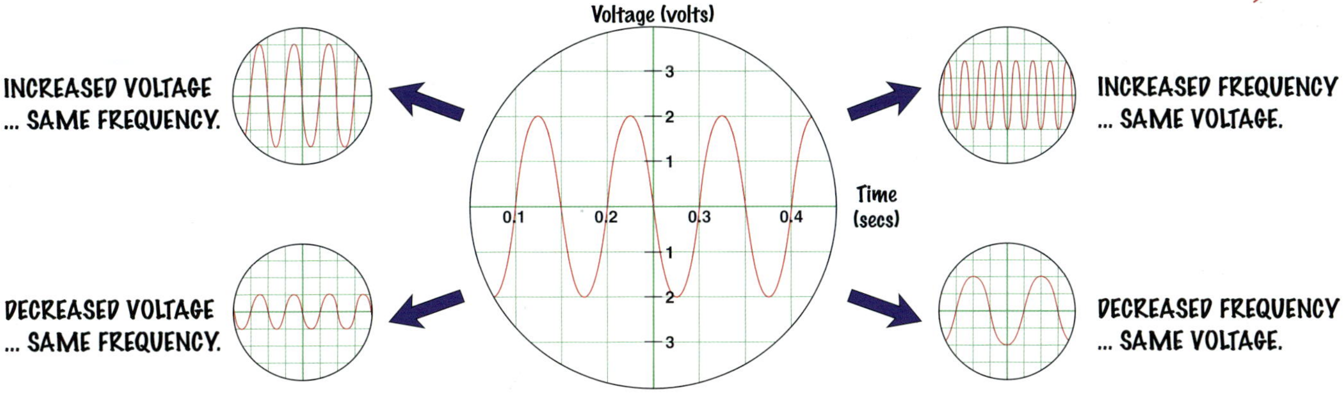

In the main example above, the peak voltage is 2 volts and the frequency is 10 cycles per second since one complete cycle takes 0.1 seconds.

Direct Current

This type of current always flows in the same direction. Cells and batteries supply d.c. We can use an oscilloscope to compare the voltage of different d.c. supplies.

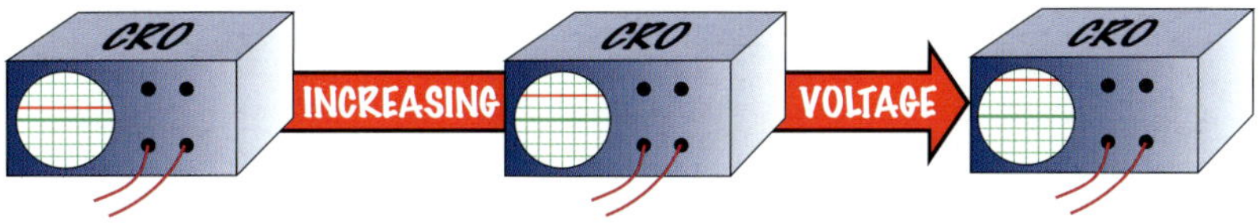

Fuses

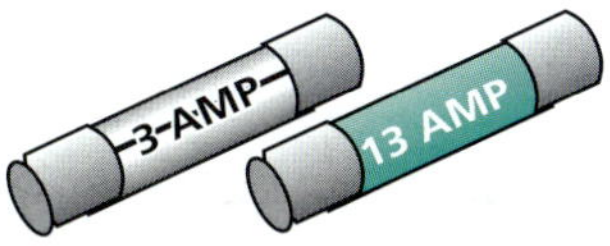

A FUSE is a SHORT, THIN piece of WIRE with a LOW MELTING POINT.
When the CURRENT passing through it EXCEEDS the CURRENT RATING of the fuse, ...
... the fuse wire gets HOT and MELTS or BREAKS.
This PREVENTS DAMAGE to the CABLE or the APPLIANCE through the possibility of OVERHEATING.

CURRENT LARGER THAN CURRENT RATING OF FUSE → FUSE BURNS OUT → CIRCUIT IS BROKEN → NO CURRENT FLOWS → CABLE OR APPLIANCE IS PROTECTED

However ...
- For this safety system to work properly the CURRENT RATING of the fuse ...
- ... must be JUST ABOVE THE NORMAL WORKING CURRENT of the appliance (see P.85)

Example Of A Fuse In Action

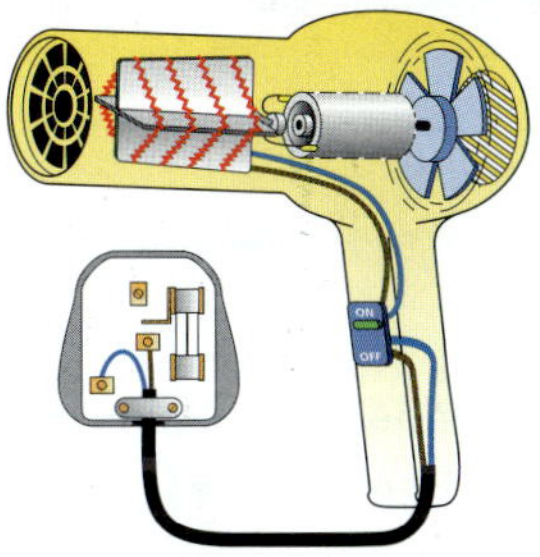

Normally the current flowing ...
... is BELOW the current rating ...
... of the fuse ...
... and the appliance (hairdrier) ...
... works properly.
However ...
... a fault occurs inside the appliance ...

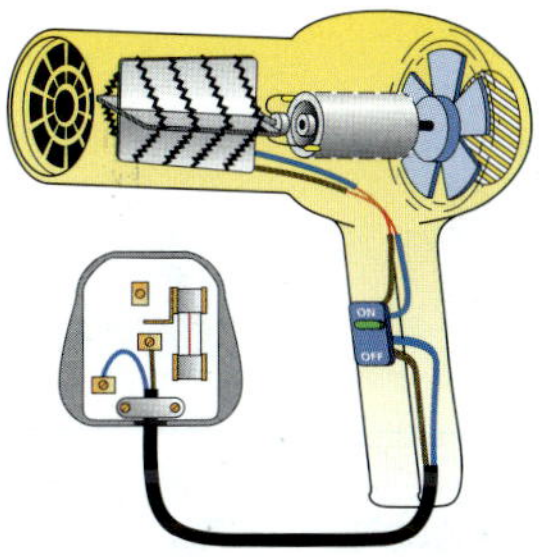

... and the live wire makes contact ...
... with the neutral wire.
The current now flowing is ABOVE
... the current rating of the fuse ...
... because there is less resistance.
This causes the fuse wire to get ...
... hotter and hotter until ...

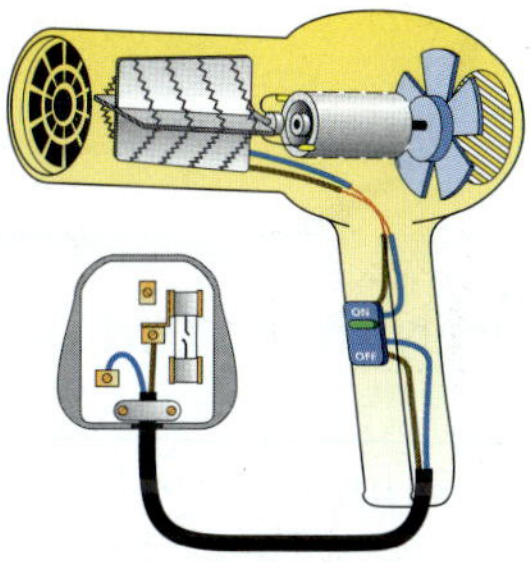

... it gets so hot ...
... it melts!
The circuit is now broken.
No current flows and ...
... there is no danger of ...
... further damage to the appliance ...
... or injury to the user.

Circuit Breakers

Most modern houses tend to have **CIRCUIT BREAKERS** rather than rely on fuses in the consumer unit.

- They depend on an **ELECTROMAGNET** which separates a **PAIR OF CONTACTS** ...
- ... **WHEN THE CURRENT BECOMES HIGH ENOUGH.**
- They work **MORE QUICKLY THAN A FUSE,** ...
- ... and are **EASILY RESET** by pressing a button.

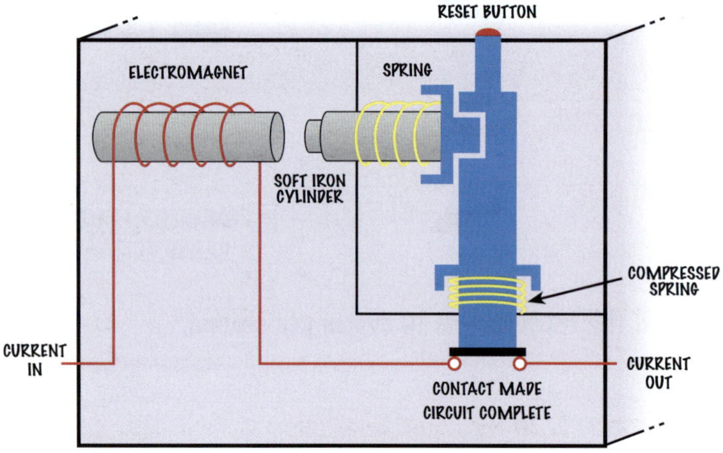

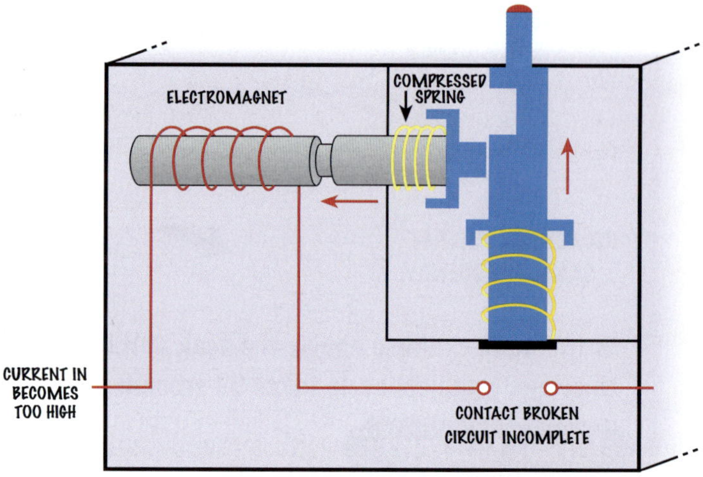

CURRENT BECOMES TOO HIGH → ELECTROMAGNET ATTRACTS SOFT IRON CYLINDER → PAIR OF CONTACTS ARE SEPARATED → CIRCUIT BROKEN → CABLE OR APPLIANCE IS PROTECTED

Many houses though still have consumer units ...
... that rely on ordinary fuses. In these cases, ...
... it is advisable to use an **ADAPTER PLUG** ...
... which contains a circuit breaker ...
... when using certain appliances ...
... such as a lawnmower or hedge cutter.

Earthing

All electrical appliances with outer metal cases **MUST BE EARTHED.**
The outer case of the appliance is connected to the **EARTH PIN** in the plug through the **EARTH WIRE** ...

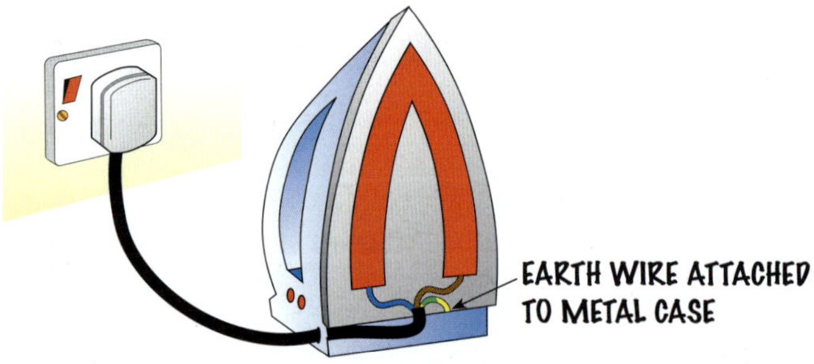

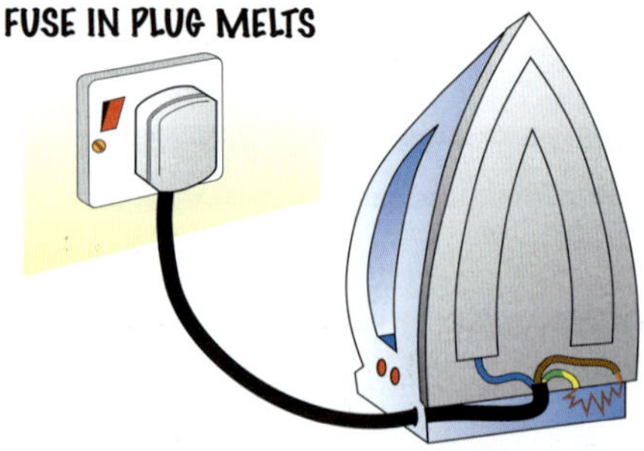

- Normally the current flowing ...
- ... is BELOW the current rating ...
- ... of the fuse.
- The appliance (iron) ...
- ... works properly.

However ...

- ... if a fault in the appliance connects the live wire to the case, then the case will become **LIVE!**
- This current will 'run to earth' through the earth wire, because this offers less resistance ...
- ... and this **OVERLOAD** of current will cause the fuse wire to melt (or a circuit breaker to trip).

'LIVE' CASING → SHORT CIRCUIT → CURRENT 'SURGES' TO EARTH → FUSE MELTS → CIRCUIT BROKEN → CABLE OR APPLIANCE IS PROTECTED

Power And Energy Transfer

An electric current is a flow of charge which transfers energy from the battery or power supply ...
... to the components in the circuit. If the component is a resistor, electrical energy is transferred as heat.
The RATE of this ENERGY TRANSFER is the POWER of the component or appliance ...
... and is measured in joules/second or WATTS (W) where 1 watt is the transfer of 1 joule of energy in 1 second. Power is calculated using the following formula ...

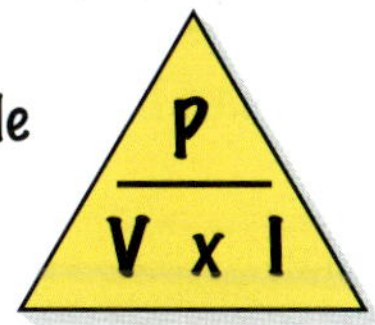

POWER (W) = POTENTIAL DIFFERENCE (V) x CURRENT (A)

Most appliances have a rating plate on them which gives us their maximum power and their working voltage. We can then calculate the current passing through the appliance and therefore the ideal current rating of the fuse in the circuit.

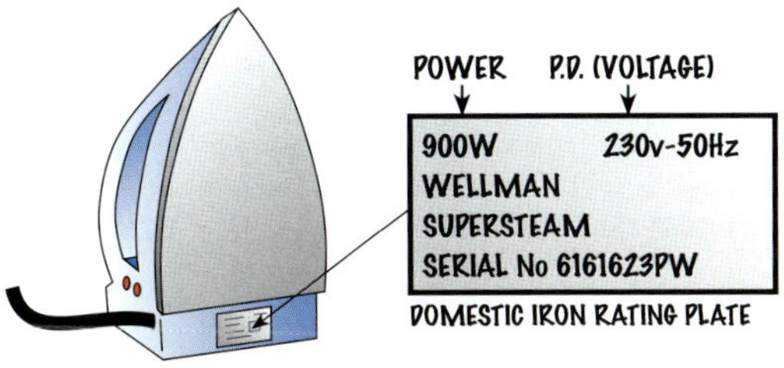

Using our formula:
(rearranged
using formula triangle)

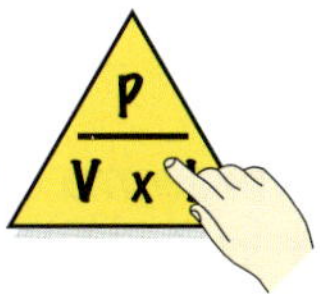

$$\text{CURRENT} = \frac{\text{POWER}}{\text{POTENTIAL DIFFERENCE}}$$

$$= \frac{900\text{W}}{230\text{V}}$$

= 3.9 amps.

And, the CURRENT RATING of the fuse should be 5amps. Ideally it should be as close as possible to (but HIGHER than) the normal current which flows through the appliance (see P.83)

Charge And Energy Transfer

The amount of electrical CHARGE which passes ANY POINT in a circuit is measured in Coulombs (C) and depends on ...
... the CURRENT that flows and the TIME for which the current flows.

Charge, current and time are related by the formula:

CHARGE (C) = CURRENT (A) x TIME (s)

Here is a simple circuit ...

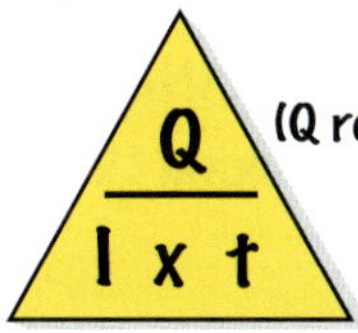

(Q represents charge)

If the circuit above is switched on for 40 seconds and a current of 0.5 Amps flows, then ...

... using the formula: CHARGE = CURRENT x TIME
= 0.5 A x 40 s
= 20 coulombs

... THIS AMOUNT OF CHARGE GOES PAST ANY POINT IN THE CIRCUIT IN THE 40 SECONDS.

However ...
As this CHARGE PASSES THROUGH THE BULB AN ENERGY TRANSFER TAKES PLACE.
The amount of ENERGY TRANSFERRED BY EVERY COULOMB of charge depends on the SIZE of the SUPPLY VOLTAGE!
THE GREATER the SUPPLY VOLTAGE the GREATER the ENERGY TRANSFERRED by EVERY COULOMB OF CHARGE.

Energy transferred, potential difference and charge are related by the formula:

ENERGY TRANSFERRED (J) = POTENTIAL DIFFERENCE (V) x CHARGE (C)

If we go back to our circuit above which was switched on for 40 seconds then ...

ENERGY TRANSFERRED = P.D. x CHARGE
= 1.5 V x 20 C
= 30 joules ...

... THIS AMOUNT OF ELECTRICAL ENERGY IS TRANSFERRED BY THE BULB TO LIGHT AND HEAT ENERGY.

REMEMBER The charge has gained this energy from the supply voltage ie. the battery ...
... which it then transfers to the bulb in the 40 secs the circuit was switched on!

Magnets

All MAGNETS have a region of space around them called the MAGNETIC FIELD...
... which exerts a force on any magnetic material (eg. iron, steel) or on any other magnet, which enters it.
This force can be ...

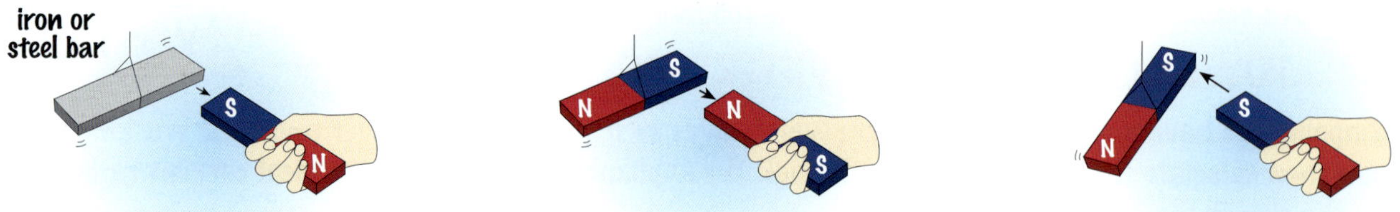

... ATTRACTIVE ... REPULSIVE

Electromagnets

If an ELECTRIC CURRENT flows through a COIL OF WIRE a MAGNETIC FIELD is formed around the coil...
... creating an ELECTROMAGNET. This is a MAGNET which can be SWITCHED ON and OFF.

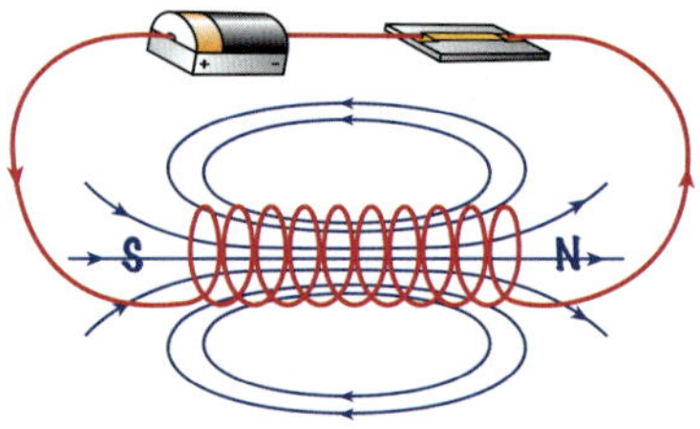

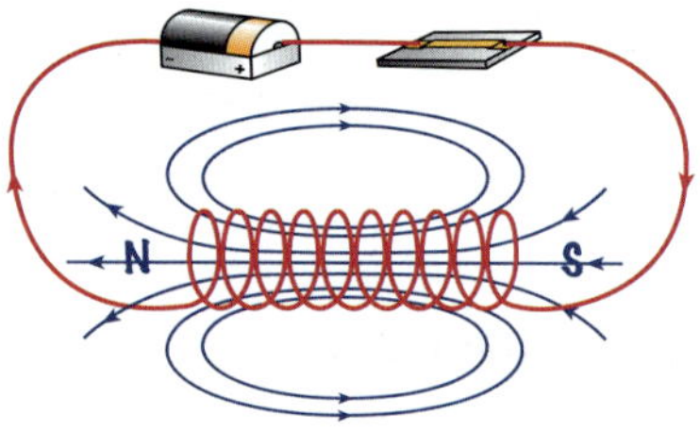

When the switch is closed...
... a current flows and a magnetic field is formed...
... which is very similar to that of a bar magnet.
One end becomes a north-seeking (N) pole...
... and the other end a south-seeking (S) pole.

However...
... if we reverse the direction of the current...
... this reverses the poles ...
... of the electromagnet formed.

NB
When the switch is open...
... a current no longer flows...
... and the magnetic field disappears.
The electromagnet is switched OFF.

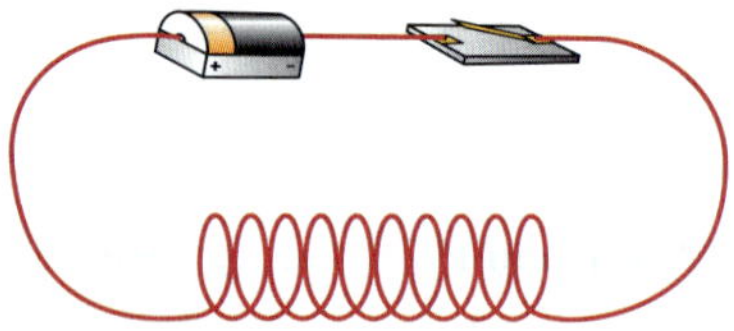

The Circuit Breaker

This is a safety device which uses an electromagnet.

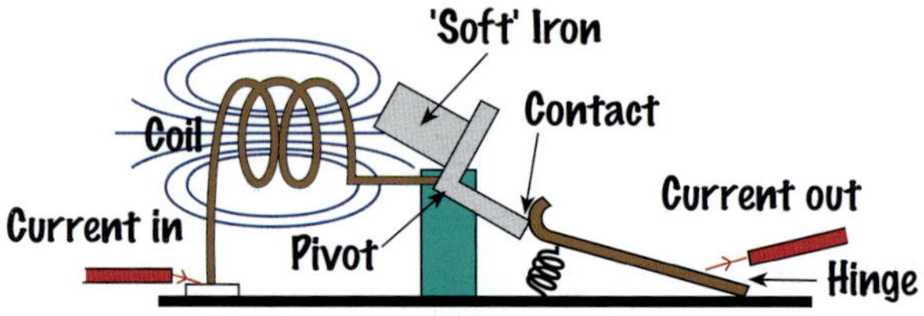

When the current through the COIL gets TOO HIGH...
... the strength of the magnetic field...
... generated by the electromagnet INCREASES until...
... it is strong enough to ATTRACT the SOFT IRON rocker.

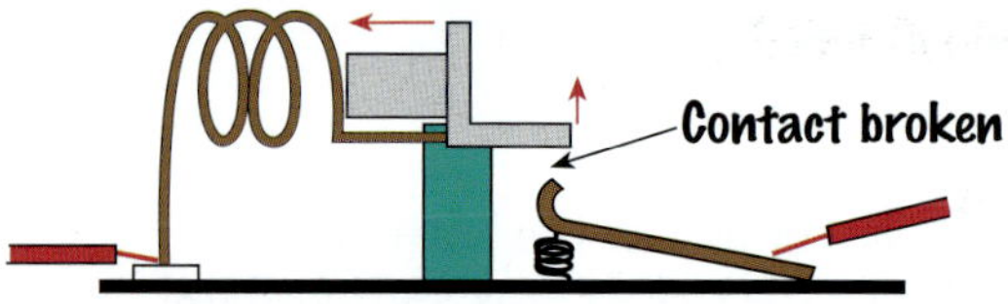

This causes the CONTACT TO BREAK...
... SWITCHING OFF THE CURRENT.

* See P.84 for an alternative diagram of a circuit breaker.

The Principle Of The Motor Effect

- When a wire carrying an ELECTRIC CURRENT is placed in a PERMANENT MAGNETIC FIELD...
- ... the magnetic field formed around the wire ...
- ... interacts with the permanent magnetic field...
- ... causing the wire to experience a force which causes it to move.

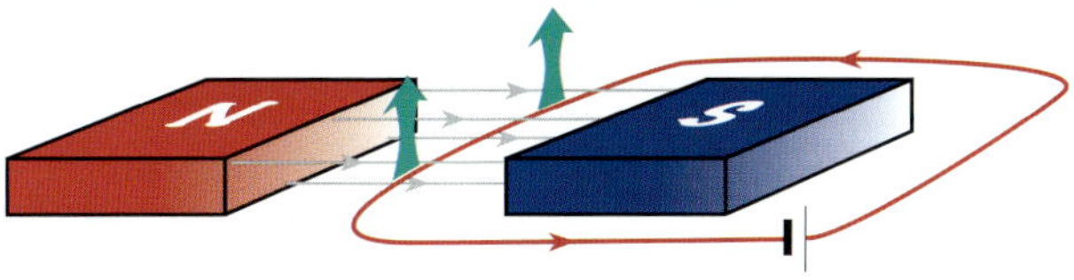

- The **SIZE** of the force on the wire can be increased by...

... INCREASING THE SIZE ...
... OF THE CURRENT ...
... (have more cells).

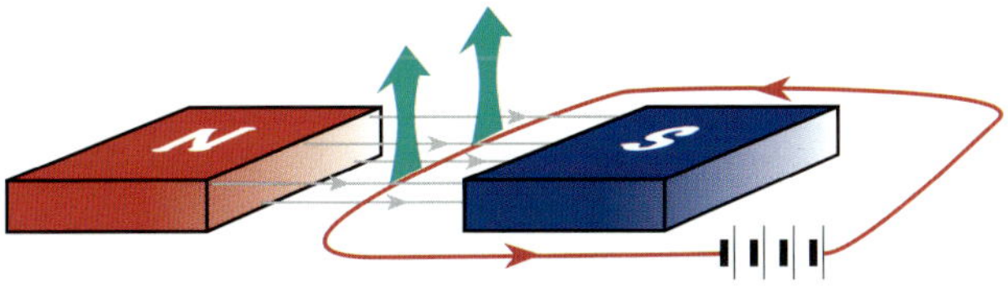

... INCREASING THE STRENGTH ...
... OF THE MAGNETIC FIELD ...
... (have stronger magnets).

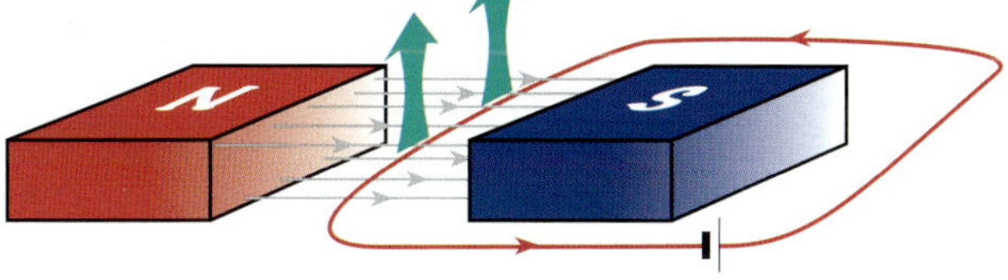

- The **DIRECTION** of the force on the wire can be reversed by...

... REVERSING THE DIRECTION ...
... OF FLOW OF THE CURRENT ...
... (turn your cell around).

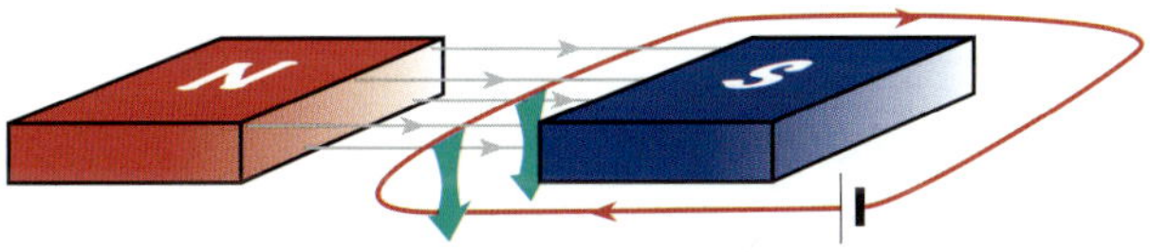

... or REVERSING THE DIRECTION ...
... OF THE MAGNETIC FIELD ...
... (swap your magnets around).

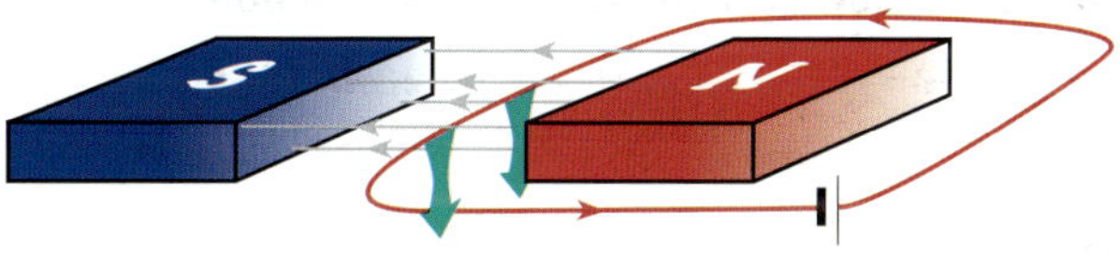

The Direct Current (d.c.) Motor

Electric motors form the basis of a vast range of electrical devices both in and out of the home. These rely on the principle of the motor effect.

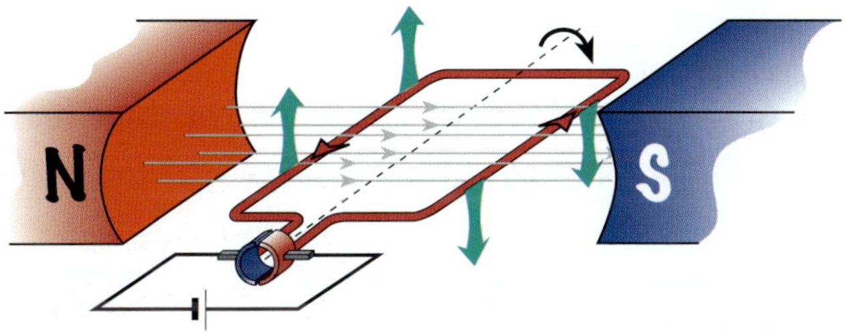

As a current flows through the coil a MAGNETIC FIELD is formed around the coil...
... creating an ELECTROMAGNET.
This magnetic field INTERACTS with the PERMANENT MAGNETIC FIELD...
... which exists between the TWO POLES, N and S.
A FORCE acts on both sides of the coil, which ROTATES THE COIL...
... to give us a very simple motor.

Making Electricity By Electromagnetic Induction

- If a wire or a coil of wire cuts through the lines of force of a magnetic field, or vice versa, ...
... then a **VOLTAGE IS INDUCED** (produced) between the ends of the wire ...
... and a **CURRENT** will be **INDUCED** in the wire if it is **PART OF A COMPLETE CIRCUIT.**

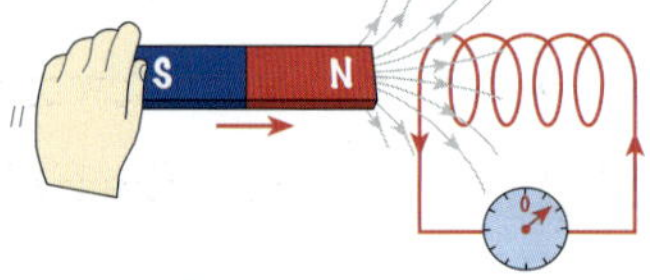

- Moving the magnet **INTO** the coil ...
- ... induces a current in one direction.

A current can be induced in the opposite direction ...

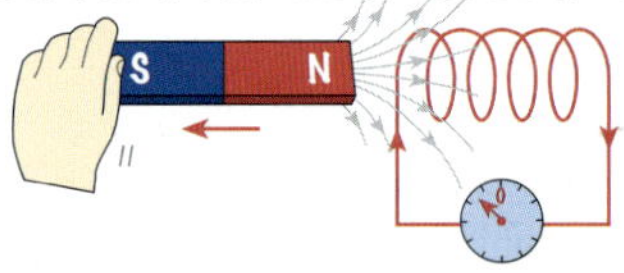

... by moving the magnet out of the coil OR ...

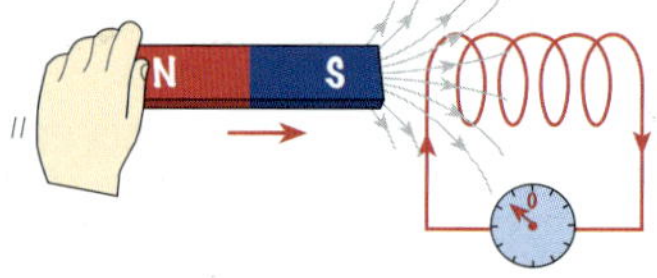

... by moving the other pole of the magnet into the coil.

- Generators use this principle for generating electricity by ...
... **ROTATING A COIL OF WIRE WITHIN A MAGNETIC FIELD OR ROTATING A MAGNET INSIDE A COIL.**
Both of these involve a magnetic field being cut by a coil of wire, creating an induced voltage.
However, if there is NO movement of magnet or coil there's no induced current.

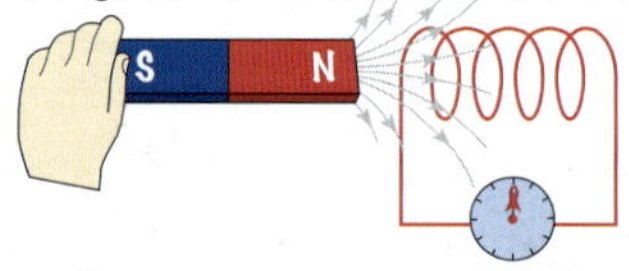

> In Electromagnetic induction, **MOVEMENT PRODUCES CURRENT.** This is really the opposite of what happens in the motor effect where **CURRENT PRODUCES MOVEMENT.**

Increasing The Size Of The Induced Voltage

The size of the induced voltage can be increased if we ...

1. Increase the **SPEED OF MOVEMENT** of the magnet or the coil.

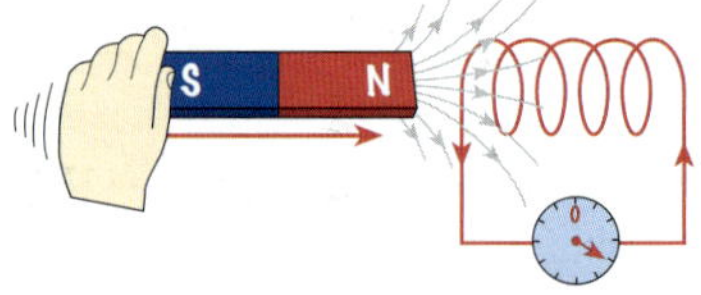

2. Increase the **STRENGTH OF THE MAGNETIC FIELD.**

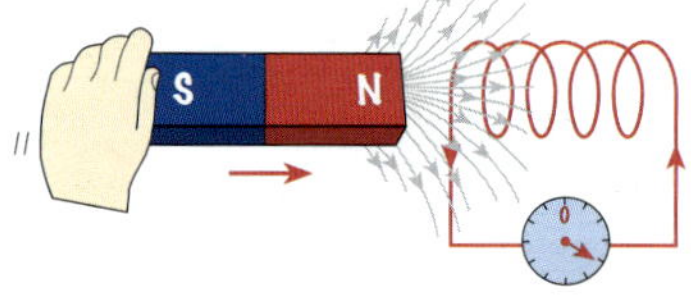

3. Increase the **NUMBER OF TURNS** on the coil.

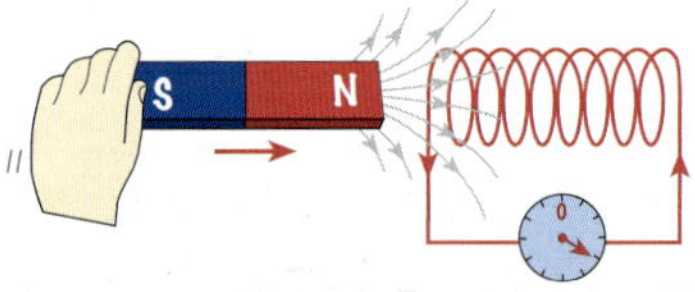

4. Increase the **AREA OF THE COIL.**

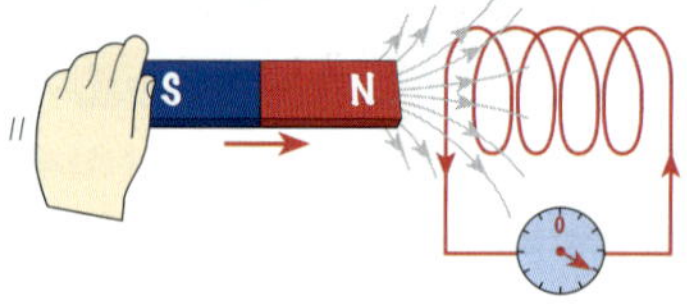

The Alternating Current Generator

Very simply, **A COIL OF WIRE IS ROTATED IN A MAGNETIC FIELD,** and the same four principles for increasing the size of the induced voltage apply.
As the coil cuts through the magnetic field a current is **INDUCED** in the coil ...

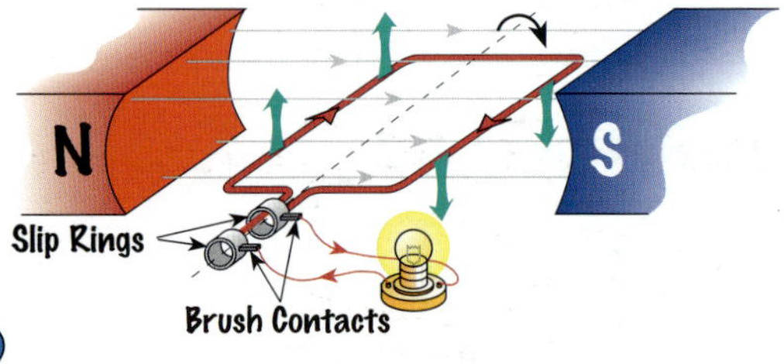

... which is **ALTERNATING** ie. it reverses its direction of flow...
... every half turn of the coil, as can be seen below...

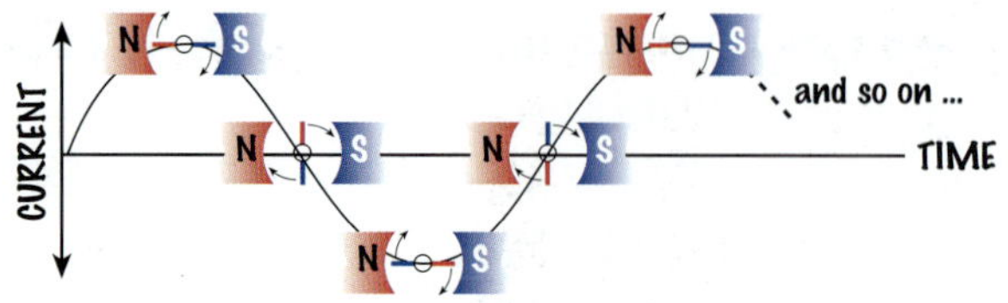

NB

THE BRUSH CONTACTS are spring-loaded so that they push gently against the **SLIP RINGS** in order that the circuit remains complete. Gradually they wear away and have to be replaced.

Distributing Electricity

Electricity generated at POWER STATIONS is distributed to homes, schools, shops, factories etc. all over the country by a network of cables called the NATIONAL GRID. Transformers are used to change the voltage of an a.c. supply, and are used both before and after transmission through the grid.

- Before transmission onto the GRID ...
  - ... TRANSFORMERS are used to 'STEP-UP'...
    - ... the VOLTAGE of the electricity generated.

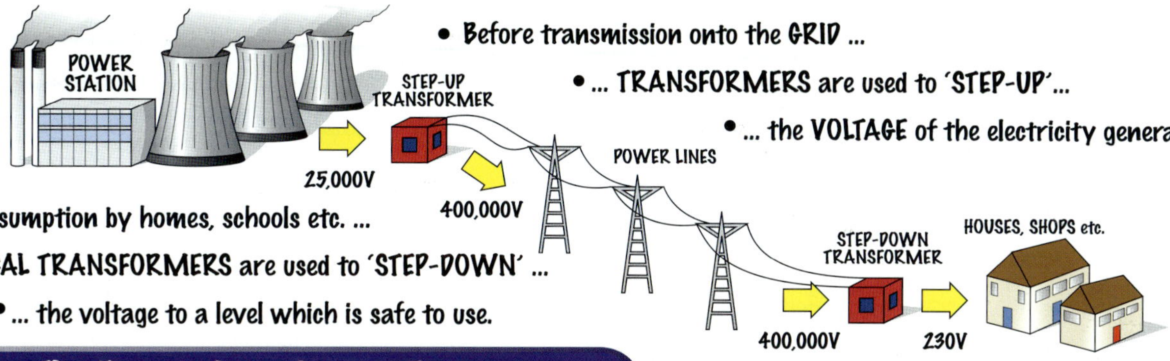

- Before consumption by homes, schools etc. ...
  - ... LOCAL TRANSFORMERS are used to 'STEP-DOWN' ...
    - ... the voltage to a level which is safe to use.

Reducing The Energy Loss During Transmission

The HIGHER the CURRENT that passes through ANY WIRE the greater the AMOUNT OF ENERGY LOST AS HEAT FROM THE WIRE. So we need to transmit as low a current as possible through the POWER LINES.

But since, POWER = VOLTAGE x CURRENT (see P.85) ...

... the smaller the current, the higher the voltage, needed to transmit energy at the same rate! This is where transformers come in.

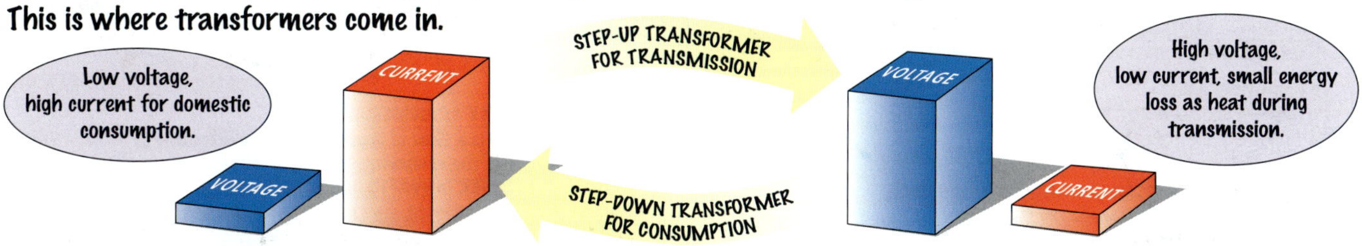

How Transformers Work

Transformers consist of ...

- Two COILS called the PRIMARY COIL and the SECONDARY COIL wrapped around a SOFT IRON CORE.

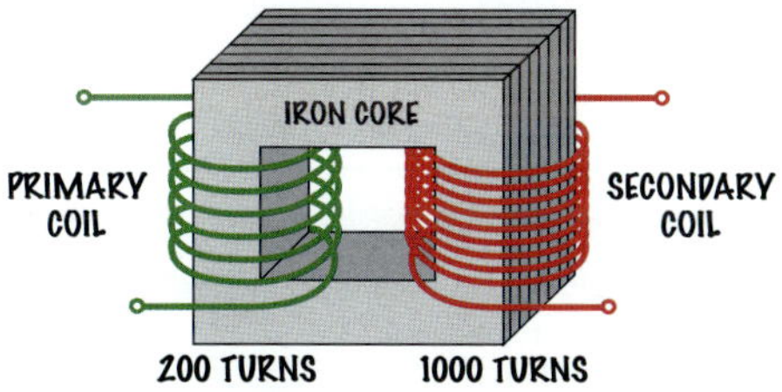

... an example of a STEP-UP TRANSFORMER.

Transformers work because ...

- An ALTERNATING INPUT VOLTAGE across the PRIMARY COIL ...
- ... causes an ALTERNATING CURRENT (a.c) ...
- ... to flow through the PRIMARY COIL.
- This alternating current creates a continually changing ...
- ... MAGNETIC FIELD which expands and collapses across ...
- ... the SECONDARY COIL INDUCING an ALTERNATING OUTPUT VOLTAGE.

THE SIZE OF THE OUTPUT (OR SECONDARY) VOLTAGE DEPENDS ON THE RELATIVE NUMBER OF TURNS ON THE PRIMARY AND SECONDARY COILS.

In general the formula is ...

$$\frac{\text{VOLTAGE ACROSS PRIMARY (V)}, V_p}{\text{VOLTAGE ACROSS SECONDARY (V)}, V_s} = \frac{\text{NUMBER OF TURNS ON PRIMARY}, N_p}{\text{NUMBER OF TURNS ON SECONDARY}, N_s}$$

EXAMPLE

A voltage of 230V is applied to the primary coil in the above diagram. What is the voltage across the secondary coil?

Using our formula: $$\frac{V_p}{V_s} = \frac{N_p}{N_s}$$

$$\frac{230V}{V_s} = \frac{200}{1000}$$

(if we rearrange) $$V_s = \frac{230 \times 1000}{200} = 1150 \text{ volts}$$

... OR, since there are five times more turns on the secondary coil, V_s will be FIVE TIMES V_p ... ie. $V_s = 5 \times V_p = 5 \times 230V = 1150V$

P.D., CURRENT AND RESISTANCE

The amount of current flowing through a component depends on ...
- ... the P.D. across the component, and ...
- ... the RESISTANCE of the component.

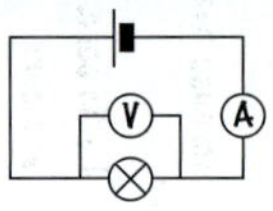

P.D. is measured by a VOLTMETER connected in parallel;
CURRENT is measured by an AMMETER connected in series.

STANDARD SYMBOLS

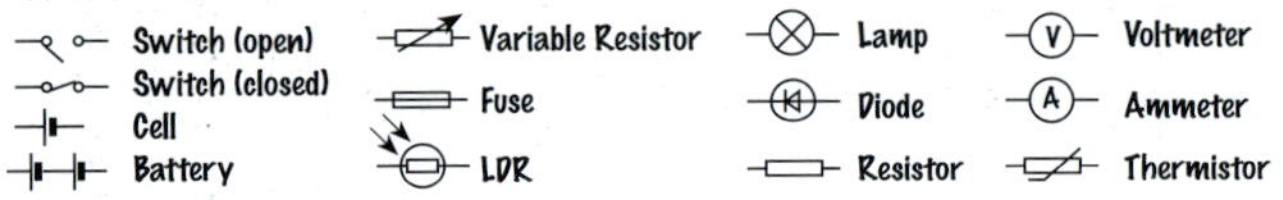

RESISTANCE ...

POTENTIAL DIFFERENCE (V) = CURRENT (A) x RESISTANCE (Ω)

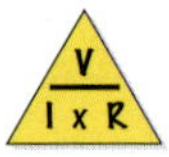

RESISTANCE OF COMPONENTS ...

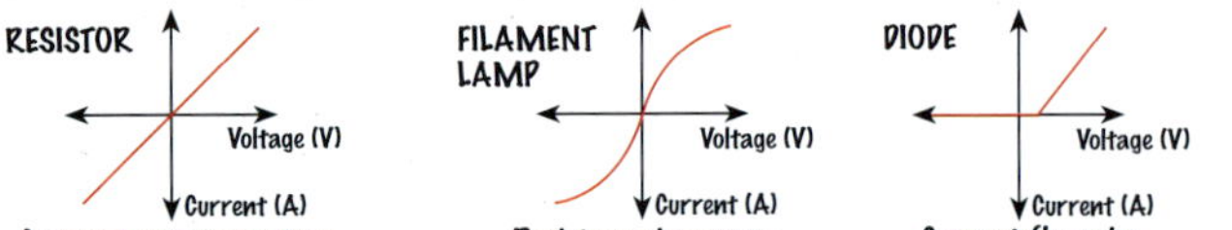

At constant temperature I is proportional to V

Resistance increases with temperature

Current flows in one direction

- In LIGHT DEPENDENT RESISTORS resistance decreases as light increases.
- In THERMISTORS resistance decreases as temperature increases.

SERIES AND PARALLEL CIRCUITS

IN SERIES CIRCUITS ...

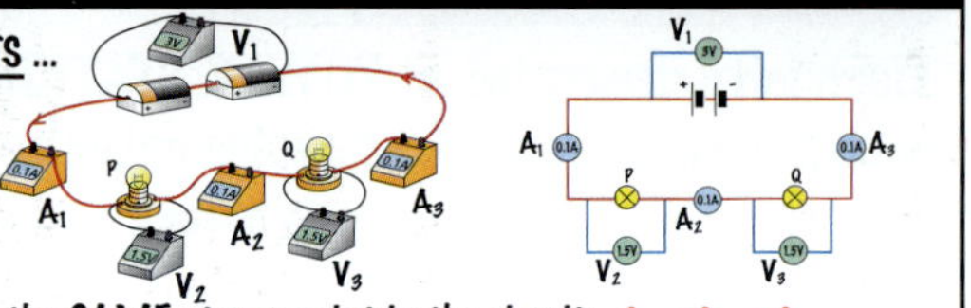

- The CURRENT is the SAME at any point in the circuit. $A_1 = A_2 = A_3$
- The P.D. is shared between the components. $V_1 = V_2 + V_3$
- The TOTAL RESISTANCE is the sum of the separate resistances. $R_{TOTAL} = R_1 + R_2$

IN PARALLEL CIRCUITS ...

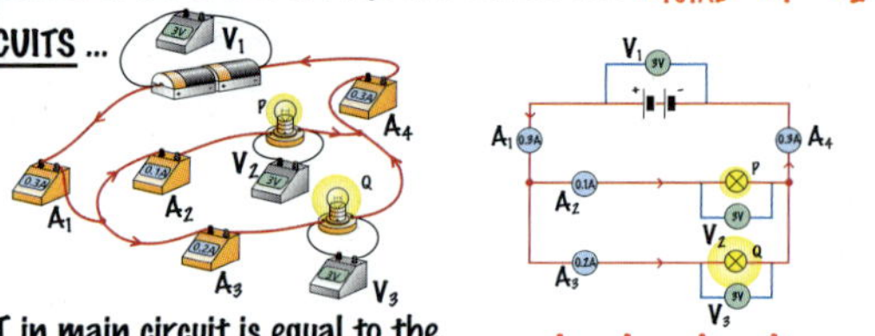

- TOTAL CURRENT in main circuit is equal to the sum of the currents passing through each component. $A_1 = A_2 + A_3 = A_4$
- The P.D. across each component is the same. $V_1 = V_2 = V_3$
- The current through each component depends on its RESISTANCE.

CELLS ...

Total P.D., when connected in series, is the sum of the P.D's of each separate cell.

STATIC ELECTRICITY

Electrons can be transferred between different materials. Gaining electrons results in a negative charge while losing electrons results in a positive charge.

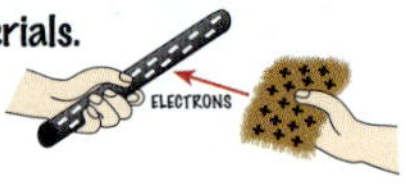

DISCHARGE ... can be achieved by connecting an object to EARTH via a conductor.

THE PHOTOCOPIER ...
(a) Copying plate is electrically charged.
(b) Image is projected onto the plate to leave an 'electrostatic impression'.
(c) This charged impression attracts the ink powder. This powder is then transferred from plate to paper and heated to fix the image.

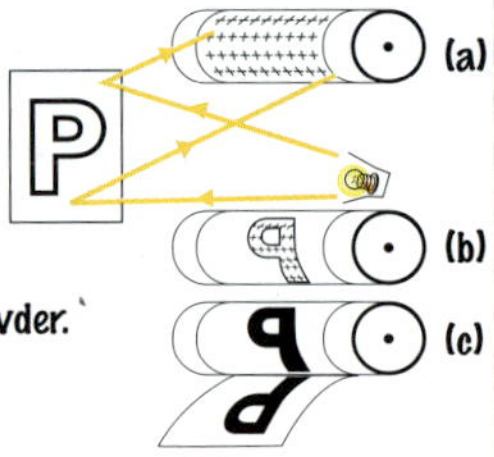

ELECTROSTATIC SMOKE PRECIPITATOR ...
solid smoke particles become charged and are attracted to oppositely charged collecting plates to form layer of 'soot' which is regularly knocked loose.

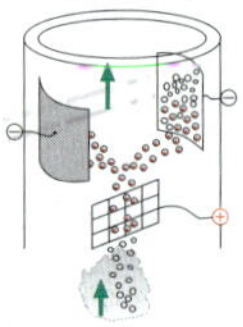

DISCHARGING UNSAFE STATIC ...
during refuelling of planes, the fuel gains electrons from the fuel pipe making the pipe POSITIVELY CHARGED and the fuel NEGATIVELY CHARGED. In order to prevent discharge and a spark, the plane is earthed or the tanker and the plane are connected via a copper wire.

ELECTROLYSIS/ENERGY IN CIRCUITS, POWER AND CHARGE

ELECTROLYSIS ...
some substances produce ions when dissolved in water or melted. This allows them to conduct electricity due to NEGATIVE IONS MOVING TO THE +ve ELECTRODE and POSITIVE IONS MOVING TO THE -ve ELECTRODE, resulting in simpler substances being released at the two electrodes.

QUANTITY OF SUBSTANCES RELEASED (g) ... is proportional to ... < THE CURRENT / TIME FOR WHICH CURRENT FLOWS

POWER AND ENERGY TRANSFER ...
An electric current is a flow of charge which transfers energy from the power supply to the components in the circuit. The rate of this energy transfer is the POWER in WATTS (joules/sec.).

POWER (W) = POTENTIAL DIFFERENCE (V) x CURRENT (A)

CHARGE AND ENERGY TRANSFER ...
Charge is measured in COULOMBS and is given by the formula:

CHARGE (C) = CURRENT (A) x TIME (s)

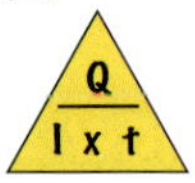

The greater the supply voltage, the greater the energy transferred by every coulomb of charge. This is given by the formula:

ENERGY TRANSFERRED (J) = POTENTIAL DIFFERENCE (V) x CHARGE (C)

eg. If a current of 2A flows for 10 seconds ...
CHARGE = 2 x 10 = 20 coulombs, ...
At a P.D. of 6V, ...
ENERGY TRANSFERRED = 6 x 20 = 120 joules

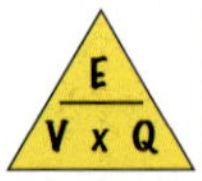

MAINS ELECTRICITY

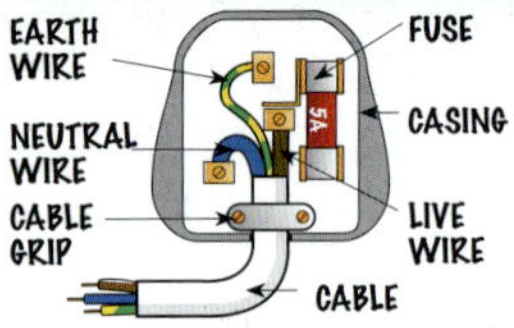

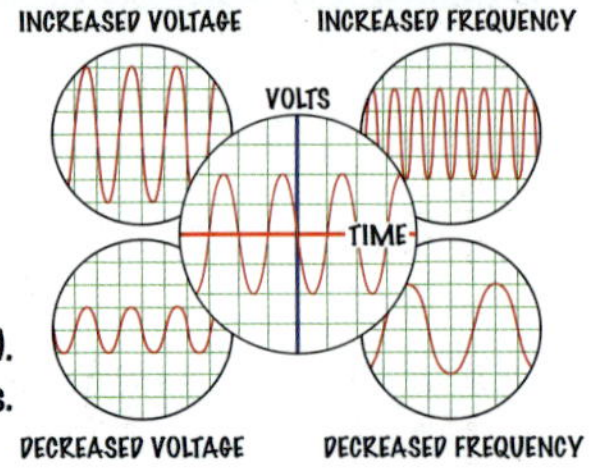

- a.c. changes direction continuously (50Hz).
- d.c. one direction only. Cells and batteries.

FUSES ...

CURRENT LARGER THAN CURRENT RATING OF FUSE → FUSE BURNS OUT → CIRCUIT IS BROKEN → NO CURRENT FLOWS → CABLE OR APPLIANCE IS PROTECTED

CIRCUIT BREAKERS ...

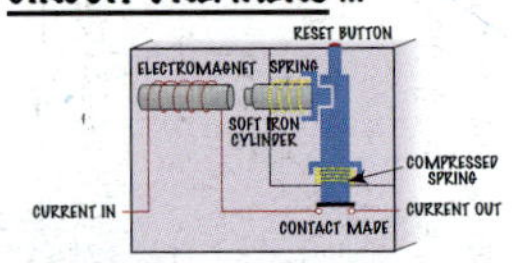

- Current too high ...
- Electromagnet attracts cylinder ...
- Contacts separated ...
- Circuit broken ...
- Appliance protected.

EARTHING ...

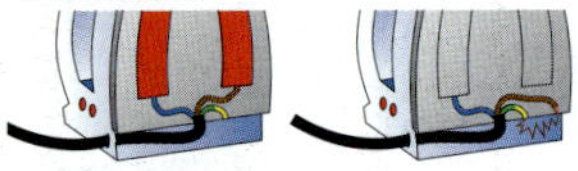

- Casing becomes 'live'...
- Short circuit ...
- Current surges to earth ...
- Fuse melts ...
- Circuit broken ...
- Appliance protected.

ELECTROMAGNETS/MOTOR EFFECT/GENERATORS/TRANSFORMERS

ELECTROMAGNETS ... are coils of wire around which a magnetic field forms when a current flows.
See MAINS ELECTRICITY for use in circuit breakers.

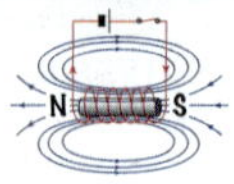

THE MOTOR EFFECT ...
- A current-carrying wire in a magnetic field experiences a force, the size of which can be increased by ...
  INCREASING THE MAGNETIC FIELD STRENGTH,
  INCREASING THE SIZE OF THE CURRENT.
- The direction of the force is reversed by reversing current or field direction.

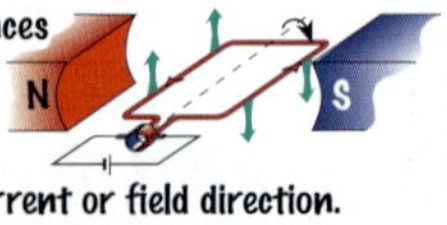

ELECTROMAGNETIC INDUCTION ... occurs when a wire or coil of wire 'cuts though' a magnetic field, or vice versa. This induces a voltage (p.d.) between the ends of the wire which causes a current to flow.
The size of the induced voltage is increased by ...

- ... INCREASING THE SPEED OF MOVEMENT.
- ... INCREASING THE STRENGTH OF MAGNETIC FIELD.
- ... INCREASING THE NUMBER OF TURNS ON THE COIL.
- ... INCREASING THE AREA OF THE COIL.

TRANSFORMERS ... 'step-up' and 'step-down' voltage.
Because POWER = VOLTAGE x CURRENT, increasing voltage reduces current and therefore energy wastage.
- An alternating primary voltage induces an alternating secondary voltage - an example of electromagnetic induction:

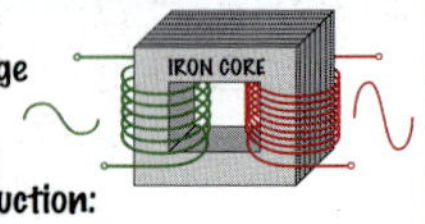

$$\frac{\text{VOLTAGE ACROSS PRIMARY COIL (V)}}{\text{VOLTAGE ACROSS SECONDARY COIL (V)}} = \frac{\text{NUMBER OF TURNS ON PRIMARY}}{\text{NUMBER OF TURNS ON SECONDARY}}$$

1. Look at the circuit diagram and choose words from the list to complete the labels.
A. LAMP.
B. VOLTMETER.
C. CELL.
D. AMMETER.

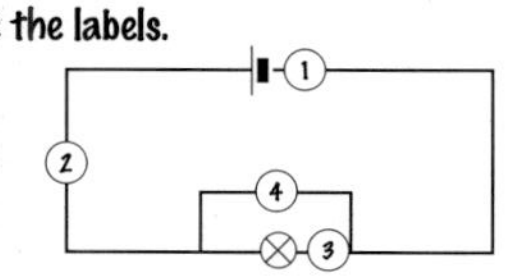

The ---1--- transfers energy to other components in the circuit. The ---3--- transfers electrical energy as light and heat. The ---4--- measures the p.d. across components in a circuit. The ---2--- measures the current flowing in the circuit.

2. The diagram shows a T.V. set. Choose words from the list for each of the spaces in the sentences.
A. CURRENT.
B. VOLTAGE.
C. RESISTANCE.
D. HEAT.

To make the T.V. set work, a ---1--- must be applied across it so that a ---2--- flows through it. Electricity doesn't flow easily through the T.V. set because it has ---3---. This causes some of the electrical energy to be transferred as ---4---.

3. The diagram shows two polythene rods which are repelling each other. Which two of the following statements relating to this diagram are true?

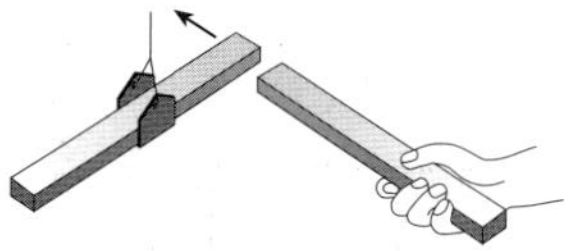

A. One rod is negatively charged and the other is positively charged.
B. Neither rod is charged.
C. Materials with the same charge repel each other.
D. These rods are made of different materials.
E. These rods both carry the same type of charge.

4. Look at the circuit diagram below.

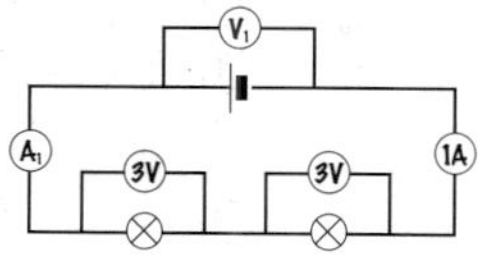

4.1 What reading would show on the ammeter A_1?
A. 3A.
B. 1A.
C. 2A.
D. 6A.

4.2 What reading would show on the voltmeter V_1?
A. 3V.
B. 1V.
C. 6V.
D. 7V.

4.3 What is the resistance of each of the bulbs in the circuit?
A. 3 Ohms.
B. 6 Ohms.
C. 1 Ohm.
D. 7 Ohms.

4.4 What is the power of each of the bulbs?
A. 100 watts.
B. 60 watts.
C. 6 watts.
D. 3 watts.

5. As a fuel tanker fills up a jet plane, the fuel becomes highly negatively charged and the fuel pipe positively charged?

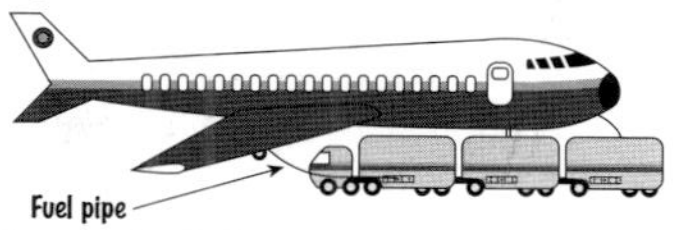

5.1 Why does the fuel become negatively charged?
A. Because electrons are flowing from the fuel to earth.
B. Because electrons are transferred from the pipe to the fuel.
C. Because electrons are transferred from the fuel to the pipe.
D. Because of electromagnetic induction.

5.2 Why could this situation cause a serious accident.
A. The fuel may spill from the tanker.
B. Discharge may occur in the form of a spark.
C. Negatively charged fuel may catch fire.
D. The fuel pipe becomes hot because of the positive charge.

5.3 The chances of an accident can be reduced by ...
A. Earthing the fuel tank.
B. Only half filling the tank.
C. Refuelling more slowly.
D. Connect a copper wire from the fuel pipe to the fuel tanker.

5.4 The greater the potential difference between two objects, one of which is earthed ...
A. The greater the magnetic field.
B. The smaller the magnetic field.
C. The smaller the charge they hold.
D. The greater the chance of discharge occurring.

6. The diagram below shows a transformer which is used to change the potential difference of an electrical supply.

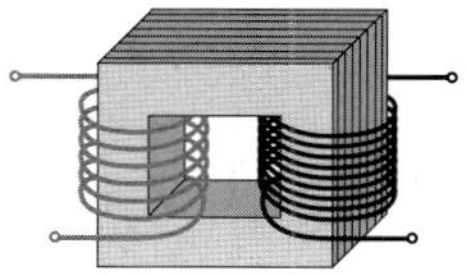

6.1 Why are transformers used to step-up the voltage to over 400,000 volts before electricity is transmitted through overhead cables?
A. So that more energy is transmitted per volt.
B. So that the same power is transmitted with less wasted heat energy.
C. So that more energy is transmitted per amp.
D. So that the same power is transmitted more quickly.

6.2 Transformers will only operate with ...
A. A 50 Hz supply.
B. A 240 V supply.
C. An a.c. supply.
D. A d.c. supply.

6.3 An industrial transformer increases the 230 volts supply to 9200 volts. This transformer has ...
A. 8970 more turns on the secondary coil than on the primary.
B. 2,116,000 more turns on the secondary coil than on the primary.
C. 40 times more turns on the primary coil than on the secondary.
D. 40 times more turns on the secondary coil than on the primary.

6.4 An industrial transformer has a primary input voltage of 230 volts and has 350 turns on the primary coil and 5250 turns on the secondary coil. What will the output voltage be?
A. 3450 volts.
B. 15.3 volts.
C. 22.8 volts.
D. 7980 volts.

7. The diagram below shows a simple direct current motor.

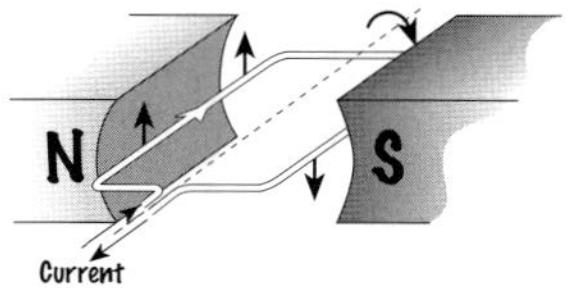

7.1 When the motor is connected to a d.c. supply, ...
A. The coil spins due to the build up of static charge.
B. Each side of the coil produces a magnetic field which interacts with the permanent magnet.
C. Each side of the coil produces a magnetic field which attracts the other side.
D. Each side of the coil produces a magnetic field which repels the other side.

7.2 Which one of the following will increase the size of the force on the wires of the coil.
A. Wrap them around a heavy plastic core.
B. Wrap them around a light plastic core.
C. Reduce the current in the coil.
D. Increase the strength of the permanent magnets.

7.3 What would happen if an a.c. supply was used instead of a d.c?
A. The motor would reverse its direction of spin.
B. The motor would vibrate about a central position.
C. The motor would turn more quickly.
D. The motor would turn more slowly.

7.4 Electromagnets are used in many everyday appliances. Which of the following would NOT increase the strength of an electromagnet?
A. Increasing the number of turns on the coil.
B. Increasing the size of the current.
C. Placing a soft iron core inside the coil.
D. Increasing the frequency of supply.

LIST OF FORMULAE

You are expected to be able to **RECALL** the following formulae for the following modules.

Energy

FORMULA						PAGE No.
Change In Gravitational Potential Energy (joule, J)	=	Weight (newton, N)	x	Change In Vertical Height (metre, m)	$gpe = mg\Delta h$	68

Electricity

FORMULA						PAGE No.
Potential Difference (volt, V)	=	Current (ampere, A)	x	Resistance (ohm, Ω)	$V = IR$	78
Power (watt, W)	=	Potential Difference (volt, V)	x	Current (ampere, A)	$P = VI$	85, 89
Energy Transferred (joule, J)	=	Potential Difference (volt, V)	x	Charge (coulomb, C)	$E = VQ$	85
Charge (coulomb, C)	=	Current (ampere, A)	x	Time (second, s)	$Q = It$	85
Voltage Across Primary (volt, V) / Voltage Across Secondary (volt, V)	=	Number Of Turns On Primary / Number Of Turns On Secondary			$\frac{V_p}{V_s} = \frac{N_p}{N_s}$	89

Lonsdale SCIENCE REVISION GUIDES

All you need for the **Tested Modules ...**

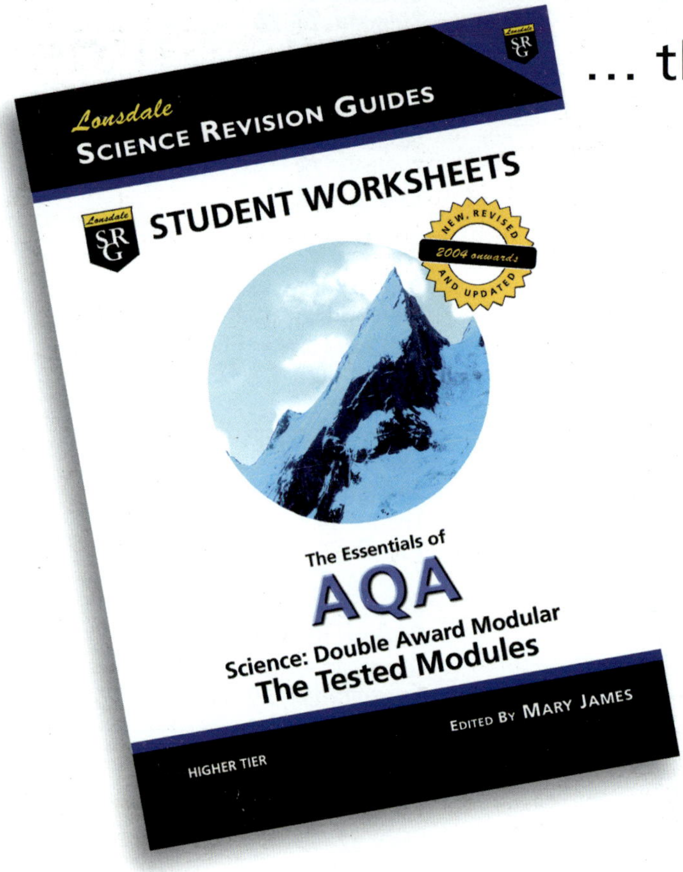

... the **Student Worksheets**

The Essentials of AQA
Science: Double Award Modular
STUDENT WORKSHEETS

- Completely updated and revised for the new AQA specification
- Series of student worksheets to reinforce understanding of the Tested Modules
- Every worksheet is cross-referenced to this revision guide
- Also available at **FOUNDATION LEVEL**

... and the **Modular Test Papers**

- Two practice tests for each Tested Module
- Test and answer grid layout is the same as the actual tests - to provide the ideal experience
- Answers included
- Also available at **FOUNDATION LEVEL**